BALZAC ON THE BARRICADES

Balzac on the Barricades

The Literary Origins of an Economic Revolution

❧

Rebecca Terese Powers

University of Virginia Press
Charlottesville and London

The University of Virginia Press is situated on the traditional lands of the Monacan Nation, and the Commonwealth of Virginia was and is home to many other Indigenous people. We pay our respect to all of them, past and present. We also honor the enslaved African and African American people who built the University of Virginia, and we recognize their descendants. We commit to fostering voices from these communities through our publications and to deepening our collective understanding of their histories and contributions.

University of Virginia Press
© 2024 by the Rector and Visitors of the University of Virginia
All rights reserved
Printed in the United States of America on acid-free paper

First published 2024

1 3 5 7 9 8 6 4 2

Library of Congress Cataloging-in-Publication Data
Names: Powers, Rebecca Terese, author.
Title: Balzac on the barricades : the literary origins of an economic revolution / Rebecca Terese Powers.
Description: Charlottesville : University of Virginia Press, 2024. | Includes bibliographical references and index.
Identifiers: LCCN 2024003290 (print) | LCCN 2024003291 (ebook) | ISBN 9780813951393 (hardcover) | ISBN 9780813951416 (paperback) | ISBN 9780813951409 (ebook)
Subjects: LCSH: French literature—19th century—History and criticism. | Labor in literature. | French literature—Economic aspects. | Literature and society—France. | BISAC: LITERARY CRITICISM / Semiotics & Theory | LCGFT: Literary criticism.
Classification: LCC PQ292 .P69 2024 (print) | LCC PQ292 (ebook) | DDC 840.9/008—dc23/eng/20240206
LC record available at https://lccn.loc.gov/2024003290
LC ebook record available at https://lccn.loc.gov/2024003291

Cover art: Detail from *Révolution de Paris,* anonymous, c. 1830. (Musée Carnavalet, Histoire de Paris)
Cover design: Cecelia Sorochin

To Josephine and Matilda, my real babies

The Provisional Government of the French Republic promises to guarantee the worker's livelihood by his labor [*l'existence de l'ouvrier par le travail*]. The Government promises to guarantee work to all workers. It recognizes that all workers must be able to associate among themselves in order to benefit from the fruit of their labor.

—"Declaration of the *droit au travail*," February 25, 1848

The right to work is that every man has a right to live by working. Society must provide work to able-bodied men who cannot obtain it otherwise, with all productive and general means available to it and those that will later be organized.

—Article 7 of the first draft of the Republican Constitution, June 20, 1848

The Republic must, through fraternal aid, ensure the existence of its needy citizens, either by providing them with employment within the limits of its resources, or by giving assistance to those who are unable to work and who do not have family who can support them.

—Article 8 of the Republican Constitution, November 4, 1848

CONTENTS

	Acknowledgments	xi
	Introduction	1
1.	Between Two Revolutions	21
2.	Balzac's Literary Labor Theory of Value	49
3.	The Worker as Hero: Constructing a Bourgeois Narrative	81
4.	A Literary Identity for the Worker-Writer	112
5.	Building Character: A Formula for Success	140
	Epilogue: The Writers' Republic, February–June 1848	173
	Notes	183
	Bibliography	197
	Index	211

ACKNOWLEDGMENTS

This book has taken me longer to write than expected, and through these many years, I have received support, feedback, and encouragement from a great many colleagues, mentors, friends, and family members. I will try to include as many of them as I can here.

I began working on this book immediately after I defended my dissertation in May 2016, and I was very lucky at that time to land at the University of California, where mentors like Catherine Nesci, Didier Maleuvre, and Jody Enders generously read and commented on what probably seemed like endless chapter drafts and book prospectuses.

During this time, I also had the immense fortune to find a group of fellow first-book writers, whose stories, snacks, smiles, and sometimes, quite simply, presence in the room was an enormous inspiration to continue writing, even when the task seemed overwhelming. Elana, Heather, Mona, Summer, and Swati, you are the best.

Thank you as well to Sarah Sussman at Stanford University Libraries for inviting me to work in the Gustave Gimon Research Collection, where I was able to access rare and fascinating works and engage in vibrant discussions about my project with brilliant academics in the Bay Area.

I'm also extremely grateful to the members of the Groupe de Recherches Interdisciplinaires sur l'Histoire du Littéraire and to the L'École des hautes études en sciences sociales for welcoming me as a visiting researcher during the fall of 2019. A very special thank you to Judith Lyon-Caen and Dinah Ribard for reading chapter drafts and sharing their incredibly extensive knowledge on virtually every aspect of French literature, culture, and history that this book touches on.

I'd also like to thank my "Economic Fictions" students at UC Santa Barbara and Sciences Po Paris-Reims for allowing me to test out many of my ideas in the classroom. Your careful readings, pertinent questions, and general enthusiasm for the subject helped me to think about my research in ways that I never would have thought of.

A special word of gratitude goes to Eric Brandt at the University of Virginia Press, who believed in this project many years ago, and who has shown more patience than I would ever have expected. Thank you as well to the editorial team at UVA Press who have been a pleasure to work with.

Finally, of course, I must thank all of the friends and family members who have listened to me talk about Balzac at Christmas dinner and social gatherings for over a decade now. And above all, a very special "merci, mon amour" to Clément, who has been my faithful sounding board and number-one cheerleader throughout it all, and without whose boundless optimism this book would never have come to completion.

BALZAC ON THE BARRICADES

Introduction

On November 1, 1834, an open letter appeared in the respected literary magazine *Revue de Paris*, signed by the prolific but financially struggling author Honoré de Balzac. The letter was addressed to "French writers of the nineteenth century," but, as the passage below makes clear, he really meant to reach a wide variety of artists and intellectuals. "And so, gentlemen," he begins, listing off their professions: "you poets, you musicians, you dramatists, you prose writers, those who live by their thoughts, those who *work* for the glory of the country, those who must *forge* the century!" (emphasis added).[1] What did these various creative professionals have in common, according to Balzac? They were all laborers, and it was imperative that they demand the same legal protections that he imagined business owners and manual laborers all around him were enjoying.

Balzac hails his fellow writers and artists as those who "work for the glory of the country," and "forge [*pétrir*] the century." Within these sweeping statements about the importance of creative work, the author's choice of the verb *pétrir* was particularly meaningful. Although it has been translated here as "to forge," its more technical equivalent in English would be "to knead," as in the universally appreciated labor of the baker. To equate the musician and the novelist with the *boulanger* was to frame their creative works as the most essential of goods. It was also a reminder that, in the past, the French people had not hesitated to protect their most basic products from the vagaries of the free market. In Balzac's day, it was widely held that a shortage of bread had been the primary cause of the French Revolution, and, although modern historians would consider this explanation far too simple, there is no doubt that fears of hunger played an important role in stoking popular unrest. Caused by both natural disasters and early attempts to liberalize and industrialize food production, famines—or the threat thereof—were a constant source of concern during the eighteenth century. Under Louis XV, bread had become an ideological flashpoint as free marketers like the physiocrat Anne Robert Jacques Turgot clashed with those in favor of strict government oversight over the best way to ensure a constant and reliable food supply. In the streets, women called for "Bread or Death," fearing both hunger and "the breakdown of government."[2] Even as late as the 1830s and 1840s, there were reports of bakers being assaulted when the price of bread became too high for the ordinary worker to afford.[3] At the same time, bakers managed to defend their craft from the onslaught of industrialization, even as other sectors were trading in skilled human labor for automation and cutthroat competition.[4] To compare the creative artist to the *boulanger*, therefore, was to frame him as a workingman's hero, threatened by, but triumphant over, the laissez-faire policies of Louis-Philippe's so-called July Monarchy government (1830–48).

Balzac's letter reveals how important the question of labor had become in the literary culture of his day and hints at the growing role that literature was playing in political and economic discourse. Just four years earlier, in July 1830, a group of printworkers facing lay-offs due to new censorship laws had organized labor protests and were quickly joined by unhappy citizens from across the social spectrum. Their movement would eventually lead to the ouster of Charles X, the last of the Bourbon monarchs. Following these events, leaders from all sides, realizing the revolutionary power of the working classes, had begun to listen to their concerns, or at least pretend to do so. By stressing the economic value of literature and by pointing to its laboriousness, Balzac was hoping that his grievances would also be heard. Primary among these grievances was what he saw as the government's failure to enforce copyright law, despite its commitment to upholding property law, a subject in which, as a former law student, Balzac felt he had some expertise.[5] "THE LAW," he writes emphatically, "protects the land, it protects the home of the proletarian, who sweats; [but] it confiscates the work of the poet who thinks. THE LAW [is] so respectful of the merchant's bundle, of the gold earned through labor, as long as it is in some way material, and often [acquired] through vile means" (64, capitalization in the original). In his eyes, even the lowly workshop employee or factory worker—whose pitiful living conditions had begun to attract the attention of social and moral reformers like those associated with the Académie des sciences morales et politiques—had more protections than the artist or author. And yet, as he makes clear, few work harder than those very artists and authors. Balzac offers himself as an example of such industriousness, describing himself as: "a man who has so much work to do that the days do not suffice" (63). The writer, we are to understand, works as hard as any sweatshop laborer or highly skilled artisan.

In his critique of the liberal July Monarchy government, Balzac—an avowed Catholic and monarchist who had added the aristocratic *particule* "de" to his name—found himself in common cause with radical republicans and socialist organizers. He reasoned that the best way for artists and authors to defend their financial interests, increasingly diminished by publication taxes (*timbres*), weak copyright laws, and numerous counterfeit operations, would be through "association," modeled after the "maternal societies that give aid and assistance [to the laborer] in his moments of distress" (79). Balzac's use of "association" as the paradigm for his call for reform is quite significant. Best known as one of two key elements of Louis Blanc's plan to link industrial workers more closely with the products of their labor (the other one being "organization"), the act of "association" was already being promoted by politically minded artisans and even educators in the early 1830s.[6] Balzac was calling on his fellow writers and artists to come together to fight for the right to literary property, and, in the socialist spirit of the time, he saw that the way to do this would be through collective action.[7]

For Balzac, the process of creating literature was just as important as any other type of work, and its practitioners would have to organize themselves like other sectors of the labor force in order to survive the new social, political, and economic realities of the nineteenth century. Among these "new realities"—which included technological advancements, industrialization, demographic changes, growing international trade, and many others—it was the problem of economic liberalism that associations were best equipped to address. The pro-industry policies of Louis Philippe's July Monarchy government meant that artisans and other manual laborers had little protection from falling wages, deskilling, and unsafe working conditions. Balzac's argument was that the government's refusal to enforce copyright law was equally harmful to the artistic and intellectual laborer. In both cases, then, association was a way to restore a level of protection from both the vagaries of the free market and the harmful effects of cutthroat competition. When workers called for the "right to work" in February of 1848, they were demanding that the government assume full responsibility for providing this protection.

If manual labor was the foundational paradigm for Balzac's attempts to promote the economic value of intellectual and artistic labor, it is unclear to what extent this paradigm was metaphorical. Did Balzac truly consider his efforts as a literary author comparable to those of an artisan or a factory worker? Or was this merely an opportunistic analogy, linking him up with what he saw as the zeitgeist of the early years of the July Monarchy? It is unclear what he was privately thinking in 1834, but we can be sure that, in later writings such as his unpublished "Lettre sur le travail" (1848) and the *Parents pauvres* (*Poor Relations*) novels (1846–47), he would express a decidedly anti-working-class sentiment, portraying artistic—and, in particular, literary—efforts as the *only* type of labor that was truly valuable. Nonetheless, there is a good deal of evidence to suggest that, perhaps unbeknownst to him, the message of cross-class worker solidarity that he helped to construct in the early 1830s would become the rallying cry of a popular revolution in 1848.

A Failure?

Balzac was not the only prominent novelist to take an active interest in the question of labor during the 1830s and 1840s, and the conspicuous role that literary figures and literary tropes played in the Revolution of 1848 has long been a topic of scholarly interest. Usually, it is presented in negative terms, given as a cause of the Second Republic's precipitous failure, or as one example of how France's nineteenth-century revolutions were disconnected from reality. Contemporary observers were doubtful that a political movement so closely aligned with the literary world could bring about sustained revolutionary change. As early as April 1848, the socialist Pierre-Joseph Proudhon complained that "this revolution had taken place for no other reason than to give us a comedy in the middle of the street, as if all of Paris were a theater in which to play out the old revolutionary drama."[8] Two months later, a young Karl Marx, who had spent several years living among the working classes in Paris, charged that any social progress in terms of workers' rights won during the February Revolution had "won only a joyous existence, an existence of phrases, or words," and that once "things [had] taken the place of phrases" in June 1848, these ideals were quickly discarded. Qualifying February as the "beautiful" revolution and June as the "ugly" one, Marx affirms that only the second could ever have any real effect.[9] Two years later, Marx's *Class Struggles in France* (1850) presented a damning assessment of the February Revolution as a farcical restaging of the original French Revolution of 1789. For both Marx and Proudhon, who famously disagreed on many other points, it was clear, from the outset, that the literary nature of the revolution spelled its doom.

Similar critiques came from within the literary world. Indeed, some of the most memorable depictions of the 1848 Revolution have been handed down to us in a novel, Gustave Flaubert's *L'Education sentimentale* (1869), where the revolutionary movement is the object of searing derision, similar to his skewering of Romantic literature in his earlier *Madame Bovary* (1857). Loosely based on Flaubert's personal experiences, *L'Education sentimentale* is a retelling of history through the eyes of Frédéric Moreau, a romantic young man from the provinces who arrives in Paris in the early 1840s. He soon joins a group of self-styled poets, Republicans, and proletarians who participate (to varying degrees) in the events leading up to the Revolution of 1848. Flaubert's ironic depictions of the people and the situations in which they find themselves leave the reader unsure whether to laugh or cry. In the end, however, the protagonist experiences the Revolution and its repression as a trauma that he will never accept and never overcome.

Frédéric's superficial flirtation with various social movements of the July Monarchy reveal these well-intentioned causes to be first inane and then dangerous for the senseless violence they ignite. This transition from insipidity to deadliness is embodied by the character of Sénécal, first described as an imposing but somewhat ridiculous "hard-headed man with Republican convictions," who gradually descends into ideological extremism, and finally assassinates his friend, Dussardier, the only truly heroic figure in the novel.[10] Like Marx and Proudhon, then, Flaubert saw the empty (Romantic) phrases of the July Monarchy as an enabling force for false revolution and the eventual silencing of the working-class movement during Napoleon III's repressive dictatorship.

Throughout the twentieth century, historians and critics continued to describe the Revolution of February 1848 as a literary event. Commemorating the revolution's centenary in 1948, for example, Georges Duveau dubbed the period immediately following the uprising a "Lyrical Illusion," a label that has stuck.[11] This way of characterizing the effusive but unrealistic way the public had hailed the revolutionary events pf their time implies that they believed that, much as Romantic poets like Victor Hugo used language and imagery to bring together the sublime and the grotesque, Romantic politicians would be able to employ those same techniques to bring social classes together. This analogy was embodied in the figure of Alphonse de Lamartine, the poet-turned-politician whose rhetorical finesse helped to unify disparate factions in the early days of the Republic. However, if we are to follow Duveau's interpretation, this belief was delusional. The "extraordinary sense of freedom, joy, and plenty . . . the depth and intensity of this feeling," he explains, could not withstand the test of reality.[12] It was merely, as another historian puts it, "the last flames of a Romanticism which had tried to erect a political system out of confused thought and sentimental outpourings."[13] According to the dominant historiography of the twentieth century, then, the February Revolution was, at best, a failure, at worst, a scam.

The field of twentieth-century literary studies took a slightly different approach to the 1848 Revolution, framing it as a rupture rather than a failure. Admitting that most of the movement's political ambitions were indeed unsuccessful, literary critics were particularly interested in how this failure gave rise to a new era in literary production. In 1953, a young Roland Barthes argued that 1848 must be seen as a turning point—a "degree zero" as he calls it—in the way novelists perceived their relationship to society. The act of writing (*écriture*, understood as the moral and social relationship of writers to the world around them) could no longer be seen as an "intelligible pact," such as the one Balzac sought to establish, but rather a relationship of "dissociation" or distance, exemplified by the irony we find in Flaubert's works. Balzac's understanding of his role as a novelist, says Barthes, was authoritative and even world-building, like the work of a historian like Jules Michelet. For both men, he continues, the narration of a (hi)story in the third person singular represents "the most important means [the writer] has of building the world in the way that he chooses" (31). Beginning in 1848, says Barthes, writing takes on a tragic aspect: "Under the weight of History, Literature became dissociated from the society which consumes it. Between the third person as used by Balzac and that used by Flaubert, there is a world of difference (that of 1848): in the former we have a view of History which is harsh, but coherent and certain of its principles, the triumph of an order; in the latter, an art which in order to escape its pangs of conscience either exaggerates conventions or frantically attempts to destroy them" (33).[14]

Although Barthes would soon shift his scholarly attention from social and historical analyses to more structural ones, this early insight about how the "weight of History" acts upon the practice of writing (the moral relationship between the writer and the world), would lead to a different kind of revolution, this time, in the way literature was studied in the Francophone world. According to Claude Duchet, Barthes's definition of *écriture* was foundational to two major schools of literary criticism: his own sociocriticism movement that had emerged in the 1970s, and the more recent social discourse analysis, an approach that continues to gain in influence. "We were all born with *Writing Degree Zero*," says Duchet, "with the notion of writing [*écriture*] defined as a form of collective expression . . . for Barthes, the term *écriture* pointed to the social nature of every literary gesture."[15] In the eyes of Barthes, Duchet, and many others, then, the close relationship between literature and the sociopolitical world that characterized July Monarchy France contrasted sharply with the retreat from these realms that literary authors seemed to take after 1848. The Second Republic was not merely a failed political experiment, it also marked a new chapter in literary history. From then on, under the authoritarian censorship regime of the Second Empire (1852–70), most literary authors would pointedly try to distance themselves from political and social controversies.

According to the sociologist Pierre Bourdieu (in *The Rules of Art*, 1992), the removal of social and political content from literary production also entailed avoiding any direct criticism of economic problems like labor practices or inequality. This was due not only to political prudence but also to an increased desire by some writers to establish themselves as artists in an autonomous literary field. Bourdieu takes Flaubert as an especially interesting example of an author who eschews the bourgeois productivist worldview of his upbringing to help define literature as an artistic practice that does not enter into the utility-focused logic of commerce. "Nobody is rich enough to pay us," Flaubert complains, snobbishly. "Right now I manage to pay for my paper, but not the errands, trips, and books that I need for my work; and, in the end, I find that all right (or I pretend to find it all right), because I don't see what relation there is between a five-franc coin and an idea. You have to love Art for Art's sake; otherwise, the humblest job is worth more."[16] Echoing Balzac, Flaubert points to the laborious nature of his literary efforts and hints at the injustice of his insufficient pay. Unlike his predecessor, however, Flaubert simultaneously affirms that no one could pay him what his work is worth, suggesting that the products of his labor are essentially priceless. His inability—or unwillingness—to calculate the value of his labor points to an ambivalence about his own economic situation, indicative, perhaps, of a more general apathy toward political and social questions. Both Flaubert and Balzac argue that their work is difficult and worth more than they are paid for it, but the contrast between

Balzac's earnest call to action and Flaubert's detached resignation could not be more pronounced.

Because of the dominant narrative of failure and rupture that Marx, Flaubert, Duveau, Barthes, Bourdieu, and many others have helped shape over the years, it can be easy to forget or belittle the significance of the February Revolution of 1848 and what it *did* accomplish. Seen through the lens of the present, with our knowledge of the traumatic June Days, the coup d'état, and the return of an autocratic emperor named Napoleon who was even less welcoming to socialist ideals than the government of the July Monarchy had been, the victories of 1848 are easily forgotten. It's only thanks to a decidedly discursive turn taken by historians, philosophers, and (perhaps somewhat belatedly) literary critics that scholars have come to recognize the February Revolution not merely as a point of rupture, nor as a "Lyrical Illusion," that would inevitably lead to the violent June Days, but as the result of an interlocking network of political, social, and cultural processes, successful in their own right. By the 1970s and 1980s, the historiography of 1848 had expanded to include the experiences of men and women from various social classes and geographical locations, thanks to work by social and cultural historians like Maurice Agulhon, William Sewell, and Joan Scott, who presented the February Revolution as the culmination of decades of reflection and discussion about labor since the Old Regime. More recently, the political scientist Samuel Hayat has further explored the discourse of the 1848 moment, attributing the failure of the new Republic not to an overly idealist or "lyrical" social zeitgeist, but to a necessary working-out of different definitions of what the term "republic" actually meant, in concrete terms, to various revolutionary actors.

In the field of literary criticism, we have been suspicious of the political and social leanings of many July Monarchy authors, as well as their desire for commercial success. It was, after all, during this very moment that the connected phenomena of the serial novel, the cheap newspaper, and the imagery of an "industrialized" literature were emerging. For a long time, scholarship focused primarily on a few canonical authors—Hugo, Stendhal, Balzac, and several others—whose genius seemed to allow their writings to rise above the materialistic concerns of the day. Their Romantic belief in the poet's higher calling and their desire to bring beauty into existence through the power of words provided inspiration to the revolutionaries of the 1830s and 1840s, and the connection between the two was seen as so strong that the failure of the Second Republic also marked the end of Romanticism.[17] Interestingly enough, it was a specialist of

Second Empire literature who was among the first to offer an alternative to this strict periodization. In his 1997 work *Le Spleen contre L'Oubli*, Dolf Oehler begins with an investigation into "the language of forty-eight," gathering evidence from a variety of sources, including newspapers and other periodicals, that lay out the tropes, signs, and images that helped contemporary observers understand the bloody days of June 1848.[18] He shows that, far from forgetting the socialist elan of February 1848, modern authors like Flaubert, Baudelaire, and Heine internalized it, and continued to long for it, albeit through the tragic lens of June. Since Oehler's work, which was republished in 2017, scholars have been more open to seeing the literary production of 1848 not as the swan song of the doomed Romantic movement, but as a creative force with far-reaching influence. Taking a literary approach to the journalistic innovations of the time has provided an especially fertile ground for cultural investigation, and several edited volumes have demonstrated the richness of 1848 as a meeting point for historians and literary researchers.[19]

The philosopher Jacques Rancière, known for his extensive work on worker-poets and working-class writings, has also paved the way for a reconsideration of the meaning of 1848 by proposing a new periodization of literary history. Arguing that the rupture that critics (like Barthes) have tended to locate in the mid-nineteenth century had its beginnings toward the end of the eighteenth century, Rancière identifies important changes in the early days of Romanticism. For the philosopher, a major—albeit "silent"—shift took place with "the ruin of the generic principle," when literature became the art of expressing emotions and ideas rather than adhering to strict generic and formal rules.[20] In this way, he argues, literature became a more democratic phenomenon, no longer limited to the informed audience of salons and the highly educated readers who would have been familiar with such codes. In this view, the difference between Balzac and Flaubert, so central to the young Barthes and to the field of sociocriticism, is minimized. While it is true that the contrast between Balzac's earnest call to action and Flaubert's detached resignation could not be more pronounced, a Rancierian reading of the two would find that the ideas and emotions they express are more similar than not. Indeed, much of the ennui that Flaubert expresses above comes from the fact that his work is difficult and insufficiently compensated. It is, in short, a continuation of the complaints that proliferate in Balzac's fiction, nonfiction, and personal correspondence. The difference in their style is less important than the similarities in what they are saying.

What the most recent explorations of nineteenth-century literary history have shown is that, despite the dominant narratives portraying 1848 as a literary—and therefore failed or futile—revolution, the relationship between literature, politics, and economics was never so simple. As Anne O'Neil-Henry argues in her *Mastering the Marketplace* (2017), the cut-throat publishing environment of the nineteenth century was as central to the stylistic and topical choices made by authors of the July Monarchy as were their ideological convictions. The average author, just like any *homo economicus*, needed to figure out how to put food on the table, and an understanding of the tastes and habits of his or her potential readers—a growing number of whom were workers—was essential to making a living. This should not, however, lead us to interpret the interest that literary figures took in the working classes during this same period as purely opportunistic. In *Inventing the Popular: Printing, Politics, and Poetics* (2018), for example, Bettina Lerner has demonstrated that a solidarity between working-class writers and their Romantic interlocutors of the 1830s and 1840s did indeed exist, even if it was quite "vexed" from the beginning, describing their relations as a complicated "network of multitudinous and contradictory affiliations and repudiations."[21] Another important work that looks at how popular culture, literature, and politics came together in the mid-nineteenth century is Eliza Jane Smith's *Literary Slumming: Slang and Class in Nineteenth-Century France* (2021). Smith's sociolinguistic study examines how, throughout the nineteenth century, prominent literary figures adopted the language and style of marginalized social groups in order to present them to a mainstream bourgeois audience, often in the service of selling books or making political statements. Smith's analysis demonstrates that those traits of the underclasses that had once denoted criminality, sexual deviance, or social injustice could be transformed, through these literary and other cultural interventions, into the parlance of fashionable society. By taking seriously literary works that have often been dismissed as popular or dogmatic, O'Neil-Henry, Lerner, and Smith have exposed the complexity of the literary environment of the July Monarchy and just how aware its authors were of the political, economic, and cultural import of their productions. My book draws on this research to argue that, if we see these literary actors as savvy participants in the social, political, and economic discourse of their time, then we cannot discount the central role that literature played in the "production" of the 1848 Revolution, as a result of the creative and productive force of July Monarchy literature and its practitioners.

Droit au travail!

As we saw in Balzac's letter, he, like many writers of his day, worried that they would no longer be able to make a living from their labor. This was an economic anxiety they shared with the working classes, and it is perhaps not surprising, then, that the rallying cry of the Revolution—*droit au travail!*—was enthusiastically adopted by protesters across the social spectrum, by playwrights and shoemakers alike. Because of its centrality to the 1848 Revolution, it is worth taking a moment to reflect upon the significance of the phrase *droit au travail*. The noun *travail*, which may be translated as "labor" or "work," has carried a variety of meanings throughout its history, and its definition was far from fixed in the mid-nineteenth century. The verb *travailler* had first appeared in Old French in the eleventh century, coming from the Latin *tripaliare*, meaning to torture with a certain tool called a *trepalium*. For centuries, the substantive retained these connotations of pain and submission (also found in the English "travail"). It wasn't until the Enlightenment that philosophers, with John Locke (1632–1704) first among them, truly began to celebrate labor as the basis of private property, the most fundamental of all rights. Yet, even Locke, who saw labor as the source of nearly all value, could not separate the act of working from pain and suffering: "it is not barely the ploughman's *pains*, the reaper's and thresher's *toil*, and the baker's *sweat*, is to be counted into the bread we eat" (emphasis added).[22] Locke's ideas were popularized in France by Jacques Turgot (1727–1781), finance minister under Louis XVI. In one of his famous edicts of 1776, Turgot argued in favor of what would later be termed the *droit du travail*, basically the freedom of the individual to work without being regulated by the guilds, *jurandes*, and corporations. These institutions had governed work practices since the Middle Ages and were seen as promoting an old system of privileges that was out of step with the liberal ideals that many French intellectuals had come to embrace. As accounts of government proceedings that took place in the fall of 1848 demonstrate, Turgot's *droit du travail* would prove to be more appealing to nineteenth-century moderates than the *droit au travail* demanded by workers.[23]

By the mid-nineteenth century, *travail* still retained its connotations of fatigue and pain, but it was increasingly used to indicate productive activity, as well. A comparison of different editions of *Le Dictionnaire de l'Académie Française* demonstrates this shift. From the late seventeenth through the late nineteenth centuries (in editions published in 1694, 1762,

1798, 1835, and 1878), the Académie defines *travail* as "Labor, fatigue, pain that one takes on in order to do something." However, in the next edition of the *Dictionnaire*, published in 1932, the painful connotations have been removed from the primary definition: "Labor, attention to a task, sustained effort for doing something."[24] The complete transformation in the way labor was seen—from a punishment (a "pain" that one submits to) to an intentional exertion of creative energy (an "effort" directed toward building or improving something)—did not register in the lexicography, then, until almost a century after the "right to work" was declared. Keeping in mind that the dictionary (especially the one published by the decidedly conservative Académie Française) would be slower to take into account linguistic changes than everyday speech such as the kind used in newspapers and popular fictions, these entries help us understand that the call for the right to work was at odds with the way labor was seen—at least officially—in the years preceding and following the events of 1848. The transformation of labor from drudgery to point of pride was instead a shift that took place gradually, helped along by Enlightenment-era ways of thinking about both property and, as we shall see, suffering.

In the early nineteenth century, the more constructive ("effort") sense of labor—where a positive relationship is established between the suffering of the laborer and the object created from that labor—was most readily applied to what was beginning to be seen as intellectual labor. While Locke had focused on the role that manual tasks like farming and shepherding had played in the early days of humankind, passing from the state of nature to a state of civil society, French scientists began to take a special interest in the intellectual pathologies of so-called "men of letters" (*gens de lettres*) near the end of the eighteenth century. These great philosophers and literary authors (many, like Voltaire and Rousseau, were both) had brought new and exciting ideas into the world, and yet, it was remarked, many of them seemed to suffer psychologically, physically, or both. Observing this strange phenomenon, the vitalist anatomist Xavier Bichat (1771–1802) theorized that "a person's aptitude for a given profession was determined by the organ that he or she exercised most frequently"; he suggested that men of letters performed what could be called "brain work" and that an overworking of this organ could lead to illness. Bichat shows little concern for the working classes: his idea of an occupation that requires "muscular prowess" includes "dance, equitation, and the [skilled] mechanical arts," but does not mention what we would call manual labor. However, the figure of the noble writer, sacrificing his physical well-being to the creation of new ideas, was a powerful argument for the moral value of labor. In 1834, the hygienist Joseph-Henri Reveillé-Parise (1782–1852) wrote a treatise on *The Physiology and Hygiene of Men Devoted to the Labors of the Mind* (*Physiologie et hygiène des hommes livrés aux travaux de l'esprit*), where he "portrayed intellectuals as living in a state of mental intensity that was both devastating and sublime: although it overwhelmed their nerves and depleted their material bodies, it was also the motor of civilization and social progress."[25] Reveillé-Parise was awarded the distinguished Montyon Prize for the work, and it was reprinted several times through the end of the century, attesting to its popularity. Long before the dictionary would codify such a shift, then, the scientific community had begun to consider intellectual labor a morally and materially productive undertaking, and an activity to be valued. By process of analogy, a new appreciation for manual labor was not far off.

That the "right to work" became a political objective during the February Revolution was something of a surprise to many, even those who had already shown support for the idea. In 1844, for example, the poet-turned-statesman Lamartine had waxed poetic about the "right to work," equating it with the "right to live."[26] He was celebrated as a champion of the workingman, but, soon after the Revolution was declared a success, he found himself brushed aside by workers impatient with his speechmaking. In a memorable scene recounted by the historian Georges Duveau, on February 25, just one day after the king had abdicated and the Republic had been declared, a crowd of workers invaded the proceedings of the Provisional Government: "An armed delegation presented themselves, led by a worker named Marche, who demanded the immediate recognition of the right to work. Lamartine began to make a speech, but he was interrupted by Marche: 'Enough patience, the people are waiting.... They have sacrificed three months of misery for the sake of the Republic.'"[27] Each detail in the historian's somewhat theatrical account gives us insight into the dramatic atmosphere of the early days of the Second Republic. The setting of the event—a government building, taken over by force, and now occupied by the loose coalition of the mostly inexperienced politicians who made up the Provisional Government—reveals the chaotic tenor of the situation and the high stakes of failure. The actors on the scene, despite their shared support of the Revolution, are presented as adversaries: the delegation of workers, led by Marche on the one hand, and the self-appointed governors, many of whom were writers, on the other.[28] The dynamic of their exchange (the workers threaten, the celebrity poet is silenced), points to the fragility of the worker-writer relationship that was thought to have been formed. Indeed, although there would be much talk of cooperation and solidarity between bourgeois *littérateurs* and working-class militants, Duveau indicates that, from the start, this apparent unity was tinged with moments of intimidation and coercion, supporting his "Lyrical Illusion" theory of the event.

Beyond providing evidence for a more nuanced understanding of the relationship between workers and writers in 1848, however, Duveau's account also shows us how central the *droit au travail* was to the revolutionary project of the workers. Before the right to vote was even mentioned (universal suffrage was not even discussed until March 2), the people were demanding the right to work. In their declaration of the *droit au travail*, composed immediately after Marche and the other workers had stormed the meeting of the Provisional Government, Louis Blanc and his Leftist allies promised to "guarantee the worker's livelihood by his labor," "guarantee work to all workers," and "recognize that all workers must be able to associate among themselves in order to benefit from the fruit of their labor."[29] Unsurprisingly, as it came from the author of *Organisation du travail*, Blanc's declaration was sweeping and comprehensive, promising good wages, abundant work opportunities, and, of course, the right to association. Even as late as June 20, two weeks after the conservatives had prevailed over the radicals in a second round of parliamentary elections, the government was still speaking about the right to work in its most positive and forceful sense: "The right to work is that every man has a right to live by working. Society must provide work to able-bodied men who cannot obtain it otherwise, with all productive and general means available to it and those that will later be organized."[30] This first draft of the Constitution, which included language that affirmed the right to work, was read by the president of the Assemblée Armand Marrast on June 20, 1848, just two days before the National Guard (no longer sympathetic to the populist cause) would ruthlessly squash another workers' rebellion, a bloody show of government force known as the June Days. This strange disconnect between the government's words and its actions can help us understand that, while the "fears of the consequences of the implementation" of right-to-work policies were widespread, there was nonetheless a certain "agreement on principles" as to the value of the *droit au travail*.[31] In other words, there was no lack of support for the right to work as an ideal, but its impracticality as the basis of government policy was too severe to overcome.

Travail as Production

Such widespread agreement that labor should be recognized socially and perhaps even politically should not be surprising. After all, labor was the source of all production, and productivity was the catchword of the day. Indeed, politicians, philosophers, and social observers from across the ideological spectrum held up production as the key to bringing France into the modern world. Liberal scientists, for example, thought that economic output (production) might be used as empirical data to assess the well-being of society, an otherwise tricky measurement to take. In 1830, the liberal medical doctor and *enquêteur* René Villermé compared mortality rates in different Parisian neighborhoods in order to prove that "productive" wealth was statistically linked to lower mortality rates than "unproductive" wealth (he was less enthusiastic about the other conclusion that could be pulled from his research, namely that poverty was statistically linked to high mortality).[32] He and other members of the future Académie des sciences morales et politiques (reinstated in 1832) adhered to what Michelle Perrot has called an "industrial mentality," that is, a worldview in favor of progressive policies that cultivate the twinned values of economic growth and public morality.[33] According to this worldview, which we might call "moral productivism," the creation of new goods and ideas was held up as the life force that would allow a society not only to exist but also to grow and progress. Increasingly detached from its biblical and Classical connotations, then, labor was associated with what it could bring to society, rather than by how much suffering it caused the individual.

The historian Anson Rabinbach rightly defined productivism as "the belief that human society and nature are linked by the primacy and identity of all productive activity, whether of laborers, of machines, or of natural forces," but his focus on scientific discourses has led him to locate the phenomenon later in the century than I do.[34] For Rabinbach, the productivist worldview was the result of a series of scientific discoveries of the mid-nineteenth century (and in particular the formulation of the Second Law of Thermodynamics in the 1850s) that reached its height in the second half of the nineteenth century. My analysis does not assume that political ideas rely on scientific discourse, allowing me to focus on the popular interpretations of what it meant to be productive in July Monarchy France. In this context, productivism refers to the belief that the future of the nation depended on its ability to increase production, and I will show that this political and economic paradigm was already the object of much interest and often a source of anxiety in the literary world decades earlier. Literary authors (that is, writers who use both narrative and specifically literary techniques such as imagery and character to express a theme) recognized that a new barometer for understanding social and economic value had emerged, and their participation in the productivist discourse of the period helped to shape the social, economic, and cultural changes that led to the Revolution of 1848.

Among the most influential promoters of a moral-productivist worldview was Henri Saint-Simon. Having observed the events of the French Revolution of 1789 and its aftermath firsthand, Saint-Simon was convinced that it was time to usher in a new era. In order for French society to rebuild itself after the necessary but devastating revolutionary period, he argued, an entirely new social system would have to be erected. In this new society, industry and, more fundamentally, productivity would be valued above all else. Those who work to "produce useful or agreeable things," he writes in 1817, are the only "legitimate members" of society. These producers, he continues, must be protected from "the activities of idlers [*fainéants*]."[35] Saint-Simon's imagining of a society-wide conflict of workers versus idlers would become an important reference point for the budding labor movement.

Saint-Simon's writings remained largely obscure until 1819, when he wrote a short text elaborating on his definition of what it meant to be productive. In this so-called "parable" (it was republished as *La Parabole de Saint-Simon* by his disciple Olinde Rodrigue in 1832), the author communicates a simple moral message: those who produce are good, those who merely consume are bad. The narrative is largely composed of a series of lists: first, he enumerates those members of society whom he considers "*Producteurs*" and imagines the ruin that the country would face were they to disappear. Then, he makes a list of the "*Oisifs*," or idle members of society, singling out the members of the royal family by name, an insolence that earned him a trip to the *cour d'assise* for insulting the crown and subverting social order.

It is notable that in his *Parabole*, Saint-Simon's list of those "Frenchmen who are most essentially productive" includes not only artisans, factory owners, and doctors, but also sculptors, musicians, and a group he calls *littérateurs*.[36] "*Littérateur*" was a vague term that referred to anyone who "made" literature, including not only novelists and poets, but also editors and publicists. The Enlightenment philosopher Voltaire had insisted upon the distinction between the inspired genius of the poet and the scholarly knowledge of the *littérateur*, but the two types of creative process became one and the same for Saint-Simon.³⁷ This indiscriminate mixing of the different understandings of literature, as well the inclusion of the commercial aspects of publication into the domain of the literary, would prove problematic later on. However, for the early followers of Saint-Simon, the idea that literary creation and production should be seen as integral parts of the productivist economy was as natural as it was novel. The idea was formalized in an essay titled *Aux artistes* (1830), written by a professor of rhetoric named Emile Barrault. The piece depicts a harmonious relationship between literature and social reform. In a coming era of synthesis, states Barrault, "the true and the beautiful will be reconciled [and] ... poetry will be the sublime expression of these two universes reconciled."³⁸ Perhaps unwittingly, Saint-Simon and his followers were setting the stage for the revolutionary moment of 1848, when so many novelists, poets, and journalists took up the cause of the workers' movement.

Despite the notable participation of so many literary figures, the events of 1848 were far from "lyrical," and, as Marx and other critics have convincingly argued, their presence may have done more harm than good to the political cause of the workers. Nevertheless, they were there: speaking at banquets, publishing articles, giving financial support to worker-poets, and even occupying the seats of power. The aim of this book, therefore, is not to determine whether or not the revolution itself was literary. To answer in the affirmative, as Marx does, does a disservice both to the revolutionary movement (by dismissing it as some sort of imaginary romance) and to literature itself (by judging it according to its ability to effect political change). To answer in the negative is to ignore historical facts. Instead, I am interested in understanding how the practices of reading and writing literature were so crucial to its coming about. How is it that literature— a form of culture that today has been relegated to the classroom and, occasionally, the Sunday newspaper—played such an outsized role in a historical event that was above all social, political, and economic? What role did literature play in disseminating the idea of labor as a value and a political right to be claimed *through* revolution?

To answer the fundamental question of this book—that is, how literature led to a revolution that was not *only* literary but also economic, social, and political—a series of other questions must be addressed: What did early fictional representations of the worker say about popular conceptions of the working classes? How did liberal reformers and socialist utopians alike come up with the same figure of the idealized worker as the hero and the future of society? What led artisans to believe that they would achieve better working conditions through writing poetry? How did serial novels like Eugène Sue's *Mystères de Paris* (*The Mysteries of Paris*) come to be read as pleas for social reform despite their authors' ambiguous personal politics? And how did all of these developments translate into a truly popular social movement, as workers and writers joined together briefly to defend the "right to work"? By 1848, it seems, a paradigmatic shift had already taken place (*pace* Barthes) in the way the relationship between society and literature was viewed. Influenced by the Romantic emphasis on the emotions and the liberal focus on productivity and material comfort, a belief that the individual's imagination and his or her emotional life were just as important as physical and economic well-being had emerged, particularly among those who worked with their hands and with their pens.

This monograph is divided into six parts, five chapters plus an epilogue, each of which focuses on a particular element in the evolution of the complex relationships being formed, deformed, and reformed between those members of society who considered themselves workers and those who considered themselves writers. The book is therefore structured in a way that is largely chronological, but not strictly so. In chapter 1, I provide a general history of the period under discussion, linking the Revolutions of 1830 and 1848, and discussing some of the major social, economic, and cultural realities that would influence the writers under consideration. In chapter 2, I focus on attempts by the novelist Honoré de Balzac to establish, early in his career, a literary labor theory of value that would prove, once and for all, the economic value of literary creation. Drawing on his knowledge of physics and economics, and relying on analogies between physical, artistic, and intellectual types of effort, Balzac makes a scientific claim to the productive value of literature that will serve as a foundational paradigm for worker-writer solidarity.

In chapters 3 and 4, I turn my attention to the narratives of the relationship between literature and labor that come to the forefront during the years 1839–41, a period when authors of a variety of political stripes sought to paint the working classes as the creative force of a new society. In chapter 3, the focus is on bourgeois attempts to construct a working-class hero, carried out not only by socialist novelists like George Sand and Etienne Cabet, but also by liberal social reformers like René Villermé and his colleagues at the Académie des sciences morales et politiques. In chapter 4, we look at the various narratives crafted by the workers themselves, laborers who wished to participate in the literary, political, and economic discourses of their day without giving up their identities as laborers. The narratives examined in chapters 3 and 4 share many ideals: each of them attempts to celebrate the unique talents and perspectives of the French worker, all bring focus to the productive values these workers bring to society, and all reveal a desire to establish some form of cross-class solidarity between bourgeois and working-class members of society.

In chapter 5, I take stock of the relationship between literary and manual labor on the eve of the workers' Revolution of 1848 through the lens of the *roman-feuilleton*, the French serial novel, a new fixture in the media landscape. In the works discussed here, the market-savvy *feuilletonistes* Eugène Sue and Honoré de Balzac use heartbreaking depictions of the suffering laborer to develop compelling characters and establish themselves as able novelists, but they also present manual labor as incapable of producing economic value. In the Epilogue, I return to the events of the 1848 Revolution in order to examine how the literary nature of the Revolution was expressed by those living through it. The toppling of the monarchy had indeed been a joint effort by *littérateurs* and manual laborers alike, and, for a few months, at least, there was a belief that their interests could be aligned: the new society would accord literary creation the same social value as manual labor while granting the manual laborer access to the emotional and imaginative experience of producing and consuming literature.

Each of the works analyzed in this monograph used literary techniques that helped to establish a new definition of *travail*, or labor, over the course of the 1830s and 1840s. Balzac—the physiologist of modern French life—was one of the first authors to attempt a definition of modern labor as an integral part of the postrevolutionary society. Focusing on the mysterious nature of work-energy that functions as a form of currency, more meaningful than gold, Balzac's allegorical and panoramic texts served as a preliminary gesture toward a modern understanding of *travail*. Soon after, bourgeois writers like Sand, Cabet, and Villermé would define labor—carried out dutifully and intelligently—as the marker of the modern nobility, the foundation for the new elite of democratic society. Simultaneously, the worker-poets and contributors to the worker press would try to define labor as a purely physical activity, relegating literary production to a type of spiritual activity, just as *feuilletonistes* like Sue and Balzac sought to portray their own literary labor as the only type of effort that is valuable. By 1848, then, the act of defining *travail* had become a collective undertaking, carried out not only by bourgeois academics, politicians, and journalists, but also by poets, novelists, women, and workers, in short, by a wide variety of social actors who dared to take their ideas to print, despite a perilous media environment. The interaction of their diverse approaches to writing about labor transformed the still-unstable signifier, *travail*, from a negative force to a positive one. No longer did the workers—whoever they were—submit to labor as an obligation or duty. Now they would claim it as a right.

To show where writing was unable to impose a much-desired equivalence between producing ideas and producing objects, I pay close attention to the various aporia that appear in different stages of the defining process. If the complexity of literary language could be a fertile source of inspiration for political change, as it was in the successful toppling of Louis-Philippe, it would also prove to be a point of weakness in the construction of a new society. Literature, with its evocative images and figurative language, was both necessary to the workers' republic of 1848 and predictive of its swift collapse.

In the end, I hope to bring new insight to the processes by which an unlikely "group" of writers helped to forge a narrative of worker-writer solidarity that ultimately led to the fall of the last French monarch and the establishment of the country's Second Republic. I use scare quotes here to indicate that the members of this so-called "group" did not consider themselves as such. Espousing different (and, at times, opposing) political views, coming from diverse social backgrounds, and occupying distinct positions in the media landscape, few, if any, of the authors discussed in the pages that follow were seeking outright political revolt. Nonetheless, their use of literary techniques (such as narrative, metaphor, character, allegory, and symbolism) to construct a social definition of *travail* that included literary production would ultimately become the basis for a popular—and successful in its own right—revolution.

1

Between Two Revolutions

On February 22, 1848, after nearly two decades of watching labor conditions deteriorate and their hopes for political representation disappear, French workers took to the streets. Exasperated by years of economic stagnation, social tensions, and increasingly repressive political policies, republican leaders had begun organizing boisterous political rallies attended by huge crowds of students and workers calling for electoral reform. When, on February 21, the government decided to ban these *banquets* (as the rallies were called), this was the final straw. The organizers called for calm, but it was too late—the crowds were angry.[1] The demonstrations grew in size and intensity, and on February 24, the king abdicated, and a provisional government was quickly assembled.

Much as they had done in 1792, the protesters in 1848 demanded a republic. The precise form that it would take, however, was to be determined. The Provisional Government was composed of eleven members who worked in apparent unity, as each resolution they passed was signed by all eleven names. However, such public unanimity belied an important ideological split within the group. Most of the members were economic liberals, who represented a strain of thought held by older, more conservative politicians, known as *les républicains de la veille* (meaning, quite literally, yesterday's republicans). They saw their mission as a political and economic one: to reestablish order until elections could be held and a constitution ratified. The more socially radical members of the council would be called the *républicains du lendemain* (tomorrow's republicans, referring to their progressive ideals). In addition to political and economic reforms, they pushed for sweeping social changes including new labor protections. These latter were in the minority, but they held considerable influence as the representatives of the will of the revolutionary crowd.[2]

A new political cause took center stage in 1848. In addition to the familiar calls for liberty, equality, and fraternity, the people now demanded *"le droit au travail!"* or the right to work. Many of the protesters from the working classes believed that the new republic could not be conceived separately from this right, and they were determined not to let their new leaders forget the power they held. In his *Recollections*, Alexis de Tocqueville recalls being struck by the truly "popular" nature of the February Revolution, remarking "the complete power it conferred on the people ... who work with their hands."[3] When the armed delegation led by Marche invaded the proceedings of the Provisional Government on February 25, for example, they silenced the loquacious Lamartine, and demanded firmly "labor organization, the right to work, within the hour [*dans une heure*]!"[4] The intervention was effective. Louis Blanc and Louis Garnier-Pagès immediately set to work on their "Declaration of the *droit au travail*," and, later that day, it was released, promising, among other things, to "assure the worker's existence through labor."[5] For about a month and a half, it looked like the government would keep its promise and that a new workers' republic would be formed.

Indeed, the weeks that followed the February Revolution were characterized by a perceived sense of unity among the working classes and across other social divides. In April, the Saint-Simonian feminist newspaper *La Voix des femmes* declared: "[We] have only to show ourselves to be gentle yet incisive, and we will be heard; our message will be repeated like a joyful melody."[6] The statement sends a strikingly different message from the one found in an earlier feminist periodical, *La Femme libre* (1832–34), where the editor intones that woman has always been "a submissive slave or a rebellious slave, but never free," urging all women to break free of their yokes.[7] Instead, the editors of *La Voix des femmes* express confidence in a new era of progress and cooperation between men and women. The sense of social cohesion that inspired such hope for gender equality also seemed to make cross-class solidarity possible. A powerful motor in this perception was the so-called the Luxembourg Commission (named after the Luxembourg Palace where its members met) established by the Provisional Government on February 28. This de facto ministry of labor was something of a workers' parliament, whose elected members came from dozens of trades. Although each corporate group tended to act in its own interest, there was also an understanding that the shared task of improving labor conditions more generally united them all.[8] Composed of 231 masters and 699 laborers working together to propose new labor laws, the Luxembourg Commission was a symbol of cooperation across different classes.

There was also a special concern for cultivating solidarity between workers and writers, a partnership that was symbolized by the appearance of the elite poet Alphonse de Lamartine and an otherwise unknown machinist named Albert Martin as equal partners on the Provisional Government during the first days of the revolution. The inclusion of these two figures at the head of the new political order—each embodying one part of the government's plan for social harmony and productivity—was significant. Lamartine, a giant of the Romantic movement thanks to his poetry collections, which had attracted a wide readership in the early 1820s, was an obvious figurehead for the Provisional Government's goal of promoting cross-class unity. Beloved by readers across the social spectrum, Lamartine was an excellent orator and was able to formulate the ambitious ideas of the new republic in terms that were both moving and understandable to all.[9] Albert Martin, who was relatively unknown and signed his name on official documents simply as "Albert, the worker," served a different purpose on the government commission. Albert was an active member of several secret societies, and his presence reassured *le peuple* that their demands would be met. For a few months, the Albert-Lamartine duo seemed to signify that bourgeois writers and manual laborers, having finally realized their shared dream to topple the old order, were working hand in hand to establish a republic where all labor would be respected and recognized for its true worth.

How did labor become such a critical issue in 1848? From a sociohistorical point of view, the mid-nineteenth century was a time of great economic transformation in France. By many measures, industrialization was a bit slower to catch on in France than was the case for its closest neighbor and rival, Britain, and there was a popular belief that France needed to catch up. In 1815, for example, Britain was producing eighteen times more coal than France (16.2 million tons versus 0.9 million), and, even as late as 1840, France's railroads had only reached a meager 497 km, dwarfed by Britain's 2,390 km.[10] Despite these numbers, however, France was indeed industrializing throughout the nineteenth century, especially thanks to institutional encouragement of technological advances spearheaded by Napoleon and Jean-Antoine Chaptal, his minister of the interior from 1800 to 1804, described by one historian as "the father of the nineteenth-century French economy."[11] Disadvantaged by the interconnected problems of political instability, revolutionary wars, population stagnation, and crippling debt,

France nonetheless continued to grow economically and industrially (albeit at a slower pace) thanks to its remarkable scientific and technological innovations. When Louis-Philippe came to the throne in 1830, he and the ruling political party known as the Doctrinaires were able to set up policies that quickly generated industrial progress. Between 1840 and 1880, France had increased its railroad mileage by 500 percent (from roughly 500 km to about 25,000 km), surpassing England's 23,089 km.[12]

Artists and authors attempted to represent these changes in technology and to imagine what consequences they may have for the human experience. In 1836, for example, the Romantic painter Théodore Chassériau released a small watercolor entitled *Une forge au Creusot* (The forge at Le Creusot). This painting captures a liminal moment in the history of French industrialization under the July Monarchy. At a time when French industry was at the very beginning of its progression toward modern automation, Chassériau focuses on the male laborers in his work. There is a great deal of emphasis on their corporality: their muscles are clearly outlined, and their working bodies drive the movement of the scene. At the same time, there are already ominous signs of a coming age of dehumanization: the large wheel looming in the background is a reminder of the silent but powerful force of technology, and the protective visors worn by the some of the workers cover their faces, stripping these characters of any individuality or *personality*. These laborers are portrayed as deindividualized and dehumanized cogs in the machine.

The painting is full of phantasmagoric figures in the process of disappearing. Three of the four unmasked men in the painting are out of focus. A bare-chested boy sitting in the painting's center and several other workers in the background are pale and indistinct. Compared with the bold strokes of the three principal workers, these men appear ghostly, inhabitants of a past reality who, it seems, have not yet realized that their era is gone. The shirtless young man is especially ethereal, as he appears to float in some indeterminate space, impervious to the heat of the melted metal and barely casting a shadow. There is one figure whose face can be seen clearly, but, leaning against the wall, he is not at work. The scene, with its faceless and ghostly workers, captures the problem of *le travail* in the July Monarchy. No longer simply a question of using one's bodily force to create something, labor is now inseparable from the ability to work with and like machines. The painting is at once a testament to man's heroic ability to labor and a foreshadowing of the dehumanization that will accompany modern industrialization.

Théodore Chassériau, *Le Forge au Creusot*, 1836. (Photo © RMN-Grand Palais/Art Resource, NY)

Chassériau's choice of setting was significant. Since the Middle Ages, Le Creusot had been the site of one of France's few coalmines and had been transformed into a small-scale metalworking company in the late eighteenth century. In 1836, it was purchased by the industrialist brothers Adolphe and Eugène Schneider, who began modernizing the factory.[13] Benefitting from the new demand for iron and steel for the construction of the railroads, the company grew rapidly, and by the end of the century it was one of the largest factories on the European continent. Between 1830 and 1866, the town's population grew from 1,300 inhabitants to 23,000.[14] Chassériau could not predict in 1836 the future financial success nor the extent of technological advances that would come to Le Creusot, but he did seem to have a visionary understanding of where factory work was heading. His painting is therefore both representative of its own present and strikingly prophetic of a coming age of machines.

The fact that Chassériau chose to depict such a scene is one example of how artists, like literary writers, were anticipating a reality that had not yet come into existence. Indeed, as modest as it was, the industrial modernity of Le Creusot was quite atypical of mid-nineteenth-century France. While factory towns, engulfed in clouds of smoke, had taken over Britain's landscape by the 1820s, these were still rare in France. Nor was there the widespread displacement of artisans that was taking place on the other side of the Channel. Where factories did go up (primarily in the north and the east), numbers of artisans also increased, as they provided necessary commodities to the inhabitants of the newly constructed towns. In fact, with the exception of the textile industries, the replacement of artisanal work by large-scale manufacturing was negligible during the July Monarchy. Increased productivity was achieved in other ways, the most harmful to workers being the practices of putting-out or sweating (*confection*) and subcontracting labor (*marchandage*). *Confection* was the practice of dividing up labor tasks (piecework) to create standardized products more cheaply and efficiently than made-to-order ones. Put simply, it was less costly to pay twelve unskilled workers to perform one step each in a twelve-step manufacturing process 100 times than to pay one master-artisan to perform all twelve steps 100 times. *Marchandage* was the practice of wage bargaining, where entrepreneurs would subcontract only those laborers who were willing to work at the lowest rate. Both practices had the consequences of deskilling labor and pushing down wages.[15]

The burst of working-class unity that erupted onto the streets in 1848 was slow to form, and, for much of the July Monarchy, a working-class identity did not exist as such. There were several explanations for this. Not all artisans shared the same experiences of impoverishment caused by industrialization, nor did they necessarily see themselves as having common interests, as a deeply embedded belief held that there was a hierarchy of professions. The practices of *confection* and *marchandage* had affected different sectors of the economy unequally. Press workers were largely untouched, while shoemakers and tailors were hit hard. This unevenness, combined with the fact that workers' unions tended to be organized by profession, meant that workers in the unaffected trades saw themselves as having little in common with those who were suffering from deskilling. These latter, finding themselves with plenty of "forced leisure time," and the "intellectual freedom" of mindless tasks, were most likely to engage in politics.[16] Thus, the majority of workers urging worker solidarity across professions came from the select sectors that were feeling the worst effects of French industrialization.

Another important rift impeding social and class solidary were changes in the roles of women in working-class families. Liberal political economists like Jean-Baptiste Say had been arguing that, in a postrevolutionary society, women should be excluded from the workforce in order to maintain order and morality in the home, the family being the foundational unit of a stable society. This "male breadwinner model" was meant to exclude women from the workforce, but, especially in industrial settings, working-class families were becoming increasingly reliant on the wages earned by women.[17] Indeed, although women had always been essential to the functioning of the urban economy (running boarding houses, working as laundresses and hawkers, in addition to domestic labor performed in their own homes or in others'), this labor was unaccounted for in official reports. However, as the factory system replaced the traditional family household economy (characterized by the sharing of labor tasks within the family unit) with the industrial family wage economy (where each member sought employment outside of the home), women's work became more visible, as mothers, wives, daughters, and sisters were expected to earn wages from outside employers.[18] In particular, thanks to the deskilling practices of *confection* and *marchandage*, an enterprising clothing seller could send piecework to an unskilled woman worker who would be paid less than a male tailor. Male artisans, who blamed their financial distress on those whose willingness to accept lower pay was driving down all wages, began to see women as a threat. The conflict came to a head in 1848, when, emboldened by the successes of the February Revolution, men began demanding a return to the values of the Old Regime guild system, a primarily male form of corporatism (although some women-only guilds had existed) where skill and craftsmanship were protected and guaranteed high wages; women simultaneously called for their low-skill work to be legitimized through better pay.[19] In light of these disputes, the cross-gender solidarity expressed by the Saint-Simonian women in *La Voix des femmes* is all the more notable.

The Revolution of 1830

Lacking any substantive sense of class cohesion, French workers turned to literature as a powerful and inclusive revolutionary force. Lamartine's accession to power in 1848 was indicative of the outsized role that literature had played in political and social discourse throughout the July Monarchy. Literature's importance had already been established in July 1830, when printworkers—the literal laborers of literature—were critical actors in the overthrow of the last of the Bourbon monarchs. On July 26 of that year, Charles X's prime minister Jules de Polignac had proclaimed a new series of press laws, enforcing a harsh regime of censorship that spelled the end of many of the country's newspapers, especially those of the liberal opposition such as *Le Constitutionnel*.[20] These extremely popular papers would have had to lay off hundreds of employers. When the print workers, already suffering an economic recession, realized what this would mean for their trade, they began to organize protests, convincing other workers to strike with them. After three days of popular uprising known as the Trois Glorieuses, which saw republican students and bourgeois liberals take the side of the workers, the Bourbon dynasty was finally toppled. Louis-Philippe, a cousin of Charles X, was installed on the throne as a constitutional monarch and has been called "the first monarch to be created by the press."[21]

Despite his strict aristocratic upbringing and values, Louis-Philippe came to be known as the "Citizen King," or the "Bourgeois King," because of his association with the bourgeois majority who had finally prevailed at the close of the Trois Glorieuses.[22] His mandate was far from solid, however, as he had been placed into power as the result of a great deal of negotiation. Crucial to this victory had been a public endorsement by a group of republican leaders with the marquis de Lafayette at their head, promising the adoring crowds "a government which will owe its existence to you; morality belongs to every class; every class has the same rights; these rights are guaranteed!"[23] Workers understandably took this to mean that labor conditions would improve. Such a promise became increasingly difficult to keep, however, once the threat of absolutism was eradicated, and the differences between the liberal and republican factions who had formed the bourgeois coalition that brought Louis-Philippe to power came to the fore when order was restored. In the press industry, for instance, the calls from typesetters and other printworkers (aligned with radical republicans) for better pay and more humane working conditions ran up against moves by editors and newspaper owners (whose economic interests were more liberal) to cut costs and increase profits. Still, there was a widespread belief that the workers should be rewarded in some way. In a letter to the minister of the interior, François Guizot, a well-known bookseller named Pierre-François Ladvocat urged the new government to recognize its debt to the press workers: "All five thousand press-workers of the city of Paris spread out and instigated demonstrations all around the town, forming the central contingent which grew until it came to engulf the entirety of the working classes of the capital. These are the services they have given us, and the results are such that it is impossible for the government to forget them."²⁴ Ladvocat himself would also owe the workers a great deal. The following year, thanks to the more liberal press laws passed by the new government, he was able to publish the first volume of his successful series, *Paris; ou, Le Livre des cent-et-un* (1831–34), a sprawling collection of typologies and short sketches of Parisian life from dozens of contributors including Honoré de Balzac, Paul de Kock, and even Victor Hugo. This "editorial adventure" made a splash on the literary scene, becoming "a book that was impossible to ignore."²⁵ Ladvocat's support of the working-class protesters and his strong links to writers and critics helped to reinforce the idea that an ever-growing kinship between physical laborers and literary authors was blossoming under the July Monarchy.

Ladvocat was not the only literary figure to promote a narrative of worker-writer unity forged by the printers in the early days of the July Monarchy. The role of the press workers (and other laborers) was immortalized in Etienne Arago's vaudeville *27, 28 et 29 juillet, tableau épisodique des trois journées*, first performed on August 17, 1830, just about two weeks after the *Trois Glorieuses*. The heroism of the printers formed the subject of a catchy song:

> Nay, nay arm in arm;
> The printer's press
> Is limitless
> Nay, nay, arm in arm
> Censors cannot do you harm.²⁶

The play portrayed the extraordinary actions of revolutionary workingmen—a cooper, a printworker, a baker, and other characters described as *hommes du people* and *ouvriers*—fighting side-by-side with National Guardsmen and even an English tourist, won over by the righteous fervor of the crowd. A cowardly *rentier*—or someone who lives off his capital gains rather than working—is found hiding in a barrel. His name, Caffardin (similar to *cafard*, or cockroach), solidifies our negative impressions of such a figure. Using simple and memorable musical numbers and thanks to the general popularity of the vaudeville at the time, Arago (brother of François, astronomer and future member of the Provisional Government) made all the right choices to ensure that his tale of working-class heroism would electrify the popular imagination. The piece was an instant hit: the text was soon published as a small book by J. N. Barba and later that year in an issue of a literary subscription service.[27] Arago continued his message of worker-writer solidarity in an article intitled "La République et les artistes" (1834), where he argued for the engaged, didactic mission of art as a way to organize the working classes, and in 1847 he gave a well-publicized toast to "The people's art and their literature."[28] Indeed, throughout the July Monarchy, Arago was convinced of the power of literature to effect social and political change.

A belief that July Monarchy society would show its gratitude to the working classes was reinforced by the iconography of the July 1830 moment; a slew of inexpensive publications featuring stories and images representing the recent events in heroic fashion appeared almost immediately. These popular souvenirs emphasized the harmony among different social classes working together in the name of freedom. The motif of interclass solidarity can be found, for example, in the frontispiece to a popular children's book called *Les Enfants de Paris; ou, Les Petits Patriotes* (1831).[29] The artist depicts a trio of children dressed as major figures in the Revolution—a worker, a bourgeois, and an engineering student—standing arm-in-arm in front of the tricolor flag, embodying the type of equality that society was supposed to be enjoying. This type of "pictorial metaphor for the success of the July Revolution," as one art historian has observed, showed that "the victory of the barricades belonged to everyone: Napoleonic veterans, Polytechnicians, workers, and bourgeois youth fraternally share the triumph."[30] Such images were disseminated widely and sent a powerful message: that the role working-class men and women had played in the toppling of the Bourbon dynasty was to be celebrated and would not be forgotten.

Unfortunately, the interclass solidarity portrayed in works like Arago's vaudeville and *Les Enfants de Paris* proved more aspirational than real. For economic and political reasons, Louis-Philippe's government quickly began passing laws that ran counter to working-class and republican interests, sparking unrest in Paris and throughout the kingdom. Fed up with what they saw as unkept promises, republican rebels diverted the funeral procession of the republican hero General Jean Maximillien Lamarque and built barricades through the center of the city in June 1832 (an event that, decades later, provides the climax to Victor Hugo's *Les Misérables*). Two years later, in April 1834, another popular uprising saw barricades go up throughout the capital, culminating in the infamous events of the rue Transnonain, where numerous civilians, including women and children, were killed by government soldiers. Combined with the silk workers' uprisings in Lyon (in 1831 and again in 1834), as well as numerous attempts on the lives of the king and his family members, these events, thought to be motivated by seditious and provocative newspaper articles, resulted in growing fears of another revolution, and led Louis-Philippe to reinstate harsh press restrictions—called the September Laws—in 1835. Now, literary works that were critical of the regime—even in a satirical or mocking way—found themselves constrained by censorship and taxes, forcing them underground along with the many secret societies forming at the time, such as Auguste Blanqui's Société des amis du peuple and the Société des droits de l'homme.

The relative calm imposed by the September Laws lasted until late 1839, often seen as a turning point in the July Monarchy. Armand Cuvillier has called 1840 "one of the most curious periods [*une des periodes les plus curieuses*]" in the history of social and economic doctrines.[31] At this moment, the question at the tip of everyone's tongue seemed to be the problem of *travail*, or labor. In 1839, after several years of "quietly ruminating" "the ideas of exploitation, of association, and of the fecundity of labor," workers began to undertake acts of rebellion, starting with the uprising of the Société des Saisons in May, followed by a wave of general strikes.[32] That same year, Louis Blanc released a pamphlet that would become his best-selling manifesto, *Organisation du travail*, and the worker-run paper *La Ruche populaire* began circulating. The following year, two utopian tales celebrating the working-class hero—George Sand's *Compagnon du Tour de France* and Cabet's *Voyage en Icarie*—captured the popular imagination, and Joseph-Pierre Proudhon published his essay "What Is Property?" hailing labor as the only legitimate source of wealth. The repressive practices of Louis Philippe's government were therefore fruitful for literature-labor solidarity, as workers and writers found themselves in common cause against the forces of order. This sense of solidarity would grow over the course of the 1840s, culminating in the events of February 1848.

The Rise of the Bourgeoisie and the Productivist Worldview

Looking back from a post-1848 perspective, it is tempting to view the Revolution of 1848 as simply one more episode in a long progression of what Marx and Engels called (that same year) "the history of class struggles."[33] In a Marxist reading, the calls for the *droit au travail* must be seen as the war cry of the proletariat (those who own nothing but their own labor) against the bourgeoisie (those who own property or capital). However, this class-based interpretation ignores the complexities of French society and its economy during the first half of the nineteenth century. As mentioned above, France had not, in 1848, completely shifted to an industrial economy, and many artisans owned their own shops or at least their own tools (the means of production, in Marxist parlance), so a single worker could consider himself an *ouvrier*, a *travailleur*, and a bourgeois depending on the context. Indeed, the 1820s, 1830s, and 1840s represent a period when a variety of social actors espoused the bourgeois value system of industriousness and productivity. Not only did the ruling Doctrinaires try to appeal to "the middle classes," but the king himself walked to work carrying an umbrella, that emblematic scepter of the bourgeoisie.[34]

What did it mean to identify as bourgeois during the reign of Louis-Philippe? It is perhaps easiest to begin with what it did *not* mean. The bourgeoisie was not a coherent political party, nor did it designate those coming from a particular social milieu. Even within a single bourgeois family, beliefs could differ widely, as in the case of the radical republican Auguste Blanqui and his brother Adolphe, a liberal political economist. In theory, the bourgeois was neither working class nor aristocratic, and yet he could have close connections to both worlds. Many socialist thinkers of the period who attracted a working-class following, including Charles Fourier, Etienne Cabet, and Louis Blanc, came from bourgeois backgrounds. Henri (de Rouvey de) Saint-Simon, born into one of the most illustrious aristocratic families of the Old Regime, inspired a radical working-class movement, but he was also the author of one of the central tenets of bourgeois thought: the belief that the new elite of society could no longer be one of birth but of enterprise. Saint-Simon's ideas were the result of his experiences. Renouncing his title during the Revolution of 1789 in order to assume the working-class name Claude Bonhomme, he later went to work in a printer's shop before focusing his attention on publishing his own writings as pamphlets and periodicals.[35] In 1815, Saint-Simon, who now identified as a bourgeois, lamented the lack of any unified political program among the members of his class, and he urged the bourgeoisie to see themselves as a party, defined by their opposition to the policies of the monarchical government, newly returned to power under the Restoration.[36] His ideas shifted over time, however, and, if, in 1815, he identified his fellow bourgeois as "proprietors of national domains [*propriétaires des domaines nationaux*]," he would later prefer the term "industrialist." Saint-Simon's pointed distinction between those who lived off their *rentes*—or interest on land and other capital possessions—and those who worked for a living was indicative of the bourgeois values of hard work and productivity. During this period, then, and despite Saint-Simon's early writings, being bourgeois was more about these shared social values than any one particular political or economic program.

Indeed, a value that we may positively define as "bourgeois" was support for developing industry, a term that implies both labor (individual effort) and productivity (economic output). This industrialism was one facet of a more general worldview that I have called productivism, the belief that the future of France depended on its ability to increase output. The liberal political economist Jean Baptiste Say, for example, largely agreed with the labor theories of value proposed by British thinkers Adam Smith and David Ricardo. Significantly, however, he felt that the term "labor [*travail*]" should be replaced with "industry [*industrie*]" in order to specify that only certain *kinds* of work—what he calls "productive labors [*travaux productifs*]"—actually create (or produce) value. In his commentary on Ricardo's *Principles of Political Economy*, Say writes: "Productive labors [*travaux productifs*] are those of the scientist, who studies the laws of nature, of the entrepreneur who applies them to the needs of man, and of the worker who executes the manual labor prescribed by the two others. The word 'labor [*travail*]' imperfectly expresses all of these operations, some of which are the result of the apex of human intelligence. It is therefore fitting to give the name 'industry [*industrie*]' to the ensemble of these activities."[37] Another liberal thinker, the mathematician-turned-politician Charles Dupin, set out to establish a taxonomic understanding of labor in a work appropriately titled *Forces productives* (1827). Beginning with the "evaluation and cataloging" of different types of productive forces (natural, industrial, animal, human, physical, intellectual, and so on), Dupin concludes with a brief description of the "productive and commercial forces" of France, organized by *département*.

Productivism was embraced by a wide variety of social thinkers across the political spectrum, but there were important differences in the ways they imagined making this happen. For liberals like Say, production would increase when the individual was allowed to work in his own interest; for socialists like Saint-Simon, this would come about through better work organization and association among workers. On both sides, these theorists understood that for such society-wide changes to take place, they would need to bring a variety of people over to their way of thinking: not only lawmakers, but also business owners and, perhaps most importantly, the workers themselves. Say's *Catechism of Political Economy* (1815) and Saint-Simon's *Nouveau Christianisme* (1825), as well as Charles Dupin's *Petit Producteur français* (1827) were each written with the intention of winning over and instructing workers. A recurring practice among these authors was the encouragement of personal savings banks, mutual aid societies, and other forms of self-help among the working classes.[38]

An important factor in the emergence of a bourgeois identity was the growing influence of the Doctrinaires in political, scientific, and moralist institutions in the 1820s and 1830s. This generation of thinkers, represented by François Guizot in government and Victor Cousin in the halls of education, aimed for influence over both moral and material concerns, with the ultimate goal of putting an end, finally, to the drawn-out instability of the revolutionary period that had begun in 1789. They envisioned a new kind of aristocracy, not of birth but of what they called *capacité*, or the exceptional ability to blend intellect with action. Guizot and his fellow Doctrinaires argued that the country needed to be guided by an elite group of men who were able to embody an "alliance between intellectual activity and practical skill ... moving beyond the antagonism between action and reflection."[39] This marriage of practical materiality and the world of ideas was also a central feature of Victor Cousin's eclecticism. Cousin was reacting against the sensationalism of postrevolutionary empiricists like Etienne Bonnot de Condillac who, frightened by the powerful role that they believed the imagination had played in spurring on the excesses of the Revolution and the Terror, attempted to rein in the power of the imagination by limiting what could be considered our knowledge of the real to that which could be physically experienced. Reacting against such stark materialism, Cousin argued for a more spiritual conception of truth.[40] Both Guizot and Cousin developed for a more nuanced worldview than what had dominated French society throughout the revolutionary era, one that could incorporate reason and morality, pragmatism and ideals.

As part of their liberal ideology, the Doctrinaires preached a gospel of economic development and individual prosperity, and the nation was indeed enjoying remarkable industrial and commercial growth. Guizot captured the spirit of the times in March 1843 when he famously urged his countrymen to "*enrichissez-vous!* [enrich yourselves!]." This phrase, which was part of a larger appeal for incremental change, was soon taken out of context, and was seen to encapsulate just how out of touch the government was from the concerns of everyday people. The full sentence, published in *Le Moniteur universel*, March 2, 1843, reads: "For now, use these rights [that your fathers have bequeathed you]; establish your government, strengthen your institutions, enlighten yourselves, enrich yourselves, improve the moral and material condition of our nation." The nuance of the message, however, was lost in its popular interpretation, which the journalist Eugène de Mirecourt summed up in the following way: "[Guizot] meant that fortune alone is what earns you the respect of the world; what good is all the rest? A sack of gold is everything, honor cannot be counted. How much does a vote cost? I am ready to pay. What price do you put on your devotion? I will buy it. Enrich yourselves! Enrich yourselves!"[41] Thus, while Guizot's text encouraged social progress on a variety of fronts, many members of the public heard it as a glorification of unbridled materialism.

This unfortunate statement soon became a catchphrase for the July Monarchy's economic policy, an unrealistic assessment of the situation to workers who saw their purchasing power diminished and whose lived experience did not match up with the prosperity that was being described and prescribed. It was around this time that working-class writers, especially poets, began to publish prolifically in books and periodicals, including worker-run newspapers such as *La Ruche populaire* (1839–49) and *L'Atelier* (1840–50). Although they were of various political and social belief systems, nearly all these publications expressed a common theme: that workers were not being recognized for the important role they had played in France's incredible growth and that this was not just an economic problem but also a shortcoming in the moral and social order. Still, even these worker-run publications were not class purists. In 1841, the worker-poet Jules Vinçard even decided to hand over the direction of his newspaper to a "son of the bourgeoisie" in order to cultivate cooperation with more well-off allies.[42] The goal was not, then, to carve out a specific social identity separate from the bourgeois, but rather an attempt to claim a place for the worker among those actors who were considered productive.

The individuals and groups we have discussed so far held a variety of political beliefs but were united in a common notion that productivity should be the measure by which to determine success and that industry would be the key to progress and prosperity. Related to this was a quest for knowledge about the nature of manual labor, which was becoming an increasingly visible social phenomenon. No one who went about this task could deny the physical depletion that it caused, and yet, there was a deeply held belief that labor—in all its forms—was a moralizing force in society. The power of labor to effect these two actions at once—physical destruction and moral improvement—was a sign of its social complexity and its centrality to modern society. This tension also helped to bring the social question to the fore of public debate.

When properly managed, as the socialist Louis Blanc argued in his *Organisation du travail* (1840), labor could protect the working classes from the chaos and immoral influences of the competitive world. On the other end of the ideological spectrum, however, the threat of poverty in the context of free-market commerce was itself a powerful motivator for moral behavior. The liberal economist Charles Dunoyers held that the fear of failure, inspired by the spectacle of abject indigence, could act as a moralizing force: "It is good that there be in society places where families which behave badly may be exposed to falling and where they might rise only by dint of behaving well. Destitution is this fearsome hell. It is an inescapable abyss, placed next to madmen, squanderers, debauched individuals, and every sort of perverted man in order to contain them."[43] For Blanc, Dunoyers, and many others, the key to promoting moral order was work itself, but for many factory owners and other employers, the reverse was also true: in their eyes, morally disciplined laborers were more likely to be productive employees. Thus, throughout the nineteenth century, we see employers converting their economic power into moral influence through paternalist actions, forcing their employees to obey certain rules in order to keep their jobs.[44] As industrialization became increasingly visible and as its importance to the well-being of the nation was widely accepted, thinkers of a wide variety of political stripes and social backgrounds agreed that it was imperative to promote the fundamentally salutary nature of work.

Even the most rationalistic of thinkers had begun to include a moralist element to their logic. The mathematician Charles Dupin, for example, had long argued that empirical methods and "data" should be used to study and promote economic development in France, a method that he puts to work in his encyclopedic *Forces productives* (1827). Still, even Dupin includes an "Avant-Propos" where he makes a moral plea to those who he calls *"les notables de l'industrie."* "[You] who come to the capital to deploy the *treasures* of your ingenious creations, bring us some *treasures* that are even more *precious:* bring us proof of the *gifts* that you have spread among the working class in order to make them more *enlightened,* more *moral,* and more *religious.* . . . Show us how you benefit the lowly laborer, whose *sweat* prepares your *opulence*" (emphasis added).[45] Here Dupin downplays the purely economic value of industry to proclaim a loftier goal: the improvement of society writ large. Speaking of "treasures," "opulence," and "gifts" rather than money or charity, Dupin projects a noble image of industry that, paired with the possibility of a beatified working class (*éclairée*, *morale*, and *religieuse*), appeals to his readers' higher aesthetic sensibilities. Indeed, the language and the powerful images that he creates are decidedly literary in quality.

The Role of Literature

Dupin's appeal to the imagination and the affect to argue for social change was not unusual, and throughout the July Monarchy, there was a widespread belief among readers and writers that literature had the ability to act as a force (both negative and positive) in society. This view went hand in hand with a promotion of artistic creation and industrial production as equally important types of labor that Saint-Simon had laid out in his "Parable."[46] By counting poets and other *littérateurs* among the most productive and useful members of society—alongside bricklayers, bakers, and shoemakers—Saint-Simon had helped to establish literary writing as a form of constructive labor that helps to create the world.

Readers of *romans-feuilletons* (serial novels appearing in the cheap daily papers) were especially convinced of the demiurgic powers of literature, often using the insights gained from reading their favorite serials to better understand their own lives. It was easy to place themselves in the shoes of a particular character or imagine that they were interacting with another, treating "fictional texts as useful instruments for revealing the reality of their social experience."[47] Another literary innovation that seemed to be especially world-building was what Walter Benjamin would later call "panoramic literature." The name points to what Benjamin saw as similarities between a kind of panoramic/dioramic art installation that had sprung up in public spaces in the early nineteenth century and the literary trend that took hold soon after. Panoramic literature took the modern city experience as its object, with special attention to bourgeois social spaces, from the Bourse to the Bois de Boulogne. This type of literature, says Benjamin, is "socially panoramic," meaning that all levels of society are represented, even if most are confined to the background.[48] The origins of this admittedly nebulous genre can be traced at least back to Louis-Sébastien Mercier's *Tableau de Paris* (1788), but it was in the 1830s and 1840s that production of panoramic literature exploded. These works were published with the specific purposes of "explaining certain social codes ... that had to be deciphered in order to allow new parts of the bourgeoisie to find their place [in society]."⁴⁹ Thanks in part to new technologies in printing and papermaking, as well as to more sophisticated distribution methods, they attracted a large readership, and writers and publishers of panoramas found themselves with plenty of work to do.⁵⁰ In both inexpensive forms, like the *physiologies* (a pseudoscientific genre of literature that used humor and satire to define social types) and in more ornate bound volumes, like Ladvocat's *Cent-et-un* and a similar collection called *LesFrançais peints par eux-mêmes*, the demand for panoramic works was virtually insatiable.⁵¹ In a different type of *physiologie*, the hygienist Joseph-Henri Reveillé-Parise studied the effects of intellectual and artistic labor upon the body (*Physiologie et hygiène des hommes de livres aux travaux de l'esprit*, 1834), and the praise he received for this work was a sign that, at least within academic and institutional circles, the Romantic figure of the inspired genius was on its way out, and the ideal of the hardworking intellectual was in. Indeed, there was a growing consensus that good writing was no longer the purview of the secluded poet (à la Alfred de Vigny's *Chatterton*), but the result of hard work, craftsmanship, and social engagement, and that the effects of writing—its ability to create the world—were real and tangible.

These factors combined to lead many July Monarchy novelists to view their work as a useful art, with all the positive and negative connotations that go along with such utility. In the productivist zeitgeist of the first half of the nineteenth century, professional writers had a vested interest in promoting the ideal of literature as a form of *travail*. As we have already seen, Balzac was describing his creative efforts in 1834 as a form of labor, no less difficult and no less important than that of the baker who kneads dough for bread.⁵² In 1838, he and a group of rival writers (including his nemesis Alexandre Dumas) worked together to found the first European writers' union, the Société des gens de lettres, which still exists today. George Sand also painted herself as a worker, comparing her own literary efforts to the backbreaking but wholesome labor of the farmer, referring to her toils as a form of digging (*piocher*).⁵³ Victor Hugo was so emphatic about the laboriousness of composing poetry that he became the butt of joke, in 1842, when the poet-turned-journalist Edmond Texier took him as one of the models for his satirical *Physiologie du poète*. Here, Hugo is portrayed as a godlike but ridiculous idealist named "Olympio," depicted (by the famous caricaturist Daumier) with lines of effort pulsing from his prominent head to convey the herculean nature of his intellectual efforts.[54] Alexandre Dumas became so adept at pumping out melodramas and serial novels, says Marc Angenot, that, although his literary works were *"besogneuses"* or mediocre (the English loses its closeness to the noun *"besogne"* or hard labor), this lack of quality was made up for in quantity, and "His kindest critics ... admired his incredible rapidity, a sort of physical endurance."[55] Dumas would embrace this identity so fully that his campaign platform in 1848 (like many authors, he ran for office in the early days of the Second Republic) focused almost exclusively on presenting himself as a manufacturer of literary products and as a job-creator for bookbinders, printers, and actors.

Simultaneously, books, poems, and newspapers written by manual laborers became a growing presence in the publishing landscape. From skilled artisans like Jules Vinçard, to simple shoemakers like Savinien Lapointe, to self-described *prolétaires* like Flora Tristan, workers saw themselves as legitimate contributors to the literary field. For some time, there was even something of a sense of community among working-class and bourgeois writers. For instance, Victor Hugo supported worker-poets like Gabriel Gauny and Savinien Lapointe; Eugène Sue used his platform as a best-selling novelist to publicize issues of labor organization; and George Sand cultivated friendships with working-class writers like the mason Charles Poncy and the carpenter Agricol Perdiguier. She even went so far as to attribute to the carpenter-protagonist of *Le Compagnon du Tour de France* (1840) "a love for his profession which he understood *as an artist*" (emphasis added).[56] As working-class men and women saw themselves accepted as poets and intellectuals, and as professional writers were pointing up the laboriousness of their creative efforts, a sort of alliance could be seen to form between laborers and *littérateurs*.

Simultaneously, there was a great deal of anxiety surrounding what was seen as a growing similarity between literary efforts and manual labor. The journalist Gustave Planche sardonically wrote in 1832 that, "thanks to a strange application of Adam Smith's theory," literature was now divided into two distinct types: art and industry. While the former was far superior to the latter, he complained, it was only the industrial side of literature that ever reached an audience.[57] In reaction to this industrialization of literature, the Romantic novelist and critic Théophile Gautier wrote a manifesto, arguing for an immediate stop to the constant parallels being drawn between literary and manual labor. Writing in 1834, the very same year that Balzac called on his fellow writers to see themselves as bakers,

Gautier's disdain for such comparisons is palpable: "No, fools, no, cretins and goitrous creatures that you are, a book does not make gelatin soup;— a novel is not a pair of seamless boots; a sonnet is not a syringe with a continuous stream; a drama is not a railroad,—all essentially civilizing things and tending to assist humanity along the pathway of progress."[58] In the same text, Gautier coined the phrase "Art for Art's Sake" as the antidote to the vogue for "useful" literature and refuted head-on the literature-as-labor metaphor. He had little patience for those who would try to make literature into a practical or useful activity, and he was not alone. With the invention of the cheap newspaper that relied on the inclusion of the *roman-feuilleton* in order to subsidize printing costs (namely, Emile de Girardin's *La Presse* and Armand Dutacq's *Le Siècle*, both appearing in 1836), the debate surrounding the emergence of industrial or commercial literature occupied both countless pages in the press and hours of discussions in the chambers of parliament.[59]

Even those who profited from literature's growing commercial success could not ignore the deteriorating working conditions of writers. With the disappearance of arts patronage and the rise of the cheap newspaper, as well as a growing literate population, market forces were conspiring to change the nature of literary production. These were indeed "the origins of the modern mass-media marketplace."[60] Authors were being asked to write more quickly and for less compensation than ever before. To make a living, a journalist had to practice what Sainte-Beuve, in 1839, disdainfully christened "Industrial Literature," or the production of enormous quantities of texts, suitable for mass consumption. Even Emile de Girardin—whose need for a constant supply of *romans-feuilletons* meant that he, perhaps more than any other single person, benefited from the cheapness of literary labor—disapproved of the literary laborer's lifestyle. In 1834 he is recorded as saying: "A great many young men, victims of a university education, are recruited by the weekly and daily papers and the commercial booksellers, and, out of desperation and necessity, they must turn their own bile into a sort of daily bread, their pen into a shotgun."[61] For Girardin, the starving journalist was the victim of his own literary pretentions, nourished by his education; if he was poorly paid, this was simply a question of supply and demand: too many workers for too few jobs. This devaluing of the profession also changed the way many writers thought of their place in the world, a disenchantment that Balzac experienced himself and that he fictionalizes in *Illusions perdues* (1837–43). In this cynical depiction of the Parisian publishing industry and the authors, editors, and speculators who make it run, the reader follows the downward trajectory of Lucien de Rubempré, an idealistic, if naïve, poet from the countryside, who, over the course of the narrative, will give up all his moral and artistic standards in order to succeed in the cutthroat literary market of Restoration Paris. By the end, he has managed to understand and, indeed, dominate this media landscape, but he has been hardened in the process. Rubempré's story warns us of the moral pitfalls of comparing literary and manual labor too closely. Thus, while a shared sense of proletarianization brought some workers and writers together, literary critics and authors who sought to distance literary creation from the deskilled labor of the factory worker or unemployed artisan questioned this solidarity from the outset.

Nonetheless, the paradigm of literature as a useful political and economic activity would only grow stronger as the July Monarchy progressed. During this period, the trends of the literary market seemed to encourage an ever-growing solidarity between the worlds of labor and literature. As cultural shifts such as the rise of inexpensive newspapers and increased literacy rates helped expand readership, there emerged a very inclusive understanding of what types of writing could be considered literary. According to one critic, in the mid-nineteenth century, the word *littérature* had no less than three meanings, each one referring to a different cultural context: one institutional, another philosophical, and the third experiential.[62] In the first place, literature was seen as an art, a continuation of the estheticizing tradition of belles-lettres, a torch that was carried mainly by the proponents of *L'Art pour l'Art* or the Art for Art's Sake movement, such as Théophile Gautier. In a more modern philosophical sense, literature was understood as a way of expressing ideas, in the tradition of Enlightenment novelists like Madame de Staël and Voltaire who used fiction (among other genres) to address themselves to their "readers' intelligence." This allowed nonfiction writers like the historian Jules Michelet and the philosopher Auguste Comte to consider themselves literary writers, even though modernist and formalist definitions of literature would exclude them from the literary canon. Finally, literature was defined as a form of distraction, where any type of writing that gave pleasure and entertainment was considered literature, such as the best-selling sentimental works from the early part of the century by writers like Claire de Duras and popular theatrical productions such as Félix Pyat's miserablist dramas and Etienne Arago's vaudevilles.

This very expansive and amorphous understanding of the literary was conducive to a sense of shared culture among different sectors of society.

If works as diverse as Victor Hugo's Romantic poetry collection *Orientales* (1829), Jules Michelet's *Histoire de la Révolution française* (1847–53), and Félix Pyat's popular melodrama *Les Deux Serruriers* (1841) were all to be considered literature, then the acts of reading and writing literature were pastimes in which nearly everyone, it seemed, could participate. Authors were not required to hold a particular poetic formation or expertise, and they could touch on all manner of subjects, adopting a variety of styles. Not only could writers from diverse backgrounds and with a range of aims consider themselves *littérateurs*, but, because of the broadening of literary topics, many different social groups could now recognize themselves as characters on the pages they were reading. Literature, then, was everywhere, becoming an increasingly important channel by which cultural norms were circulated in the nineteenth century.

A major factor in the rise of literature's power in July Monarchy France was a considerable growth in literacy rates. In Paris, the stonemason Martin Nadaud recalls being asked to read the newspaper out loud to his fellow *compagnons*, indicating that even urban artisans (ostensibly more educated than rural or factory workers) were largely illiterate in the 1830s. However, the number of workers who could read and/or write was growing quickly. The Guizot Law of 1833 guaranteed elementary education to all French males, and the nationwide survey of primary school teachers that had inspired the law showed "evidence of a new age approaching . . . [an] upsurge of that social demand for education which was to transform the school itself."[63] It is not surprising, then, that during the years between 1831 to 1841, overall literacy across the nation increased by 21 percent and then again by 18 percent between 1841 and 1851.[64]

Another important development was the growing popularity of pleasure reading among the working classes and peasants. Teaching the *peuple* to read and write had been an essential component of the revolutionary project since the late eighteenth century, but most social thinkers of the time had a very specific type of reading in mind for the masses. Novels, poetry, and satire were considered unhealthy reading material because, as the Enlightenment philosopher Nicolas de Condorcet wrote in his *Troisième Mémoire sur l'instruction publique* (1791), their many allusions and stylistic devices made them unintelligible to the rural reader. Instead, useful and instructive books, like anatomy manuals or patriotic histories, or moralizing works like Benjamin Franklin's *Poor Richard's Almanac*, were to be encouraged.[65] Throughout the nineteenth century, politicians and elites continued to take an interest in what the lower classes were reading: under the Restoration, the Catholic Church began establishing libraries where readers of modest means could spend a few hours looking at Church-sanctioned *bons livres* (good books) that had been deemed morally appropriate. Under the July Monarchy, liberals like François Delessert, Emile de Girardin, and Eugène Buret promoted readings that would also teach the growing industrial working classes the basics of political economy, including some form of a labor theory of value.

Some figures in the publishing industry, including the journalist Louis de Cormenin and the editor Léon Curmer, argued that working-class readers should be able to read for pleasure. Such a radical position was perhaps somewhat self-interested, since they stood to benefit financially from a broader working-class reading public.[66] As the editor Alexandre Pigoreau remarked in 1823, "We have to publish popular novels, if I dare say so, because the people want to read novels: you need them for the artisan in his workshop, the little seamstress in her humble garret, the mending woman in her cask; you need novels for small-minded people and new editions of the Philosophers for small landowners."[67] Indeed, despite all the discussion about providing good reading material to a growing literate public, the publishing industry was driven primarily by the need to make a profit. Editors chose which works to print based not on their social or moral value but on their potential to sell.

Access to reading material was also quite dependent on market forces: the purchase of books was prohibitively expensive for all but the very wealthy, and the Church's libraries of *bon livres* were few and far between. Instead, the majority of working-class and petit-bourgeois readers consumed literary texts in *cabinets de lecture* or reading rooms. These renting libraries allowed clients of modest means to read the latest bestsellers and even newspapers without having to spend the money to purchase their own copies. Suzanne Voilquin, for example, an embroiderer and founder of France's first working-class women's newspaper, *La Tribune des femmes*, refers to the novels borrowed from her local *cabinet de lecture* as the primary source of her childhood education.[68]

Although they were open to readers of all social stripes, the *cabinets de lecture* were clearly part of the bourgeois sphere. Under the Restoration (1814–30), only those working-class readers who had direct contact with upper-class patrons or employers tended to frequent reading rooms.[69] In the 1830s and 1840s, workers and artisans began to see them as spaces for cultivating interclass relationships and business opportunities. In a letter to Eugène Sue, for example, a down-on-her-luck seamstress with two young children asks the author for money to open her own *cabinet de lecture*, framing it as a win-win situation: she will become a respectable businesswoman while Sue will find new audiences.[70] M.-J. Brisset's two-volume novel, *Le Cabinet de lecture* (1843), imagined the types of interactions that would take place when different social characters—a grisette, a bourgeois, and an apple vendor—come together in a single *cabinet*. Despite this atmosphere of social *mixité*—or perhaps because of it—the reading room remained a space of bourgeois sensibility. The type of reading that is associated with the emergence of a working-class identity, reading that is not mediated by bourgeois surveillance, did not take place in the *cabinets* but at the workplace or the local watering holes, where literate workers would read newspapers aloud to their colleagues.[71] When Martin Nadaud read Etienne Cabet's communist paper *Le Populaire* to his fellow workers in 1834, this took place "in the wine merchant's backroom."[72]

Changes to the press were also crucial to the growing influence of literature. Since 1836, when the inexpensive dailies *La Presse* and *Le Siècle* began to include *romans-feuilletons* as feature of each issue, the reading of literature on a daily basis became a widespread practice. These fictions were symbolically separated from the informational part of the newspaper with a thick black line, but both spaces were essential. The gesture was significant, as it indicated a new way of conceiving literature both as a regular part of everyday life, and as a way of understanding the world that was just as important as to the political, economic, and social discourse that populated the rest of the paper. Emile de Girardin, the founder of *La Presse*, was explicit about his intention to promote the *homme de lettres* (the man of letters) as the conscience of the nation, essentially erasing the difference between the journalist and the literary author.[73]

In short, literature, broadly understood, was becoming one of the most important means by which cultural "norms" were constructed and circulated in the nineteenth century. This had both positive and negative effects: on the one hand, literary writing was highly valued by a large portion of the population; on the other hand, literary writers began to feel as though they were being proletarianized, asked to work tirelessly for little pay. It is not surprising, then, that literary authors should be deeply involved in the construction of a new understanding of labor that became the rallying cry for political change.

Illusion and Disillusion

Within the context outlined above, it is unsurprising that so many literary figures supported the Revolution of 1848 and took on leadership roles in the early days of the Second Republic. An inclusive and expansive definition of literary writing that could include Romantic poetry, philosophical novels, historical treaties, raunchy vaudevilles, and even journalistic articles inspired many authors of various stripes to see themselves as an important force in social and political affairs. Simultaneously, the application of a productivist/industrialist paradigm to the literary field led authors to claim that they were being proletarianized, an anxiety that they had in common with artisans and low-skilled workers whose livelihoods were threatened by automation and growing competition. Finally, a blurring of the lines between fact and fiction in the daily newspapers and a growing literate population to read those newspapers made it easier than ever to propagate radical socialist politics as literature. In fact, while historians and other commentators (Proudhon, Marx, Duveau, etc.) have criticized the Revolution for its theatrical or "lyrical" qualities, the cultural context from which it arose would not have allowed it to be any other way. But does this mean that the Revolution was useless? Does the literary tenor of much of the political discourse surrounding the uprising automatically disqualify it from being taken seriously? Was the desire for change really nothing but an "illusion"?

Several moves by the Provisional Government in the early days of the Second Republic did seem to indicate that the new government would be social and egalitarian in nature and that the working classes would be playing an active role in it. On February 28, for example, Louis Blanc, one of the few socialist republicans (*républicains du lendemain*) on the Provisional Government, was appointed to head the Luxembourg Commission. The group met in the Palais de Luxembourg, the former home of *la chambre de pairs*, the upper house of parliament. This was a symbolic choice, intended to signal that the old order had been replaced by a new one. Two days later, the government declared universal suffrage, meaning that all male citizens, regardless of wealth or property-ownership, would participate in choosing the individuals who would draft the new constitution. If the size and fervor of the revolutionary crowds was any indication of how the majority of Frenchmen would vote, this seemed to favor a socialist state.

However, things did not turn out the way that the *républicains du lendemain* had hoped. The Luxembourg Commission, for example, resulted in few real policy changes. Although it brought workers from all different trades together under the overarching political ideal of labor organization, many of the debates that took place there merely served to heighten the differences between individual strains of socialist thought.[74] Each industry maintained its own distinct corporate identity. Printworkers still did not see themselves as having much in common with shoemakers. When it came time to propose a list of working-class candidates for the April elections (a second round of elections would be held in June), each trade wanted its own representative, making it impossible to rally the working classes behind a single group. Nor did the policy of universal suffrage favor the radical Left. While the urban workers who had staged the revolution in the capital were in favor of sweeping social changes, their rural counterparts—who far outnumbered them—were more conservative. When elections were finally held on April 23, and then again on June 4, the socialists found themselves in the minority of the 900-member Constituent Assembly, which included many liberals and even a number of monarchists.[75]

Perhaps the most telling sign that the workers' republic would not last was the failure of the *ateliers nationaux* (national workshops). These work programs, established in the Paris region on March 6, were based loosely on a plan proposed by Louis Blanc. For nearly a decade, Blanc had been arguing that the only way to combat the evils of competition without harming productivity would be to establish associative workshops for each industry. These *ateliers sociaux* (social workshops), as he called them, would be financed initially by the state, but directed by the workers themselves, who would be able to make the best decisions for efficient production and profitability. Blanc's plan had been widely praised among workers, and the pamphlet where he sets out these details, *L'Organisation du travail*, first published in 1839, was so popular that it was already in its fifth printing in 1847. Whether or not Blanc's *social* workshops were feasible remains unknown, however, for the program that was finally implemented, the *national* workshops, strayed greatly from his ideals.

In contrast to Blanc's proposal of a system based on association and working-class empowerment, the national workshops, directed by an engineer named Emile Thomas, were divided into militaristic regiments. Unemployed workers, regardless of trade, were ordered to complete large public works projects, and as a result, a skilled artisan like a bookbinder or a jewel cutter might find himself carrying out the brute work of digging ditches or paving roads.[76] The pay, at 2 francs per day, was better than regular unemployment benefits, and thanks to these high wages, and because the ateliers were established in Paris alone, the capital was soon overrun with *chômeurs* (unemployed workers) from across the country. The economic crisis caused by the political unrest worsened, and the numbers of *chômeurs* increased, so that Thomas was unable to provide work to everyone. A satirical newspaper titled *Potatoes by the Bushel* would later describe the *ateliers* as "a philanthropic establishment without a whit of work to offer charged with finding employment for a hundred thousand men without any either."[77] By the end of March, the program was running out of money and political support was waning. Thomas lowered the pay to 1.50 francs per day, and work was no longer required to receive it. Many of the unemployed workers spent their days milling about on the streets. Bored and increasingly dissatisfied, these workers were the target of much political propaganda from secret societies and other Leftist groups. Starting in May, they began to gather on the boulevards, discussing politics and frightening bourgeois inhabitants. It is perhaps not surprising that one of the first actions taken by the newly elected Constituent Assembly on June 21 was to close down the ateliers, requiring that workers either enroll in the military or begin working with the Corps of Bridges and Roads (Ecole des ponts and chaussées). The suppression of the ateliers, as imperfect as they may have been, marked the end of any hope for a workers' republic. The working classes—now thoroughly politicized and organized, thanks to the Luxembourg Commission and to the military-style organization of the ateliers—erected barriers and took up arms. On June 24, martial law was enacted, and by the 26th, General Louis-Eugène Cavaignac had managed to squash the uprising using violent means.[78]

The Right to Work

In the aftermath of the June Days, the members of the Constituent Assembly began asking themselves what the workers had in mind when they demanded the right to work in February 1848. This question became the subject of much discussion both in the halls of parliament and in the writings of public figures. The newspaper editor Emile de Girardin, for example, promoted a pragmatic argument for granting laborers better working conditions, without going so far as to guarantee labor for all.[79] For the liberal political economist Joseph Garnier, however, the "*droit au travail*" had to be taken literally, but defined quite differently, as the right to assistance, which, for him, would have to be strictly limited in scope.[80] In the end, the constitution that was finally adopted on November 4 was closely aligned with Garnier's assessment, promising aid only to those "who are unable to work and who do not have family who can support them."[81] In the final analysis, then, the right to work was determined to be the right to assistance, perhaps best understood as a form of unemployment insurance. This assumption was already apparent in the way the *ateliers nationaux* had been set up, but the formalization of this interpretation into law was another step away from the workers' socialist ideals.

By the end of 1848, accounts of the workers' revolution were presented as little more than a hollow joke. The satirist mentioned above who had so harshly dismissed the *ateliers* had a similar opinion of the revolutionary project writ large. Taking on the persona of a streetwise potato merchant, he concludes that the Republic was little more than vessel for producing hot air, good for heating up food, but not much else. "Believe me," he writes, "you too should be crying out 'Long live the Republic!' It might be the only way you'll be able to cook the potatoes I'm selling."[82] How was the Revolution of 1848 transformed from an exuberant celebration of worker-writer unity into the scene of a bloody massacre and, ultimately, into a bitter joke? How were righteous calls for the "right to work" translated into a law guaranteeing the right to assistance? In the following chapters, I will trace how literature, the same force that allowed the *droit au travail* to emerge as a political ideal, was simultaneously undermining the possibility of its realization.

2

Balzac's Literary Labor Theory of Value

THE VERY same year that his "Lettre adressée aux écrivains" was published in the *Revue de Paris*, Honoré de Balzac's novella *La Fille aux yeux d'or* (1834–35) began to appear in another paper. The short work was published in three installments, but it reads as a bricolage of two separate pieces of writing, one defined by sociological observation, the other focused on plot and character development. The first chapter is presented as a panoramic sketch of the different levels of the French social hierarchy, from the grotesque working classes to the sterile decadence of the aristocracy. In contrast, chapters 2 and 3 delve into specific people and places, narrating the titillating tale of Henry de Marsay, a bored Franco-British aristocrat who falls in love with an exotic courtesan named Paquita. Because of his ample fortune and rationalist upbringing, Marsay is supposed to be immune to the desire for money or sex that drives the rest of French society, and yet it is the golden color of Paquita's eyes—evoking both pleasure and luxury—that he finds irresistible. The two engage in an intense tryst, involving role-play, cross-dressing, and real and simulated violence.

Marsay's erotic adventures, recounted in the second and third chapters of the novella, seem very far removed from the concerns of the typical working-class Parisian that form the bulk of Balzac's descriptions in chapter 1, but he insists that these worlds are part of the same social system: the capitalist system of exchange. Indeed, as the title indicates, *La Fille aux yeux d'or* is a story about money. This is not particularly surprising, as Balzac's fascination—if not obsession—with money is well known. One critic has identified money to be one of two Aristotelian

"Prime Movers" of the *Human Comedy*, and, together with love, she posits, they are "the motor that puts the whole narrative system into motion, that makes the spheres revolve, rotate, and orbit." Another has argued that capital, "whether termed gold or money or whatever constituted exchange value ... was the seminal idea that served as the nucleus of forces driving this rapidly changing society."[1]

As central as wealth and possessions were to the novelist's oeuvre, however, his interest in pecuniary matters was not exclusive. In a memorable passage from the first chapter of the novella, he writes: "And so a lifetime of *labours* brings profit to children whom this lower bourgeoisie tends inevitably to raise to the ranks of the upper bourgeoisie. Thus, each social sphere projects its *spawn* into the sphere immediately above it. The rich grocer's son becomes a notary, the timber merchant's son becomes a magistrate. Not a cog fails to fit into its groove and everything stimulates the upward march of *money*" (emphasis added).[2] In this passage, it is the "labours" of the lower classes that allow them to "fling their spawn" into the social spaces above them; it is labor that "stimulates the upward march of money," facilitating the flow of energy and social mobility. In short, while money was a problematic way of measuring value, Balzac believed that labor, as a form of energy, would prove to be a constant, productive, and scientific alternative.

A Scientific Understanding of Society

The opening chapter of *La Fille aux yeux d'or* (whence the above passage is taken) was first published under the title "Physionomies parisiennes." The title was quite meaningful; it signaled to his readers that Balzac intended to carry out a scientific study of the physical traits of Parisians in order to make a precise assessment of their moral makeup. In this way, he claimed to be taking part in one of the most pressing tasks of his generation: to establish a scientific way of studying society in postrevolutionary France. Now that the old system of orders, estates, and corporate bodies had been razed to the ground, it was imperative to establish a new and more rational way of conceiving the relationship between the individual and society. The *physionomie* was a type of popular para-scientific analysis, associated with the practices of *physiognomie*, *physiologie*, and even phrenology, that had its roots in empiricism, the revolutionary theory that experience in—and most importantly, observation of—the material world was the fundamental basis for all knowledge. Like many nineteenth-century adaptations of Enlightenment theories, however, these pseudosciences (as they are now called) also contained a clear moral element. Because of this, the *physionomie* and its ilk were quite controversial in Balzac's day, the subject of heated debates about the extent to which physical matter could give access to metaphysical truths. In 1820, for example, the famed French physician Louis-Jacques Moreau de la Sarthe had tried to put an end to the materialist direction he saw scientific discourse taking by editing a new translation of a work by the Swiss theologian Johann Kaspar Lavater, titled *Essays on Physiognomy: For the Promotion of the Knowledge and the Love of Mankind* (*Essai sur la physiognomie: Destiné à faire connaitre l'homme et à le faire aimer*), originally published in German in 1775. In his preface, Moreau de la Sarthe praises its author in the following way: "No foolhardy anatomist or physiologist, [Lavater] does not try to find the material or organic cause of the disposition. He limits himself to recognizing a sign and its effects."[3]

This praise of Lavater as a pious *physionomiste* was part of a critique mounted against the German physician Franz Joseph Gall, whom he refersto as a materialist *physiologist*. Gall's countless dissections of the human brain formed the basis for his theory that the moral and spiritual character of a person was determined by his or her organic makeup. Moreau de la Sarthe characterized Gall's attempts to understand "the secrets of the human soul" as atheistic and admired Lavater's humility before a divine power.[4] Despite Moreau de la Sarthe's objections, Gall's physiological approach would come to dominate the field, serving as the basis for phrenology, which, by the 1830s, had become a popular and scientifically accepted practice throughout Europe, especially in France.

The literary vogue for *physiologies* and *physionomies* was inspired by the scientific theories of the same names and would reach its height in the early to mid-nineteenth century. Unlike Moreau de la Sarthe, their literary practitioners did not seem to draw a stark distinction between the materialist emphasis of the one and the metaphysical focus of the other. For example, in both Jean Anthelme Brillat-Savarin's *Physiologie du goût; ou, Méditations de gastronomie transcendante* (*The Physiology of Taste; or, Meditations on Transcendent Gastronomy*) (1826), which does exactly what the second half of the title promises, and Balzac's own *Physiologie du marriage* (1829), a long treatise on the state of domestic life, these authors combined metaphysical reflections on the soul with observations of physical traits, rather than sticking to the latter, as the scientific *physiologie* would demand. The same is true of Balzac's "Physionomies parisiennes" cited above (1834). By the time the wildly successful *physiologies* format took off in the early 1840s, the practice of judging character through outward appearances had become a staple of popular literature.[5]

Another budding discipline that sought to study society scientifically was political economy. The liberal thinker Jean-Baptiste Say was a pioneer of the field in the French context. Having spent many of his formative years abroad, Say was greatly influenced by British political economists like Adam Smith and Thomas Malthus. He is best known for his extremely successful *Treatise on Political Economy* (1803), where he interpreted many of Smith's ideas for a French audience. Say was particularly intent upon promoting Smith's idea that "the quantity of every commodity brought to market *naturally* suits itself to the effectual demand" (emphasis added), popularly known as the invisible hand theory. Central to this theory was the imperative that each economic player (laborer, employer, and investor) should (and does) act strictly in his or her own interest, and that *by doing so* acts "in the interests of everyone else."[6] Smith considered this to be a scientific principle, a natural law that must be recognized in order for an economic system to function efficiently.

Say was equally convinced of the scientific validity of Smith's theory and viewed it as foundational to a liberal worldview, whereby the primacy of the individual was never subsumed to the demands of living in collectivity. Indeed, for him, the nation was nothing more than a *réunion des particuliers*, a meeting of individuals who come together for a common purpose but who are not changed in any way by their encounter. The symbiotic relationship between the wealth of individuals and that of society as a whole was emblematic of this worldview and established it as a morally just one. "Wealth for the individual," Say states, "is wealth for the nation, which is nothing more than an assembly of its individual members [*la réunion des particuliers*]; this is true in the eyes of the political economist, who must not try to reason according to any notion of *imaginary* value, but according to what each economic actor—that is, all economic actors—see as value; and this is determined not by their words but by their actions." Say, who would later write a *Catéchisme* (1815), a simplified version of his ideas for a working-class audience, was already, in 1803, intent upon establishing the credibility of his theory based on experience rather than abstract reasoning. Here, he appeals to the individual's lived reality in a way that links the work of the political economist to that of a naturalist. Nothing is hidden or opaque; the way that society works is evident and observable by anyone who takes the time to look. "And this is one more *proof* that there are not two kinds of truth in the study of political economy, more than in any other *science*. What is true for the individual, is true for the government, and for the community" (emphasis added).[7] Say's language shows his eagerness to establish political economy as a science, contrasting old-fashioned "imaginary" ways of studying society with the more objective "proof" that can be found in the "science" of political economy. He would even go so far as to critique Smith for failing to define his terms "in a satisfactory manner," and generally wishing that his Scottish predecessor had been more precise in his analysis of economic concepts.[8]

As scientific as he might try to be, Say's theories were influenced by his political leanings. Liberalism—which posits that individuals, making the best decisions for themselves, will inevitably and inadvertently make the best decisions for society as a whole—can only work under a government that allows individual freedoms. It is therefore not surprising that, soon after the publication of his *Treatise* in 1803, Say was forced from public life by the autocratic Napoleon Bonaparte. He reemerged as a leading voice in the liberal opposition under the Bourbon Restoration (1814–30), and he finally saw his theories put into action under the July Monarchy, when admirers of his ideas like Louis-Philippe and François Guizot came to power. These new leaders believed that attention to economic concerns would provide political stability and that liberal policies, by empowering individuals to create wealth for themselves, would bring prosperity to society as a whole. Even after his death, Say's followers continued his work, founding the *Journal des économistes* in 1841, seeking to spread the gospel of economic liberalism, which they considered to be "a guarantee of order and security" and "a bedrock in the social edifice."[9]

Liberalism was clearly the leading political philosophy of the July Monarchy, but there were other ways that theorists sought to harness the power of science to establish a new social order. In his influential work, *Physique sociale; ou, Essai sur le développement des facultés de l'homme* (1835), the Belgian statistician Adolphe Quetelet pushed back against the liberal emphasis on individual freedom and choice. In contrast to Say's view of the nation as "an assembly of individuals [*une réunion des particuliers*]," Quetelet came up with the idea of the *homme moyen*, the average man. The *homme moyen* was not any individual person but rather a snapshot of the general trends of the entire population. For the statistician, society could be best understood as a collective mass, characterized by generalities, rather than an alignment of individual interests. Quetelet and others like him considered the unique combination of physical and moral traits found in the individual person to be a mere accident, and therefore uninteresting for scientific study. The average of those qualities, however, could indicate a kind of natural law, founded on what Joshua Cole has termed "the power of large numbers."[10]

In contrast to the ambitions of Say, Quetelet, Reveillé-Parise, and others who sought to understand society and social groups using new scientific methods, most literary authors of the early days of the nineteenth century tended to shun entirely those topics that touched too directly on the concerns of everyday life, the average person, and society as a whole. Although many figures of the first generation of French Romantics like Benjamin Constant, Germaine de Staël, and René de Chateaubriand espoused firmly held political beliefs, they eschewed questions of labor, productivity, and a scientific way of understanding society in their literary works. Instead, they were focused on achieving the Platonic ideal of Beauty.[11] The productivist tenet that value was created through effort—and, indeed, the very idea that one could assess the value of art using objective or material measurements—was an anathema to the Romantic ideal of art as the expression of nature. In Madame de Staël's *Corinne; ou, L'Italie* (1807), for example, the heroine is asked to describe how she comes up with the beautiful poetic improvisations for which she is celebrated. She describes her talent as "a literary abundance, the generosity of nature" possessed by all Italians, even simple peasants. Portrayed as a gift—something that is received without being earned—Corinne sees her creative process as a passive one: "the pure breeze of the sky and sea acts upon the imagination like the wind upon an Aeolian harp, and that poetry, like a harmony, is the echo of nature."[12] Her response encapsulates the Romantic view of the artist not as a worker but as the instrument of some higher power. For Staël and the other writers of her generation, literary creation was not the result of effort, but of nature's generosity.

Even in the second wave of Romanticism (usually considered to begin in 1830, although, as Michael Brix has argued, the difference between the two Romanticisms is more aesthetic than chronological), which was much more in tune with social questions than the first generation had been, there was a reluctance to think of artistic creation in terms of objective or material value. Alfred de Vigny's *Chatterton* (1835), for example, illustrates that any attempt to measure artistic genius (namely through monetary earnings) is deadly to that genius. The concern with coming up with a scientific way of determining literary value seemed futile, if not nefarious. In other cases, questions of productivity and labor were simply ignored. In Stendhal's "Chronique de 1830" (the subtitle of *Le Rouge et le Noir*), for example, there is little attention to the social realities of production or labor of that year. A nail factory is mentioned at the story's beginning to represent Julien Sorel's petit-bourgeois origins, but this laborious heritage is not formative but rather *deformative*. Implicitly, it is an identity that he will attempt to erase by flirting with the priesthood and making love to the daughter of a marquis. For Stendhal, then, labor looms silently as an abstraction, a social condition that one must try to overcome, even if (as Sorel's story shows us) such an undertaking is impossible.

Unlike many of his contemporaries, however, the novelist Honoré de Balzac shows a fascination for economics throughout his career, in both his fictional and analytical writings. This passion is most apparent in his posthumously published 1848 "Lettre sur le travail," described by one historian as "a veritable course on political economy ... inspired by Ricardo, Adam Smith, and especially Mathus."[13] However, the author's interest in the subject dates back at least to one of his first published works, *La Physiologie du mariage* (1829). In this analytical text, inspired in part by Brillat-Savarin's *Physiologie du goût*, Balzac signals his ambition to study society scientifically by announcing his intention to take up "the question of the influence of the bed and the part it plays in the political economy of human life."[14] Science, however, is not without its faults in Balzac's eyes, and his opinion of political economy is ambivalent, at best. For him, it is both a harbinger of modernity and a corrupting force. This ambivalence is particularly striking in the novel *Eugénie Grandet* (1833), where the moral economy of the provinces and the political economy of Paris come into direct conflict. According to E. P. Thompson, the moral economy was "a popular consensus" about fair business practices "grounded upon a consistent traditional view of social norms and obligations of the proper economic functions of several parties within the community." Proponents of political economy, conversely, saw their system as being "disinfested of intrusive moral imperatives," which could impede the natural flow of supply and demand.[15]

Eugénie Grandet tells the story of the clashing of these economies. The title character, an innocent provincial girl, falls in love with her cousin Charles, freshly arrived from Paris. A young man of twenty-one, Charles is still generous and good-natured, but, as the narrator warns us, "the seeds of this baleful political economy had been sown in his heart" and "egoism had taken deep root in his nature."[16] True to form, he seduces

Eugénie in order to obtain a part of her wealth, only to leave her when a better opportunity comes along. Eugénie, an innocent victim of the greedy Parisian, vows never to love anyone again.

For Balzac, political economy was the science of the bourgeoisie, a people without art and incapable of seeing value in anything other than that which satisfies their most basic and immediate needs. In *The Quest of the Absolute* (*La Recherche de l'absolu*) (1834), for example, he depicts the Flemish people (a society that, in his mind, has fully embraced "the civic and bourgeois way of life") as both admirable in their simplicity and horrifying in their lack of imagination: "He sees only what is visible, his thought is bent so scrupulously towards fulfilling his basic needs that in no way does he think beyond the material world. The only understanding of the future that this people has is a sort of economy of politics, their revolutionary force comes from their domestic desires to eat heartily and relax under the awning of their *steedes*" (*CH* 10:660).[17] Despite their flaws, or perhaps because of them, Balzac was fascinated by the bourgeoisie, and especially by their displacement of the aristocracy at the apex of French society. On the one hand, he seemed to recognize them as the moral descendants of the Third Estate, who, despite having caused chaos by upending the social order of the Old Regime, had the merit of understanding hard work to be a virtue. This was the argument in favor of granting more political power to the productive members of society put forth by the Abbé Sieyès in 1789: "What kind of society is it where you *lose caste* if you work? Where to consume is honorable but to produce is vile? Where laborious occupations are called *base*? As if anything but vice could be base, and as if this baseness of vice, the only true one, could be found mostly among those who work!"[18] On the other hand, as the Marxist critic Pierre Barbéris has remarked, Balzac's bourgeoisie "draws its force from the progressive accumulation of capital through exchange or transformation. But, in Balzac, it is above all exchange."[19] In other words, he sees them as a class of hoarders who exploit others' labor to maximize their own profit. This could hardly be considered a compliment coming from a writer who struggled to receive fair compensation for his creations.

As the science of the bourgeoisie, it is no wonder that political economy inspired mixed feelings in Balzac. However, it is clear that in his early fictions and analytical texts the author expresses a genuine fascination for its goal of establishing a concrete and real system of value, and, more specifically, a labor theory of value. Although many of his best-known novels focused on the bourgeoisie's attempts to move out of the ranks of the working class and into the class of *rentiers,* Balzac was deeply interested in labor as a manifestation of energetic force and as the source of value.

The Science of Energy

Throughout his career, and in ways that evolved over time, Balzac looked to science as a model for understanding the world. As the mature author of the famous "Avant-Propos" to the *Human Comedy* (written in 1842, that is, thirteen years after *The Physiology of Marriage*), Balzac declares his plan to study society the way that scientists study nature, modeling himself after naturalists like the comte de Buffon, Georges Cuvier, and Geoffroy Saint-Hilaire, who had created encyclopedic classification systems of the animal kingdom. Even more ambitious than these naturalists, however, the Balzac of 1842 sets himself the mission of providing a taxonomy of human society by observing: "the habits, clothes, words, and dwellings of the prince, the banker, the artist, the bourgeois, the priest, and the pauper" (*CH* 1:9). In the "Avant-Propos," then, Balzac takes the position of a neutral observer, declaring himself the "secretary" of his own society who merely transcribes what he sees, all while affirming that this observation allows him to draw important conclusions about the way society works as a whole.

Just ten years earlier, however, Balzac was imagining his task as a scientist/novelist quite differently, more in keeping with Lavater's pious belief that some aspects of reality are undetectable to the physical senses. In several analytical and fictional texts written in the early 1830s, the author attempts to compose a unifying theory of the world that takes into account both observable and unobservable phenomena. A striking illustration of Balzac's desire to synthesize the physical and the metaphysical can be found in a scene taken from *The Wild Ass's Skin* (*La Peau de chagrin*) (1831). The protagonist, Raphael de Valentin, has come into the possession of a magic talisman, which grants him his every desire, yet, with each wish fulfilled, causes his body to become weaker. By the end of the novel, Valentin is fantastically rich but dying from an unexplainable illness. The three best doctors in Paris are called in to examine him but are unable to agree upon a definitive diagnosis. A fourth, Dr. Bianchon, sums up their different approaches in the following way: "[Dr.] Caméristus feels, [Dr.] Brisset examines, [Dr.] Maugredie doubts. Man is compounded, is he not, of a soul, a body, and a reasoning mind? In each individual, one or other of these three primary causes is predominant, and there will always be the human element in human sciences. Believe me, Raphael, we don't effect cures, we help cures on."[20]

By taking this synthetic approach, Bianchon expresses the young Balzac's own epistemology, whereby knowledge is reached through a combination of empirical science, reason, and blind faith. Indeed, many of his early works seem to alternate between scenes or passages that promote following the scientific method of limiting one's knowledge to observable phenomena and those that express a philosophical desire to understand the world as more than what it appears to be. There is both a tension between these opposing reflexes as well as an attempt to reconcile them. In this way, Balzac was very much a man of his time; the desire to find a harmonious balance between opposing schools of thought was a concern shared by many thinkers of the day. On one side of the political spectrum, the leading thinkers of the Doctrinaire ruling party saw themselves as "the incarnation of a great synthesis between thought and action, sciences and history."[21] On the other side were the subversive Saint-Simonians who saw themselves as the priests of a new era of "complete synthesis of materialism and spiritualism."[22] Ultimately, Bianchon's prescription for Raphael is to allow nature to run its course, signaling his humility as a man of science who nonetheless recognizes the limits to his powers. Balzac's respect for the moral and the metaphysical aspects of human existence at this point in his career contrasts markedly with his confidence in the power of observation in the 1842 "Avant-Propos."

Balzac also takes a synthetic approach in the way that he treats the theme of creative destruction in *The Wild Ass's Skin*. In a very basic sense, Raphael lives in a Malthusian zero-sum world, where abundance of a resource in one place necessitates scarcity elsewhere. Every bit of material wealth or comfort that he gains entails a commensurate loss of health and longevity. Balzac would have been familiar with Thomas Malthus's *Essay on the Principle of Population* (1798) in which the British economist argued that the scourge of pauperism was primarily a problem of overpopulation. While his ideas had been slow to catch on in France, by 1840, Malthus had become "the essential reference for any social observer commenting on the troubling relationship between economic development, population growth, and poverty."[23] However, while Malthus's analysis remains at the level of material resources and bodies (his solution to the problem of poverty involved teaching the working classes to curb their sexual desires), the resources that are reallocated in Balzac's narrative are both physical and metaphysical in nature. The magic skin literally shrinks every time a wish is granted, but this change in its material substance is not limited to the physical realm; it is in fact indicative of a more mysterious metaphysical transformation taking place. The "resources" that Raphael gains in his deal with the devil (money, sex, fame) are immediately observable, but those he loses (moral strength, true love, and even physical health) cannot be measured. They are at first detectible to the reader and to Raphael through the depletion of the magic skin, which serves as a powerful allegory of energy conservation.

Indeed, the real and imperceptible forces at work in *The Wild Ass's Skin*, as in many of Balzac's early works, are energies. Although his understanding of physics was rudimentary, the novelist was fascinated by the idea, being explored in several different disciplines, that energy could be measured. For centuries, scientists had thought of energy as a mysterious and indestructible substance (what Allen Thiher has called an "imponderable," a force that could not be measured), and it was only in the 1820s that the physicist Sadi Carnot had begun to theorize that heat could be measured as a form of kinetic energy.[24] In the analytical *Physiologie du mariage* (1829), Balzac describes energy as a type of human capital, a constant that moves from place to place, from body to body, retaining its volume, but shifting form: "Man possesses a given amount of energy. . . . the amount has a limit which cannot be exceeded. . . . This force is a unique force, and whether it expends itself in desires, in passions, in labours of the mind, or in bodily works, it hastens at its master's call. A boxer expends it in punches; a baker in kneading his bread; a poet in moments of ecstasy; a dancer lets it pass into his feet."[25]

For the novelist, then, energy is the unifying force that brings all the different human "species" of the human comedy—the boxer, the baker, the poet, and the dancer—into the same system. This theory of energy as a constant substance in all human activity is what allows Balzac to bring his own literary labor into comparison with the essential work of the baker in the 1834 "Lettre adressée aux écrivains," and, indeed, it is the basic assumption that underlies every aspect of his social theory.

An Economy of Energy

Within the universe depicted in the *Physiologie du mariage*, each character is endowed with a limited amount of resources—that is, of energy—that they must conserve or spend as they see fit. There is, then, a system of energy allocation in Balzac's narratives that reflects the dominant economic thought of July Monarchy France; both, as one critic has noted, are "capitalist, individual, and inegalitarian, as the quantity [of energy, like wealth] that each of us possesses is not the same."[26] According to the novelist, energy, like wealth, was a scarce resource, accumulating in the hands of some while running through the fingers of others. Such scarcity explains the longevity of the eponymous usurer in Gobseck (1830), who "economized the vital movement and concentrated all the human sentiments on the I."[27] On the other end of the spectrum, the *prolétaire* of the "Physionomies parisiennes" does not "spar[e] his vital resources," as he should, but instead "overtaxes his strength, harnesses his wife to some machine or other, and exploits his child by gearing him to a cog-wheel," thereby expending the energy reserves of the next generation. Even in his leisure time, the narrator tells us, the laborer overdraws his resources, spending his weekends in "a form of exhausting debauchery . . . [that] lasts only two days but steals tomorrow's bread."[28] We can almost see the transfer of energy as it flows from the workers' constant movements, through the hands of savvy industrialists and desire-driven aristocrats like Henry de Marsay, and eventually into the motionless body of the hoarder Gobseck.

If, in the above examples, the economic energy of Paris appears to follow the laws of physics as Balzac understood them by existing in only one place at a time, many of his other narratives pass into the realm of metaphysics. This assessment is perhaps nowhere more true than in *The Quest of the Absolute* (1834), where the author's belief that energy is a force that is at once physical and metaphysical is mirrored by his protagonist's quest to transform charcoal into a diamond and therefore prove that all earthly objects contain the same elements (CH 10:719). Under the spell of a mysterious alchemist, Balthazar Claës undertakes a series of expensive and dangerous chemical experiments in his home laboratory. His goals are both spiritual and temporal: first, by demonstrating that two very different materials are in fact made of the same substance, he will prove the existence of God. As a secondary effect, the transformation of charcoal into a precious stone will recoup the enormous sums of money spent on the experiments. Tragically (or ironically, depending on how you read it), at the very moment that Balthazar solves the problem (signaled by a triumphant shout of "Eureka!"), he drops dead, recalling the theme of creative destruction found in *The Wild Ass's Skin*. Only in death does the scientist accomplish his life work, proving his hypothesis that "all life necessitates combustion," and that each productive action depends upon a certain amount of destructive force.

Balthazar's fantastical quest contrasts sharply with the realist setting of the novel. He and his family are described as typical middle-class residents of Douai, known as a quiet and thoroughly bourgeois Flemish town, yet his home laboratory is a furnace of consumption and production where the physical and the metaphysical coincide. Although far from removed from the capital city, then, the quiet domestic hearth in a provincial town becomes the mirror image of the churning streets described that same year in the "Physionomies parisiennes." Here, the narrator emphasizes the physical properties of heat and energy exchange. "It is not only in jest that Paris has been called an inferno. The epithet is well deserved. There all is smoke, fire, glare, ebullience; everything flares up, falters, dies down, burns up again, sparkles, crackles and is consumed. Never in any country has life been more ardent, more intense" (309–10).

Indeed, the capital city of the *Human Comedy* is a real social space where the laws of physics must be obeyed, but the moral and metaphysical implications are clear. This hellish environment is likened to the mythical realm of Vulcan's smithy. Vulcan, whom Balzac calls "the emblem of this strong and ugly race of men, superb in its mechanical skill" (312), was not only a god, but an artisan, skillful enough to weave an invisible net out of bronze to ensnare his adulterous wife, Venus. Like Vulcan's workshop, then, Paris is a space of ingenuity and invention, powered by trickery and deceit. Ultimately, its destructive nature is the source of its seemingly endless creative energy.

Although he insists upon the mimetic nature of his narratives (and their respect for the laws of physics), Balzac's allusions to hell and to the god Vulcan also point to the existence of a mysterious and immaterial realm of reality. In fact, many of Balzac's early texts alternate between realist and metaphysical modes of representation in a way that reveals what Thiher has called his "quest for the totalization of knowledge."[29] His understanding of energy as a hybrid physical/metaphysical substance is central to this unifying theory of the world. Nonetheless, even if these works abound with descriptions of energy as a constant substance in all human activity, its exact makeup is difficult to define. The metaphysical nature of energy in Balzac's unifying theory is perhaps most evident in his conception of the *vis humana*: the manifestation of energy circulating in the body. He had pulled this idea from a corpus of scientific texts that could generally be divided into two camps, the materialist *Organicistes* like Jean-Baptiste

Nacquart and François Broussais who practiced phrenology, and the more metaphysically inclined *Vitalistes* such as Xavier Bichat who were greatly influenced by the animal magnetism of Franz Mesmer.[30] The *Vitalistes* asserted that there existed one life principle (*le principe vital*) common to all living things, from a blade of grass to a human heart. They also subscribed to a theory of "limited vital energy," according to which each organism contains a limited amount of energy, which is spread out unevenly across the different parts of the organism. This theory of "limited vital energy" is attributed to Bichat, who held that one could only have so much intelligence throughout one's organism and that one could not be equally energetic in each of one's organs. "Arguing that a person's aptitude for a given profession was determined by the organ that he or she exercised most frequently, Bichat divided human occupations into three general classes . . . [defined as] fields that mainly used the senses, like painting, music, sculpture, the arts of the perfumer, and haute cuisine . . . professions that involved brain work . . . [and] professions that required muscular prowess, such as dance, equitation, and the mechanical arts."[31]

Balzac was fascinated by this energy, which he called the *vis humana*, and which seemed to cross the physical and metaphysical realms of existence. He explores most fully its dual nature in "La Théorie de la démarche," an analytical text published in 1833. Here, he proposes the existence of a vital substance that is at once material and mystical. Its hybrid nature is manifest in the way that, on the one hand, the individual can "direct," "economize," and "amass" it (like Gobseck), or spend it recklessly (like the *prolétaire*); and, yet, on the other, it remains "an invisible fluid" and a "constant phenomenon," beyond the control, it seems, of any individual person (*CH* 12:270). The text itself is a hybrid: at times it reads like a *physiologie*, an attempt to discern the moral character of individuals through their movement; and, at others, it is a series of meditations on how those movements could act upon the exterior world. The narrator pretends to take a materialist approach to his observations but often finds himself philosophizing. "If the *vis humana* cannot be at once in the head, in the lungs, in the heart, in the stomach, in the legs; / If the predominance of *mouvement* in one part of the body excludes *mouvement* in the others . . . / And, well, if the lack of *mouvement* enfeebles intellectual force, if all repose kills it, why does the man looking for energy seek it in rest, in silence and in solitude?" (*CH* 12:301).

The paradox at the end of the passage is a witty way to expose the folly of trying to explain the world using physics alone. How *can* we find a resource (in this case, energy) precisely where there is none (in inactivity)? Putting aside what scientists already knew at the time—that the body produces its own energy from food—Balzac ostensibly casts doubt onto his own theory of energy conservation, but he resolves the problem, through his use of the term *mouvement*. Synonymous in many ways with the English "movement," the French *mouvement*, according to the 1835 edition of the *Dictionnaire de l'Académie française*, also included "the different impulsions, passions, and affectations of the soul."[32] It may, therefore, simultaneously obey the laws of physics (by existing in only one place at a time) and transgress them (by appearing, as if by magic, where previously absent), because of this mystical quality.

The term *mouvement* also introduces the question of labor into Balzac's text (although not a labor *movement*, as the 1835 definition did not include any reference to political or social organization) that is itself somewhat mystical. "The *mouvements* of man" he posits, "set loose an animic fluid. His sweat is the smoke of an unknown flame" (CH 12:294). *Mouvement* produces sweat because it requires effort, or an expenditure of energy. It is, in other words, labor. Like the *vis humana*, labor functions as an organic force, bringing life with its presence and leaving sterility and decomposition where it is not, and yet, as the images of the "animic fluid" and the "smoke of an unknown flame" indicate, the true nature of labor remains mysterious. By existing in only one space or vessel at a time, labor obeys the rules of physics, but it carries a significance that goes beyond mere materiality.

For Balzac, labor energy is embodied by the working classes. Again, we turn to the "Physionomies parisiennes" for an example. This sweeping view of Parisian society begins with the manual laborer, who is defined through a series of chaotic and somewhat fantastic images which bring attention to the excessively physical nature of the worker's existence. Balzac first does this through an enumeration of body parts, presenting the so-called *prolétaire* in fragments: "*The artisan, the proletarian, the man who toils with foot, hand, tongue, back, his strong right arm or his ten fingers to gain a living.* This man, who should be the first to think of sparing his vital resources, overtaxes his strength, harnesses his wife to some machine or other, and exploits his child by nailing [*le cloue*] him to a cog-wheel" (emphasis added) (CH 12:311). The unevenness of the sentence structure is revelatory. The subject clause (in italics), which takes up about two-thirds of the passage, is composed of an accumulation of labels ("artisan," "proletarian," "man," and again "this man"), as if Balzac were not quite sure what to call this particular individual. The worker is portrayed as an agglomeration of body parts—feet, hands, tongue, back, arm, fingers—which seem to be in constant movement. The worker's movements appear contradictory, simultaneously spending ("overtaxes his forces" and "exploits") and confining or hoarding ("harnesses" and "nailing") his labor energy, representing both directions of the flow of energy into and out of the human body. Yet, a closer reading reveals that those forms of energy that are constrained by the worker are really those of his wife and child, with the aim of better channeling them into productive labor.

The working body is little more than a furnace of energy consumption and production. Energy enters the body and then leaves it in order to become the multiplicity of things in the material world. We find once again the theme of creative destruction that haunts *The Quest of the Absolute* and *The Wild Ass's Skin*. In the "Physionomies," however, there are as many types of labor as there are products: "these puppets who with grimy hands *model* and *gild* the potter's clay, *stitch* coats and dresses, *beat out* iron, *shave* and *plane* wood, *temper* steel, *spin* and *weave* hemp and flax, *burnish* bronzes, *festoon* crystal with floral decorations, *embroider* woollens, *train* horses, *plait and braid* harness, *cut out* copper, *paint* carriages, *pollard* aged elms, *steam-dye* cotton, *dry out* tulle, *polish* diamonds and metals, *foliate* marble, *round off* precious stones, *give thought a graceful form* in print, *deck it out* in colour or plain black and white" (emphasis added) (*CH* 12:311). Here, the enumeration of tasks creates a sense of constant movement, the writing style once again mirroring the activity of the worker. However, as each task is attached to a product, this passage conveys an additional theme of productivity and abundance. In contrast to the image of the worker who destroys his body by expending his energy, this passage focuses on what is gained: the creative power of labor upon the exterior world. Thus, the loss of one's labor force is not inherently *bad*, and, in fact, at the level of society, it is a good thing. It is thanks to labor that humanity has been able to achieve an ever-improving material well-being. For Balzac, labor's most important characteristic was its ability to produce the objects that furnish modern life, the plethora of keepsakes, gadgets, accessories, devices, instruments, and other items that filled the rooms and streets of the capital city. In a sense, Balzac was concluding that manual labor was making not just *things*, but also *identities*. This was especially true for the proletarian, who, although he had worked his own body to near destruction, could now be a part of the "society of things" that, as one critic has posited, was fast becoming just as important as the society of humans.³³ If the identity of Balzac's laborer was directly tied to how he channeled his energy into producing things that were not him, the individual loss of energy that he might have experienced was outweighed by the social material that he created.

Labor's flow from the working individual to the objects of modern society follows the laws of physics as Balzac understood them. This flow also allows energy to circulate throughout the social panorama, even in spaces that are supposed to be free of labor, such as the boudoir. By comparing the capital to "a vast cornfield whose waving stalks are incessantly swayed this way and that by the winds of self-interest" (CH 12:309) and "a battlefield of interests and passions" (CH 12:326), Balzac evokes a horizontal landscape, but the movement of this field is in fact vertical. The upward movement of money and labor propels each generation of workers into a higher social class, and the laboring masses seem to provide a limitless supply of productive energy. This up-and-down panorama of contemporary society, which moves from the stinking hovels of the working classes to the "purified air and space" of the aristocracy is proof of the connectedness of Parisian society and that the laboring proletarian is part of the same organic system as the debauched aristocrat Henry de Marsay.

The porosity of labor energy that we see in *La Fille aux yeux d'or* is a recurring theme in Balzac's *Thirteen* trilogy, of which it was a part. Another *Thirteen* tale, *Ferragus* (1833), for example, opens with a young aristocrat, Auguste de Maulincour (an associate of Marsay), who follows a mysterious woman walking hurriedly on the streets of the capital. His pursuit leads him across Paris, where each neighborhood has a distinct social character, described in terms of energy production and consumption. Not only do the working-class *barrières* at the edge of town "shake [*se secouer*]" and "move their arms [*ses bras se remuent*]," but even the bourgeois Bourse quarter is described as "babbling, active, and hustling [*babillarde, active, prostituée*]" (CH 5:796–98). After traversing these various spaces, the mysterious woman finally stops at a "mean" and "vulgar" building, and, just as he finally gets a glimpse of her face, Maulincour is promptly smacked by a wooden plank carried on the shoulder of a construction worker (CH 5:799). During this time, decades before the Baron Haussmann's famous project of urban renewal, the city was already undergoing extensive renovations, as much of the city's infrastructure systems, like the sewers, were being modernized. Labor was everywhere, ready to consume and destroy everything that impeded its drive to produce new things. Rather than apologizing, the workman who has smacked Maulincour growls at him to pay attention, and in this way, the young man realizes that labor's driving force does not respect social caste.

Nor is the beautiful Clémence Desmarets, the object of Maulincour's pursuit, free from the effects of labor energy, despite her relatively privileged social status. Within the privacy of her ornate dressing room, this seemingly pristine bourgeoise demonstrates the laboriousness of feminine grooming, working hard to construct an aesthetically pleasing façade for her husband. Balzac uses the language of labor when describing her primping as "a woman's craft [*ce métier de femme*]" and enumerates the tools of her trade: a sheer peignoir, a partially opened bodice, perfume, velvet slippers. With the skill of an artisan who expertly handles his instruments, Clémence uses these tools to embellish the different parts of her person (*CH* 5:840–41). Thus, even the boudoir is revealed as a space of labor. The corset that Clémence never takes off, even when going to bed, establishes a permanent material link between herself and the working world. This world is personified by the figure of a hardworking *grisette*, or needleworker, named Ida Gruget, who, as Catherine Nesci has suggested, may have sewn the very girdle that gives Clémence her seductive form.[34] A *grisette*, a ubiquitous social type of the early nineteenth century, by the 1840s had come to embody the contemplative, vulnerable, and hardworking needlewoman of the July Monarchy. If, in the 1820s, Henry Monnier's lithographs entitled *Les Grisettes dessinées d'après nature* depicted the *grisette* as opportunistic, superficial, and cruel to her lovers, Louis Huart's *Physiologie de la grisette* (1840) portrayed her as the epitome of the working woman in Paris. Ida provides an interesting link between these two extremes.[35] Like all *grisette* types, she is characterized by a seemingly boundless supply of energy, even in the face of immense economic and romantic setbacks. This quality shines through even in her love letters to Ferragus, which contain "no commas, no pauses [*repos*]" (*CH* 5:818). Ida takes no rest; she expresses herself only through labor.

As labor flows from space to space, it brings life and beauty where it exists and leaves behind decay where it is not. This is demonstrated in the contrast between Ida and her mother. Ida, the energetic *grisette*, is beautiful, while her mother, a slovenly drinker, is hideous. Thoroughly shaped and processed by her labor, Ida is compared to "the water of the Seine which is manufactured [*se fabrique*] in Paris' great reservoirs, filtered ten times before being delivered in faceted carafes" (*CH* 5:850). Like the river water, which comes to Paris brown and polluted from both industrial and natural causes, the working-class *grisette* needs a bit of refinement.

It is only with the help of some "manufacturing" in the form of grooming and pruning that, properly "delivered" in the right accoutrements, she takes a more aesthetically pleasing form, suitable for visual consumption. Like the miraculously clean drinking water that comes from the muddy Seine, Ida's pretty figure is a sign of the wonders of industrial labor. The *grisette* embodies the violence and force of manual urban labor, which is both the source of her flawed nature and the solution to her blemished appearance.

Like her daughter, Madame Gruget is a member of the working class, but her character is formed less by work than by vice. The narrator, through the eyes of Jules Desmarets, is horrified by the woman's physical appearance. Her "yellow" face (*le visage jaune*) is a mass of grotesque features, the result of years of neglect. "Her grey eyes, lacking eyebrows and lashes, her toothless mouth, her black-toned wrinkles" (CH 5:869). This repulsiveness may at first seem to be the result of overwork, but another cause suddenly "rises up." Jules surveys the contents of her worktable, "loaded with plates and bits of silk, pieces of work in cotton and wool, and in the middle of all of this rose up [*s'élevait*] a bottle of wine" (CH 5:869). In this meaningful tableau, the bottle appears to loom over the unfinished bits of work strewn across the table, an allegory of how the woman's drinking habit dominates all her other productive activities. Her hideous appearance is caused not by labor then, but by a lack thereof: vice.

Women workers were often a flashpoint in discussions of the relationship between labor and vice.[36] However, the signs of labor on the male worker's body were also of great interest, and Balzac addresses this question directly in "La Théorie de la démarche." The narrator, in the process of using outward appearances to understand an individual's moral makeup, finds his project thwarted by the appearance of a sickly-looking passerby. The amateur physiologist wonders: "Were these vices or work which had deformed him? Sad thought! Work, which edifies, and vice, which destroys, produce the same results" (CH 12:286). He cannot tell, based on the outward signs, whether this is a laborer who has simply worked himself sick, or an idler who has engaged in too much carousing. Balzac expresses dismay ("Sad thought!") at the idea that two completely opposite forces—labor and vice—could be confused with one another, but this also gives us insight into the novelist's understanding of labor power as a moralizing force. When, either by working too much or by not working at all, individuals are completely lacking in labor energy, they become immoral.

Balzac was certainly not sympathetic toward what we would today call the working classes, and, indeed, they are largely absent from the *Human Comedy*. For the most part, Balzac's worker characters are essentially depicted as fragmented bodies, as we saw above in the *prolétaire* of the "Physionomies parisiennes." A similarly inhumane description of the worker appears in one of his earliest works, the analytical "Traité de la vie élégante" (1830): "[The worker] becomes *un moyen* . . . some kind of winch, mixed up with the wheelbarrows, shovels, and spades. . . . Similar to steam engines, all men ruled by work take on the same shape; they have no individuality. The man-instrument is a kind of social zero, of which the greatest possible quantity will never compose any sum unless it is preceded by another number" (CH 12:212). This collection of fragmented images presents the working class as a homogenous mass. Instead of a person, the worker is *un moyen*, a term that may be read in two slightly different ways: either as a means to an end, like a shovel or a wheelbarrow; or as an average, an ordinary person who eschews extremes and is indistinguishable from the person next to him. This second definition is somewhat akin to the *homme moyen* that the statistician Adolphe Quetelet would propose several years later, but, while Quetelet's average man was a purely agnostic figure, used as a tool for measuring trends in society, Balzac's was an insult. Neither comparison he makes—to the uniform products of a steam-powered assembly line (which all take on "the same shape") or to the steam-machine itself—allows the worker any individual value. For the young Balzac, workers were not only indistinguishable from one another but also from the products of their labor, a perspective that simultaneously promotes the value of the material object (the "thing") and lessens the value of its creator (the human).

And yet, as we see in the comparison between Ida Gruget and her mother, Balzac does value labor itself, and surely, he believes, it is better than idleness. Even the aristocratic idler, who, in the persons of Henry de Marsay, Auguste de Maulincour, and others, looms so large in the author's early fictions, is the object of some criticism. As the title implies, "Le Traité de la vie élégante" aims to conduct a philosophical study of the world of style and leisure, but the narrator struggles to define "elegance" in any positive terms. Instead, as his "Aphorismes" make clear, elegance can only exist where labor is completely absent: "The man who is accustomed to labor cannot understand the elegant life" and "to be *fashionable* [Balzac uses the English word as a nod to that particularly British embodiment of elegance, the dandy], one must benefit from rest [*repos*] without passing through work [*travail*]" (*CH* 12:215). Leisure is defined not as something in its own right but as what it is not, namely, labor. The words *travail* and *occupé* and their variants appear no less than thirty-two times, while the different forms of *repos* and *oisif* occur only eighteen, giving us an idea of the importance of labor in Balzac's social theory.

As he does elsewhere, Balzac expresses in this "Treatise" a productivist worldview. Society, he claims at the start of his analysis, has a tripartite structure, composed of workers, thinkers, and idlers who lead lives that are described, respectively, as "busy," "artistic," and "elegant." However, the "thinking" or "artistic" class quickly disappears from the panorama, as the author begins to speak in terms of just two social groups: those who labor and those who do not. He characterizes this breakdown in different ways, "people who *produce* [versus] people who *consume*" (emphasis added) (*CH* 12:217), and, several pages later, "those who have *bought* the right to be idle [versus] those who *try* to acquire it" (emphasis added) (*CH* 12:223). As he would develop further four years later in his "Lettre adressée aux écrivains," Balzac believes that the thinking/artistic class are rightfully a part of the busy/working class, and together they form a single category of producers and "tryers" whose interests seem to be diametrically opposed to the class of consumers and "buyers." In this binary system, the social distinction between the proletarian (*"Un laboureur, un maçon, un soldat"*), the bourgeois professional (*"le médecin, le curé, l'avocat, le notaire"*), and the artist (*"vous poètes, vous musiciens, vous dramatistes, vous prosateurs"*) is negligible. They are all "tryers," workers, and producers, and, because of this, they are morally superior to their idling compatriots.

The moralizing force of labor is often overshadowed by the threat of corruption in Balzac's Parisian tales, but it is quite clear-cut outside of the city walls. For example, in *The Country Doctor* (*Le Médecin de campagne*) (1833), Balzac tells the story of a brilliant Parisian doctor named Benassis who has dedicated his life to bringing economic and agricultural progress to a struggling community of peasants in the distant countryside of the Isère. Balzac, through Benassis, constructs an imagined society that has been driven forward in time through the power of labor. The narrator notes the prosperity and efficiency of the transformed village conveyed by the houses' exteriors:

> Little cottages, scattered here and there, with their gardens full of blossoming fruit trees, call up the ideas that are aroused by the sight of *industrious poverty*; while the thought of *ease, secured after long years of*

toil, is suggested by some larger houses farther on, with their red roofs of flat round tiles, shaped like the scales of a fish. There is no door, moreover, that does not duly exhibit a basket in which the cheeses are hung up to dry. Every roadside and every croft is adorned with vines ... whose leaves are stripped off to feed cattle. (emphasis added)[37]

With gardens full of fruit, baskets of cheese, and even roofs that look like tasty fish, these houses exude a sense of bounty. Such wealth is directly connected to hard work: the poor are "industrious," and the rich have earned their comfort through "years of toil." Indeed, the prosperity of the town is the direct result of Benassis's efforts to instill a sense of hard work and practicality in its citizens. These efforts, which he undertakes as a form of penance for a sin committed as a young man, demonstrate his axiom: "my prayer takes the form of the active work to which I have set my hand, and which I love—the work of sowing the seeds of happiness and joy" (258). This form of prayer through work depends upon a belief in the mutability of work, that labor is defined not only as physical effort, but also intellectual work, be it spiritual, artistic, or scientific in nature.

For Benassis, as for Balzac, labor is defined quite broadly as any effort that produces something, whether that product be material (like baskets of cheese) or immaterial (like "happiness and joy"). He does place a special emphasis on the intellectual work performed by doctors, lawyers, and priests, however, reasoning that "if civilization is to spread itself, and production is to be increased, the people must be made to understand the way in which the interests of the individual harmonize with national interests" (70). In a way that continues the pedagogical mission of Jean-Baptiste Say's *Catechism of Political Economy* (1815) or Saint-Simon's *The New Christianity* (1825), the "three black robes" (as Balzac calls them) take on the task of convincing the people that it is in their best interest to work toward the good of society. In this way, says Benassis/Balzac, and despite his lack of material productivity, the bourgeois professional must therefore be recognized as the constructor of modern society.

Elsewhere, Balzac focuses on the laboriousness of artistic efforts. In the 1831 novella *The Unknown Masterpiece* (*Le Chef-d'œuvre inconnu*), for example, the author imagines a meeting between the famous painter Nicolas Poussin and a fictional master named Frenhofer. When the young Poussin goes to observe the latter at work, his creative process is described in terms of struggle and effort. "The little old man turned back his sleeves with impatient energy.... He worked with such passionate fervor that beads of sweat gathered upon his bare forehead; he worked so quickly, in brief, impatient jerks, that it seemed to young Poussin as if some familiar spirit inhabiting the body of this strange being took a grotesque pleasure in making use of the man's hands against his own will."[38] The image of the artist being overtaken by some force that is greater than himself appears, at first, to follow the Romantic conception of genius expressed by Madame de Staël in *Corrine*. However, there is certain physicality and an insistence upon the effort that goes into artistic creation—manifest in the beads of sweat and the focus on the painter's hands and arms—that ultimately goes against the Romantic ideal of art. This contradiction becomes clear when, obsessed with his own ideal of representation, the Pygmalion-like Frenhofer begins to work on a painting that, he hopes, will be so realistic that the woman represented comes to life. After three months of struggling with the piece, the painter falls ill from overwork. When, in a final burst of energy, he completes the work, his friends can see only "a dim, formless fog" (30). Immediately after, Frenhofer burns the painting and kills himself. Much like Balthazar's scientific labors deplete the chemist of all energy, leading to his death, Frenhofer's artistic efforts exhaust him to the point of extinction.

We can see how, in these early fictions and analytical writings, Balzac was imagining labor as a form of energy that could take on many different forms while obeying the laws of physics as he understood them (that is, by existing in only one place at the same time). He was not alone in thinking of labor as a form of energy, however, and much of what he claimed to know simply by observing society was already being tested in laboratories. In 1824, the physicist Sadi Carnot had helped to establish "the modern concept of work as the equivalent of energy originally consumed," and by the 1830s, other scientists like Claude-Louis Navier, Gaspard-Gustave Coriolis, and Jean-Victor Poncelet had begun to refer to "puissance de travail" as the standard measure for the energy yield of machines. Later, Hermann von Helmholtz's 1847 theory of *Kraft*, or energy, as a universal force present in all matter would lead to the use of the term *Arbeitskraft* (labor + energy) as a way to express the quantifiable abstract power of the workforce.[39] However, even before scientists began focusing on proving the physical existence of the non-observable phenomenon of *Arbeitskraft*, Balzac's theory of work energy moved seamlessly between the physical and metaphysical realms. Throughout the early nineteenth century, he and his fellow French thinkers were framing labor not as a destructive force, or a dreary activity, but as a powerful resource to be harnessed for the good of society. Still, we must assume that Balzac's writings reached a wider readership than those of his scientific compatriots.

For Balzac, labor was the manifestation of energy in the *social* body, just as the *vis humana* was the manifestation of energy in the *human* body. In a way that anticipates later theories of *Arbeitskraft* or labor energy, Balzac saw labor as a force that could assume many different forms, while remaining intact. In contrast to physicists like Helmholtz, however, Balzac held that labor was *also* moral in nature: those who had no labor power (either by working too much or by not working at all, as in the haggard man observed in "La Théorie de la démarche") became immoral, whereas immoral people and places could become moral through labor.

The examples of Balthazar, Frenhofer, and Benassis demonstrate that, for Balzac, intellectual effort (be it scientific, artistic, or spiritual) was a form of labor, and one that could allow the individual to understand metaphysical truths. In this way, his worldview was in line with the eclectic philosophy of Victor Cousin. By the 1820s, Cousin had become one of the most popular lecturers at the Sorbonne, and once the Doctrinaires came to power with the July Monarchy, he was charged with redesigning the national curriculum. Cousin held that there were three elements of consciousness—sensation, reason, and volition (the most important of which was the third)—and that the individual psyche could be developed only by cultivating all three faculties. Cousin's psychological method for forming a new generation of responsible and free citizens, which Jan Goldstein has described as a form of "observationally based metaphysics," demanded that the student undertake the difficult and labor-intensive task of self-reflection in order to come to metaphysical truths about the universe.[40]

Balzac enjoyed mocking Cousin and his school of thought for being pedantic, but a Cousinian eclectic method—whereby one tries to reconcile opposing truths by assuming a "general attitude of objectivity"—was central to his understanding of the world.[41] The influence of Cousin on Balzac is perhaps nowhere more apparent than in *The Wild Ass's Skin*. In the opening pages, for instance, Raphael meets an ancient antiquarian, who, at 102 years of age, reveals the secret of self-preservation using a tripartite breakdown of human faculties similar to Cousin's: "The exercise of the *will* [*vouloir*] consumes us; the exercise of *power* [*pouvoir*] destroys us, but the pursuit of *knowledge* [*savoir*] leaves our infirm constitution in a state of perpetual calm. So desire or volition is dead in me, killed by thought. Movement, or power, has been dissolved by the natural play of my organs. In short, I have invested my life, not in the heart, so easily broken, nor in the senses which are so readily blunted, but in the brain, which does not wear out and outlasts everything."[42] The sage tells Raphael that, by cultivating one faculty—*savoir*, or knowledge—over the others, the individual can avoid the seemingly inevitable destruction that occurs as a result of emotions and desire (*vouloir*) or bodily sensations and capacities (*pouvoir*). His speech is meant to warn the young protagonist against taking the titular magic skin, which, in exchange for fulfilling all its owner's earthly desires (*vouloir*), empties him of all knowledge (*savoir*) and power (*pouvoir*). The skin itself is inscribed with an ominous warning: "Let thy wishes be measured against thy life. Here it lies. Every wish [*vouloir*] will diminish me and diminish thy days" (51), a prediction that comes true. True to its word, the skin shrinks and simultaneously depletes Raphael's life-force capital with each wish granted. Heedless of these warnings, Raphael seizes the magic skin eagerly.

Having written a treatise entitled *Théorie de la volonté*, one might think that the young man would have known better, and this irony is the narrative's driving force, its reason for being. Like Victor Cousin, Balzac held volition, or desire, to be a central element of human consciousness, but unlike Cousin, he was wary of desire's potential to cause devastation. This was a sustained anxiety, and the destructive power of desire that is so apparent in *The Wild Ass's Skin* also appears in many of Balzac's other early writings. The "Physionomies parisiennes" once again provide an excellent example of this phenomenon. Here, each social group—proletariat, petite bourgeoisie, haute bourgeoisie, artists, and idlers—is scrutinized individually, and yet they share a certain fundamental equality. Everyone, declares the narrator more than once, is motivated by one of two passions: "pleasure or gold" (309, 316). In other words, all human actions are directed toward a finality of either creation or procreation. Pleasure, here standing in for the satisfaction of libidinal desire, is the first step in the reproductive process; gold, the material manifestation of economic effort, is the motivation for all nonbiological creation. And yet desire is ultimately destructive, as when Henry de Marsay's drive to possess the courtesan Paquita (whose golden-colored eyes indicate her embodiment of *both* sexual and monetary gratification) leads to her death.

While sexual desire does play an important role in Balzac's narratives, it is the drive to obtain and to amass money that guides the majority of his characters' actions. Even those idealistic and romantic figures who believe in true love eventually accept marriage for what is really is: an institution for pecuniary stability. This is the lesson that Balzac's characters must learn time again: Eugénie Grandet from her Parisian cousin Charles, and Eugène de Rastignac from the corrupt Vautrin. This latter lesson takes place in a famous scene from *Père Goriot* (1834–35), where, using precise figures and demonstrating a clear understanding of the mechanisms of French society, Vautrin explains to Rastignac that he will never make as much money through work as he will through an advantageous marriage. An apt pupil, Rastignac seduces the wife of a banker and becomes a wealthy and popular figure in the Parisian social scene. Money is a convenient object of desire because it seems to be quantifiable, and as such it is what Fredric Jameson has called "supremely emblematic of" desire.[43] Indeed, Balzac was obsessed with money. The detailed character descriptions that he is known for are all the more realistic because they almost always include precise details of the individual's financial situation, whether they receive rent, stand to inherit, or are forced to borrow certain amounts. He gave such reliable numbers in his texts that the economist Thomas Piketty even used them to estimate the rates of income from capital in the nineteenth century, citing Vautrin's "Lesson" to illustrate how the patrimonial wealth system that reigned in pre-industrial French and British societies worked.[44]

And yet, despite the exact numbers included in his novels, Balzac holds that the real value of paper and metal currencies is arbitrary. "Everybody talks about money: nobody knows what it is."[45] As fungibles, currencies are only worth what others are willing to exchange for them. This makes money a useful tool for political economists looking to measure value across time and space, but problematic for someone like Balzac who hopes to find metaphysical truth by observing the physical world. For the *flâneur*-narrator of *Le Traité de la vie élégante* (1830), the social and moral leveling caused by money's pernicious fungibility is a root cause of France's political instability. "All of a sudden, the Revolution, forcefully reducing the wardrobe of fourteen centuries to mere paper bills [*papier monnaie*], brought about impetuously one of the greatest misfortunes that may befall a nation. The active classes [*les gens occupés*] grew tired of being the only ones required to work; they got it in their heads that both the pain and the profits should be shared, in equal portions, with those unfortunate millionaires, who knew how to do nothing other than bask in their idleness!" (*CH* 12:218–19). Putting aside, for a moment, Balzac's ironic barb at the "unfortunate millionaires," it is true that, when the Revolution put an end to the stratified system of royal privilege and social distinction of the Old Regime, it wreaked havoc in many areas of social life. If fashion seems a petty concern, for Balzac, it was not. Once the courtly practice of advertising rank and affiliation through clothing choices had been done away with, bourgeois and aristocrats alike donned identical black jackets, or *redingotes*, making it difficult to read social distinction on the street. According to Balzac, it was because they were unable to *see* the difference between themselves and their more elegant or leisurely compatriots that the working classes had begun to question the current system whereby certain members toiled and produced, while others idled and consumed. The connection he establishes between changes in fashion, social order, and paper bills (*papier monnaie*) is no doubt a reference to the assignat, a fiat money of the revolutionary period whose collapse had serious economic consequences. However, as we shall see below, it was also a more general critique of money's ability to measure value.

Balzac decries the loss of "real" social value throughout the *Thirteen* trilogy, notably in *La Duchesse de Langeais* (first published as *Ne touchez pas la hache*, in 1833), by using the language of political economy. The narrator begins his description of Restoration Paris by criticizing the aristocratic world of the Faubourg Saint-Germain for having taken on many of the habits of the bourgeoisie, and, in particular, their clamor to amass wealth. Traditionally concerned with cultivating such economically useless virtues as "courtesy," "elegance," "fine speech," and "family pride," the aristocracy was now being forced to produce revenue, by turning to "petty occupations [*occupations mesquines*]." He adds: "There was a certain intrinsic value [*valeur intrinsèque*] in these families but, when reduced to outward appearances, this merit is nothing more than a nominal value [*une valeur nominale*]" (CH 5:930). In other words, once value is measured in monetary form, it becomes nominal, or contingent (rather than intrinsic or essential). Here, Balzac is echoing the language of political economists like Adam Smith and Jean-Baptiste Say, who spoke of the opposition between nominal (sometimes called arbitrary or imaginary) value and real (intrinsic and actual) value. Unlike the political economists, however, who argued for the necessity of using socially determined conventions like money for the sake of economic exchange, Balzac found it profoundly troubling.

For the novelist, metal currency was just as problematic for measuring real value as paper money. "Each social sphere," says Balzac in the "Physionomies," "projects its spawn [*son frai*] into the sphere immediately above it" (318). The metaphor, which likens the flow of wealth and work to the sexual reproduction and associated upriver migration of certain fish species, sows further confusion between the two most common objects of desire—money and sex. The term *frai*, here translated as "spawn," which is its most common meaning, refers also to the physical wearing-away of metal currency, as in: "this coin has lost much value through [the process of] *frai*."[46] At a time when coins were often made of soft bullion, it was well known that each time money changed hands, it was subject to corrosion and that, over time, it would no longer be worth the amount stamped on its face (it was only due to social convention that it was still traded as if it were). The *frai*—which Balzac uses as a synonym for economic circulation—is a force that creates social or nominal value all while corroding and destroying the physical or real value of the money itself. It is therefore a force that, unlike labor energy, does not follow the laws of physics, highlighting the unreliability of money—even metal-based currency—as a determinant of value in Balzac's eyes.

Money was a tricky subject for many thinkers of the day. The political economist Jean-Baptiste Say, for example, was quite worried about the postrevolutionary monetary system and argued in 1803 for a return to a gold or silver standard, "which would have no nominal value [*valeur nominale*]" and, therefore, only intrinsic value. This type of currency, he explained, "would escape the caprices of legislation" and would be adopted by nations all around the world.[47] Things had not improved by the 1830s, when the instability of French currency was still a major concern. If the author of the *Human Comedy* worried about money's inability to account for social distinction, many of his more liberal compatriots saw money as *too* socially determined to support the type of equality that Republican values demanded. Postrevolutionary monetary policy had unintentionally established two different currencies. The *sous* and *écus* of the Old Regime, which were available in smaller denominations, circulated primarily among the poor and in the provinces, while the official *francs* were only used by the rich. This two-tiered system, observes Rebecca Spang, "threatened to undermine the fantasies—of progress, of liberty, of national unity, of equality before the law—that made it possible to say the time for revolutions had passed."[48] A tangible reminder that the egalitarian goals of the Revolution had not been achieved, money was seen as a problematic way of determining value among conservatives and liberals alike.

If money was flawed, how, then could real value be determined? Because Balzac (like Victor Cousin) saw volition, or desire, as the most powerful of the human faculties (more powerful than the reasoning of intellect or the sensations of the body), it may be tempting to attribute to him a hedonistic utilitarian worldview, whereby a person determines the value of a good based on how much pleasure it affords. This is essentially how Say, the most influential political economist of the day, had defined value. However, as important as Balzac thought desire was, he was also quite wary of it, as can be seen in the antiquarian's speech in *The Wild Ass's Skin*, where Raphael is encouraged to develop knowledge (*savoir*) over desire (*volonté*). Balzac did not consider volition a suitable way of determining real value primarily because it was unquantifiable. Not only did he believe that the value of an object of desire was arbitrary (this is true not only of love or sex but also money), but he also held that desire was a self-consuming—and therefore destructive—force. The allegory of Raphael's magic skin makes this abundantly clear. Instead, for Balzac, it is labor—a form of energy that creates the world of things which can then be counted and measured—that must serve as the basis for real social value.

A Labor Theory of Value

Because of the importance that he places on labor, and because of the wariness he shows toward other ways of measuring value, such as money, we can finally make the argument that Balzac was a proponent of a labor theory of value. The idea is often attributed to Karl Marx, but he was not the first to theorize that the value of an object could be determined by the amount of work that went into it. In both England and France, political economists had long pondered the question of how to best determine value and what role labor played in that calculation. Although Balzac doesn't mention these thinkers by name in his writings, it is almost certain that he would have been familiar with the basics of their thought.

Already in 1776, Adam Smith had argued in *The Wealth of Nations* that, because it "never varies in its own value," labor "alone is the ultimate and *real* standard by which the value of all commodities can—always, everywhere—be estimated and compared." In contrast, money is only able to measure the "*nominal* price" of a commodity (emphasis added). If, he continues, the worth of an object is measured in its monetary or exchange value (how many "palpable objects" can be exchanged for it), this is only for practical reasons, for the real value of labor is an "abstract notion."[49] Soon after, another British liberal political economist, David Ricardo, refuted the idea that labor was an abstract notion, arguing that the value of a product could be calculated by the hours of invested in it. This point was so crucial to his theory that, in the third edition of his *On the Principles of Political Economy and Taxation* (1821), he begins the first page of the first chapter with the following epigraph: "The value of a commodity, or the quantity of any other commodity for which it will exchange, depends on the relative quantity of labour which is necessary for its production, and not on the greater or less compensation which is paid for that labour."[50] Like Smith, Ricardo believed that labor represented real value whereas the monetary value of the wages received for labor represented nominal value. Ricardo complexified the notion, however, by adding that its real value should also take into account variables such as time, effort, and skill.

Over in France, however, Say took a more hedonistic stance, arguing that the value of all commodities was arbitrary, or nominal, but that labor was particularly unfit to act as a measuring rod because of its undesirability. "The value of labor, like all values," he says, "is determined by the mutual accord of the adverse interests of buyer and seller, and fluctuates accordingly." This leads him to conclude that the real determinant of an object's worth is its utility, defined as "this inherent fitness or capability of certain things to satisfy the various wants of mankind . . . , for the utility of things is the ground-work of their value, and their value constitutes wealth."[51] In other words, for Say, real value was determined by a type of utility that was inextricably linked to desire, and, because desire was fundamentally unmeasurable, social conventions such as money were the only practical way to approximate a measurement of and object's worth. Say's *Catechism of Political Economy* (1815), written with the intention of bringing the principles of political economy to the masses, had become a staple of popular instruction in Balzac's youth, but interestingly, the author seems to align himself with Smith and Ricardo more than with his fellow Frenchman Say.

Despite agreeing with Say's observation that economic actors are driven by desire, Balzac found his alternative to a labor theory of value unconvincing. This was not only due to the general distrust of volition that plays out in *The Wild Ass's Skin*, but also because the novelist did not believe (or did not want to believe) that social conventions had anything to do with the worth of an object. In particular, as a struggling artist himself, he could not admit that the true value of one's labor could be measured by the compensation the worker received for it. Instead, the novelist believed that the amount of effort required to produce an object was the true determinant of its value, and that this effort had to be measured according to moral and even metaphysical standards rather than purely material or social ones. Indeed, a common theme in Balzac's tales is that a "lifetime of labors" (to quote the "Physionomies parisiennes") is known to be valuable, and yet it goes unrewarded by society. This is true of both manual efforts and intellectual ones. Ida Gruget, the embodiment of working-class Paris, is unwelcome in the Desmarets' bourgeois household even as her corsets are the key to Clémence's womanly success; Frenhofer's artistic exertions result in a masterpiece unrecognizable to anyone but himself; and Balthazar de Claës's intellectual search for truth is a success only in his own mind. These are the tragic heroes offered to the reader, unrecognized by the society in which they live but held up as moral paragons by the author of the *Human Comedy*. In short, the value of a good or a service is not represented by the market price or even the social esteem it commands, but the amount of labor invested in it.

Read in this way, Balzac's early texts seem to anticipate Marx's labor theory of value, set out in chapter 1 of *Capital* (1867). In this text, Marx pushed back against classical economic systems that calculated the value of a commodity according to the labor-time invested in it. Seeing how industrialization had raised productivity and depressed wages, Marx concluded that there had to be another factor at play, namely the social context in which the commodity was produced. Marx held that, just as commodity values were dynamic—incorporating both concrete use value (real-world applications) and the more abstract exchange value—so too was the labor that produced those commodities. This led him to argue that work had to be conceived of as something "pure and simple," or "labor in the abstract," a name that could be applied to the art of making shoes as well as the act mining ore. Commodities, he writes, are what is left over from the effort put into making them. "There is nothing left of them in each case but the same phantom-like objectivity; they are merely congealed quantities of homogeneous human labor ... crystals of this social substance, which is common to them all."[52] By conceiving of human labor as a fungible good: a "social substance" that is quantifiable and exchangeable, Marx saw it as a type of currency.[53] It is striking that, three decades before *Capital*, Balzac was already depicting labor energy as a sort of currency that maintained its value even as it was exchanged for and changed into many different forms. It is incontestable that Balzac was a source of inspiration for Marx, who had plans to write a book on the *Human Comedy*.[54] He and Engels saw the novelist as a kindred spirit, describing him as "generally remarkable for his profound grasp of reality" and especially apt at demonstrating the insidious nature of the capitalist mode of production. Even in the far-off countryside, the "petty peasant" is duped into "depriving his own field of labour" by a savvy moneylender who has convinced him that the work he performed was worthless.[55] Although there is a world of difference between the society of rapid industrialization that Marx and Engels observed in England and the young Balzac's depictions of small-time hoarders and hustlers, the German philosophers were able to find a prophetic truth in the French novelist's fictions.

What stood out to Marx and Engels was that, unlike most literary figures of his day, Balzac featured labor as a central aspect of his realist-fictional world. The result of his detailed and attentive descriptions of an otherwise-neglected aspect of life in nineteenth-century France—the reality of manual, artistic, and intellectual labor—was the emergence of a new vision of the social panorama. Over the next two decades, writers from a variety of social classes would take up the theme of labor in their own fashion, developing, elaborating, and adding more texture and psychological depth to this largely unexplored aspect of social life. Their representations of work would be colored by their social origins and their political goals. Bourgeois writers like George Sand and the members of the Académie des sciences morales et politiques (discussed in chapter 3) would attempt to idealize manual labor as the foundation of modern society, while working-class authors like the contributors to *La Ruche populaire* (see chapter 4) would argue for its political importance.

Balzac's very broad definition allowed for an inclusive understanding of what it meant to perform labor. Work could include both physical toil and intellectual (spiritual, scientific, and artistic) effort; thus, literary writers could consider themselves laborers. However, even if Balzac's works focus on labor in a way that no author before him had done, this was in no way motivated by any sort of sympathy for the plight of the working classes. Instead, it was because as a scientist and as the "secretary" of his own society (*CH* 1:6), he felt obligated to portray things as he saw them. Indeed, as I will show in chapter 5, Balzac would take pains to erase the manual laborer and his work from his later novels, published in 1846 and 1847. Early on, Balzac wanted to establish a broad definition of labor, which could include writing, but, eventually, that same definition would exclude manual labor.

3

The Worker as Hero

Constructing a Bourgeois Narrative

∾

I N 1840, the journalist Eugène Buret was awarded the prestigious Prix Beaujour for his study of French pauperism, which would be published later that year as *De la misère des classes laborieuses en Angleterre et en France; de la nature de la misère, de son existence, de ses effets, de ses causes, et de l'insuffisance des remèdes qu'on lui a opposés jusqu'ici: Avec l'indication des moyens propres à en affranchir les sociétés* (On the misery of the working classes in England and France; on the nature of pauperism, its existence, its effects, its causes, and the inadequacy of remedies so-far proposed: with an indication of best ways to free societies of it). According to the selection committee's report, the competition for the award was fierce, but, in the end, Buret prevailed for his ability to "demonstrate his vast knowledge of political economy."[1] Indeed, the journalist's principal argument was that, if political economy had long been understood as the study of wealth creation, it was now necessary to investigate the other side of the coin: the nature and causes of poverty. In order to support this thesis, he provided a revisionist history of the discipline that spoke to a generation of thinkers anxiously observing the social upheavals caused by industrial take-off.

In the introduction to his study, Buret admits that the system of unregulated competition promoted by political economists like Jean-Baptiste Say and his English counterparts, David Ricardo and Thomas Malthus, may have been useful in the early days of the industrial revolution. However, he argues, now that industrialization has firmly taken root in places like Manchester, London, Paris, and Reims, it has become clear that such a hands-off approach has led to a deplorable dehumanization of the worker: "According to this theory [of laissez-faire], labor is considered abstractly, as a thing, and the economist who studies the variations of supply and demand forgets that the life, the health, and the morality of millions of men are involved in the question ... through this doctrine, the worker finds himself assimilated to an unfeeling thing, a machine from which we have the right to demand more precision, more work, and more production."[2] Balzac's trope of the worker as "winch" reappears here, not as an object of fascination, but as a cause for concern and even pity. Indeed, rather than presenting work as an abstract social force as the novelist had done, Buret promotes a humanist perspective on labor, bringing attention to the individuals who make up the working classes. More familiar with the conditions of the poor in England than in France, Buret offers a descriptive vignette of a particularly destitute working-class family that he has met in the slums of London:

> The man, the head of the family, trembled with fever; illness and hunger had reduced him to an extreme thinness, and the only parts of him that seemed to be alive were his eyes, transparent and animated by the heat of the fever, with a painful expression that was impossible to look at for long. This man, 37 years old, of English birth, and a silk dyer by profession, told us that he could earn as much as 15 shillings per week, but that he had been unable to find work for five months. The relief officer [who was with me] confirmed that this man had always exhibited good behavior and that it was neither vice nor laziness that had reduced him to such a state. (1:370)

In this passage, Buret paints the problem of industrial disorganization through a decidedly human lens. The man is described here is not a statistic but an individual, worthy of compassion. His relatively privileged background, as both a native Englishman and an artisan, makes him more relatable to his middle-class readers than the masses of rag-wearing beggars described elsewhere in the text. Additionally, with the relief officer's endorsement of the artisan's good moral conduct, the reader is given every reason to pity this man who, through no fault of his own, has found himself (and his family) in a state of dire poverty. In fact, he is depicted in almost heroic terms: the feverish look in his eyes is an allusion to the fragility of the human body—not just his, but all humans'—and the will of the spirit to overcome such physical weakness.

Even as Buret seems to be heralding the unemployed worker's heroism and critiquing the system that has permitted such suffering, the journalist is far from promoting a socialist agenda. Indeed, his essay promotes a liberal, productivist worldview that frames the problem of laissez-faire economics not only in terms of its destructive effects on the dignity and well-being of individual workers, but also, and more importantly, as a threat to the prosperity and productivity of the nation. In Buret's telling, the social disorder represented by pauperism is indicative of an industrial "neo-feudalism" that threatens to spread across society and, eventually, lead to revolution (1:58). The only way to avoid this menace, he claims, is to promote an intelligent type of production that can provide enough goods for everyone, rich and poor alike. "A people among whom the democratic element progressing," he declares, "must devote all of its efforts, all of its intelligence to encouraging the meeting of the two components of production—capital and labor—in order to ensure that production satisfies regularly the legitimate and indispensable needs of the mass of its citizens" (2:481).

Buret's attempts to balance the needs of a growing economy with the moral health of society were very much in line with the ideas of other intellectuals and administrators of his time. Another social observer, Antoine Frégier, used his experience in the Parisian police administration to write *Des classes dangereuses de la population dans les grandes villes, et des moyens de les rendre meilleures* (Of the dangerous classes of the population in large cities, and how to improve them). His imaginative depiction of a "dangerous class" was so well received that, after winning a prize from the Académie des sciences morales et politiques in 1838, the work was republished by the Royal Academy of Medicine two years later. Although he shows much less sympathy for the working classes than Buret does, Frégier does argue for a humanistic approach to understanding them, criticizing Malthusian political economists for treating the worker "like an abstraction, without realizing that this abstraction is made of flesh and blood just like us."[3] Both men sought to bring attention to the humanity of the workers they described, using their firsthand knowledge of the living conditions of the working poor.

Buret and Frégier found fame thanks to awards from the Académie des sciences morales et politiques, one of the five branches of the prestigious Institut de France, the official learned society of France. Like the other branches, its principal activity consisted in soliciting scholarly reports, reviewing said reports, and awarding prizes, but its specific purpose was to encourage the use of scientific methods to find effective solutions to social-moral problems. This emphasis on scientific methodology is apparent in the selection committee's report on Buret's Beaujour Prize, where we learn that the runners-up were also highly praised, one for having "observed at first hand some of the facts he describes," and the other for "knowing, citing, and appreciating the work of others [in the field]."[4] What makes Buret's text stand out—and earns him the first-place prize—seems to be his ability to combine empirical methodology, extensive knowledge of the field of political economy, and a concern for the moral implications of his findings. For instance, the committee singled out his long and nuanced discussion of the English Poor Laws of 1834, which he evaluates based on their measurable effects as well as their moral basis. The committee was interested in these laws not only because the workhouse system they established was seen as a way of forcing the poor to participate in the productive activity of the nation (and therefore promoting the virtues of industriousness and individual responsibility), but also because they were proof of the importance of "exact documentation [*documents positifs*] of poverty."[5] Indeed, the new English Poor Laws had been written as the result of a nationwide investigation into the living conditions of the poor and the uses of public charity. According to the report of His Majesty's Commissioners, they based their recommendations on a "considerable" number of surveys sent out to individual households across the country as well as reports from on-the-ground investigators, the pages of which "formed a large mass."[6] This attempt to collect large amounts of data to document poverty rates was particularly appealing to academicians like Rene Villermé, a hygienist who argued for the importance of using statistical methods to understand social problems. In short, Buret's text, like Frégier's and many others that received awards, were appreciated because they seemed to offer empirical proof of social and industrial theories of the academicians. In his 1827 work *Forces productives*, the future academician Charles Dupin had argued that industry and government must "spread . . . knowledge favorable to commerce and production," hypothesizing that economic growth and improved public morality should be seen as two sides of the same coin.[7] At the intersection of morality and political economy, the reports written by Buret, Frégier, and others were seen as providing proof of such a position, and labor played a crucial role in the way that the Académie des sciences morales et politiques envisioned social change.

Despite the Académie's self-proclaimed preference for empirical methods, the reports it chose to honor were littered with literary tropes and stylized descriptions that were more imaginative than what a strict observation of facts would require. For instance, in a section titled "Of the Physical and Moral Condition of the Poor Classes," Buret prepares his readers for the firsthand descriptions of destitution that will follow in a rather paradoxical way. "Before undertaking this sad pilgrimage into this hellish world, as abundant in suffering as the one described by Dante, we promise to exaggerate nothing, but to withhold nothing, either. He who desires to go down there must harden himself in advance and prepare himself to witness without fainting the most hideous of spectacles" (1:313). Despite his vow to avoid exaggeration, Buret's descriptions of the living conditions of the poor are, in fact, full of hyperbole. The sensorial experience of confronting this social underworld is so intense, he claims, that only the strongest of social observers can resist the urge to swoon. The comparison to Dante's *Inferno* evokes mythological a hellscape more than the clear-eyed account of the industrial working classes that Buret claims to be writing. The literary allusion also reminds us of Balzac's description of Paris in the "Physionomies parisiennes," where, he says, "everything flares up, falters, dies down, burns up again, sparkles, crackles, and is consumed."[8] The novelist's spectacular account of industrial Paris is also echoed in Frégier's *Classes dangereuses*, where the administrator provides a particularly theatrical tableau of what he calls the "vicious" portion of the working class. "Isn't it a painful and disgraceful spectacle of humanity to see a father and a mother, both heavy with drink, lying motionless on the floor of their boarding room, in the middle of the night, unable to turn the doorknob with their trembling hands! The first person to find them in this shameful position is their son, their own son, who, in his tender age is unable to help them."[9] Frégier does not claim to have witnessed this scene himself, but, through the use of a rhetorical question ("Isn't it a ... spectacle[?]"), presents it as a commonplace. The depravity of the incapacitated parents is brought into focus through the eyes of their son, an audience of one, and is then further amplified by the horrified readers of Frégier's text. Here and elsewhere, the social reports solicited and recognized by the Académie were often just as much an invention of the moralist imagination as they were a record of empirical observation.

In many cases, it was the academicians themselves who were producing such sensational portraits of the working classes. Perhaps more than any other figure, it was one of the Académie's founding members, the hygienist and physician René Villermé, who is best known for his *enquêtes* (on-site investigations), using empirical methods to shed light on the conditions of industrial workers. His *Tableau de l'état physique et moral des ouvriers employés dans les manufactures de coton, de laine et de soie* (Study of the physical condition of cotton, wool, and silk workers) (1840) is one of the founding works of the modern humanistic sciences. Based on two years of field research, during which time he observed firsthand the industrial centers of France, Villermé's *enquête* included statistical tables and technical descriptions of industrial processes. He did not, however, shy away from sharing his convictions regarding the importance of improving the morality of the worker, and, in fact, he believed that his eyewitness testimony would lend scientific weight to this stance. Like Buret and Frégier, however, he often went beyond reporting what he saw in the factory cities and instead relied on his literary imagination in order to argue that the destruction of the family unit necessitated stricter and more paternalistic interventions from factory owners.

Villermé insisted on the empirical method of seeing and reporting, epitomized by the repetition of the words "I saw . . . [*j'ai vu* . . .]" that abound throughout in his work. However, his interpretations of the facts often slip into the fanciful. At times, he seems to be practicing the same type of "physiological" reading of his subjects' bodies and facial features that were typical of the works of Balzac, where, as Andrea Goulet has observed, we find "a tension between abstraction and experience, idealization and physicality."[10] One description of a family of German immigrants shows this mix of what we would now consider scientific discourse and literary license quite clearly: "I saw [*j'ai vu*] on the roads, during the short time I spent [*j'ai passé*] in Alsace, some of those families who came [*qui venaient*] from Germany and dragged along [*traînaient*] with them many small children. Their tranquility, their circumspection, their way of presenting themselves contrasted [*contrastaient*] with the effrontery and the insolence of our native vagabonds. Everything about them seemed to make [*paraissait rendre*] their misfortune respectable: they weren't begging [*mendiaient*], they were merely soliciting [*sollicitaient*] work."[11] We can detect here the shift from what Goulet calls a Lockean empirical type of vision to one that is idealist. Villermé's description begins with the personal and punctual "*j'ai vu* . . ." in the *passé composé*, indicating a precise action that happened once at a specific moment. These two words (three in the French) assure the reader of the veracity of the testimony; this is the observation by an expert witness (the "I") of a singular event, indicating an empirical and subjective mode of perception. But as the sentence progresses, the verb tense shifts to the imperfect past, the tense of habitual and indefinite actions. Thus, this is not the description of one German family that the author actually saw but a *typologie* of the honest immigrant, perhaps an amalgamation of many families he encountered. What's more, Villermé's observations go beyond the physical. His gift of vision allows him to read the signs of morality. For example, he can tell, simply by looking at their faces, that they are seeking work rather than trying to avoid it by begging. In this way, the characters in the description become idealized avatars of the working poor. In the final analysis, then, his conclusions are the result not of inductive reasoning but of an a priori idea that steered his *enquête*.

Further on, Villermé offers an account of the process of the destructive effects that labor has on the body, offering a kind of narrative of alienation. In the previous passage, he had explained that when the German workers first arrived in the factory towns, they were serene, and even respectable in spite of their poverty. However, once the workers have found employment in the factories, so the story goes, their bodies quickly show the harmful traces of their new way of life: "Soon [*bientôt*] the grief, the lack of food, the continuous deprivation, the insalubrity of their new occupation, and the too-long workday degrade their health: their complexion withers, they grow thin, they lose their forces" (1:29–30). While, in the previous paragraph, Villermé had been using the past tense, here he switches to the present. The shift in tenses indicates a progression of events through time, during which the family passes from one state of existence to another, from honorable poverty to abject misery. As they devote their energy to the products of their work, their own bodies become withered and thin. This reality of factory work—the present—is placed in contrast with the more wholesome poverty of the freshly arrived family of the past. The *bientôt* indicates an inevitable future, already detectible in the present, in which the immigrant experiences the type of intense physical and spiritual pain that comes from hard physical labor, transforming a respectable worker into a decrepit shell.

Nonetheless, the moral condemnation that Villermé expresses at the sight of the alienated worker is tempered by an unmistakably miserabilist quality to his narrative, a certain delight that he seems to take in depicting the suffering of his subjects as the source of strong emotional or even sensorial feelings. This comes out most clearly in his descriptions of the female factory workers: "There are among them a multitude of women: pale, thin, walking barefoot in the mud, and who, lacking an umbrella, place their aprons or their underskirts over their heads in order to protect their faces and necks when it rains" (1:26). The erotic nature of the scene is undeniable. The image of the pale, partially undressed woman trudging barefoot through the mud, soaking wet and trying to protect her fragile neck, paints her as both vulnerable and desirable. If the *ouvrier* is represented by his arm or his hand, the *ouvrière*'s emblem is her neck, the promise of a secret and fragile sensuality beneath her rough exterior. To arrive at this precise description of the woman worker, the *enquêteur* must either have stared at her for some extended period, or else invented her. Either way, this gaze claims her as *his* creature, formed for *his* pleasure and use. She is what Michel Foucault would call a "docile body," the result not of physical violence but of a more surreptitious type of discipline, which, he explains, turns the body into "capacity" or something useful to the ruling powers.[12] In a sense, her potentially unruly sexuality becomes useful when it is channeled and transformed into a source of erotic pleasure for the bourgeois observer.

Villermé embraces the diversion of potential rebellious energy into the more constructive and productive activity of manual labor, a process he carries out discursively in his depiction of child workers. Although the unhealthy living and working conditions, lack of education, and uncertain futures of child laborers were condemned widely, in 1840 there was no consensus as to what types of laws should be put in place. Indeed, this was the subject of a great deal of debate, and a child labor law would not be passed until March 1841. As Charles Dupin laid out clearly, liberals had to balance the desire to promote morality and the need for cheap labor in the industrial sector. Finding the right way to regulate child labor was, in his words, "one of the most important subjects for the well-being of the laboring classes, for the future of industry, and for our national strength."[13] Unsurprisingly, the employment of children was to be moderated but not abolished, in part because of concerns about what children would do unsupervised while their parents were at the factory, but also because of fears about what the removal of an important portion of the workforce would do to the economy. Villermé describes the plight of child workers in a passage directly following that of the women workers. "[With the women] there is an even more considerable number of young children no less dirty, no less haggard, covered in rags, greasy from the oil of the loom that falls on them while they work. Although better protected [than their mothers] from the rain by the impermeability of their clothes, they don't seem to carry any provisions for the day" (1:26). The body of the child is above all expressed in terms of neglect, pointing to a disorderly home life: filthy, covered in grease, dressed in rags, and poorly nourished. The reader's pity for these children is evoked, but there is another process taking place, as well. The reference, at the end of the passage, to the mothers who carry their lunches to work but leave their children with nothing to eat is an indictment of the *ouvrière*'s lack of maternal instinct. Compounded with the eroticization of her body described above, and the drunken antics of their fathers (described by Frégier, Villermé, and in countless other social reports), the lamentable home life of the pauper's child was a source of great consternation. The only protection that these children were receiving, it seemed, came from their employment. If their clothes are waterproof, this is not due to any care on the part of their mothers, we are assured, but because, in the course of their labors, mechanical grease had fallen on them, making their rags impermeable. In the end, it is *work* and not family that protects the laboring child from the harsh exterior world. Lacking a real family environment, these children are taken under the wing of *travail*, and they too can be transformed into Foucauldian docile bodies.

Literary tools were necessary for liberals like Villermé, Buret, Frégier, and others to reconcile the observed physical deterioration of the industrial worker's body—which bears empirical proof that hard physical labor is damaging and even dehumanizing—with the idea of *travail* as an edifying and moralizing force among the lower classes and, ultimately, a great benefit to the economic well-being of the nation. This doubled perception of the effects of labor on the worker is latent in nearly all labor discourse in the nineteenth century and helps to explain why the physical condition of workers proved to be such a point of tension. The only way to get out of this quandary was through storytelling, working backward from the empirical observations and finding a first cause. Dominique Kalifa has argued that the social *enquête*, the genre to which many of the Académie's papers belong, is defined by its methodology, a three-step process of exploration, interpretation, and narration, the third consisting of a "retrospective telling of a chain of events which construct the truth and allow it to be read."[14] It was in this final step—narrative—that the *enquêteur* ceased to be a simple reporter of facts and turned into a teller of tales. We can see in this three-step schema the passage from the positivist act of *looking* to the visionary step of *creating* an idealized reality.

If the *enquêtes* and other reports associated with the Académie sat on the fold between scientific observation and literary invention, this was in part because many of them borrowed liberally from the tropes and types established in popular novels. Frégier's sensational depictions of an imaginary "dangerous class" and Buret's theatrical scenes, which bring the term "*misère*" to life, would have been familiar to readers of popular novels and social panoramas, which, as Judith Lyon-Caen has argued, were seen by many readers to be "an indispensable lens through which to face the terrible spectacle of pauperism."[15] Regardless of whether or not they were "real," however, the evocative descriptions in the reports of the Académie were powerful in the dominant discourse of labor in the 1840s. These depictions contributed to a way of reading the working body that Balzac had begun in the early 1830s. Similar to the "winch" imagined by Balzac, the figure of the worker here is a tool for advancing productivist values rather than a complete human being.

Despite the similarities in the way they depict the living conditions of the working poor, it is important to note a very important distinction between *littérateurs* like Balzac and *enquêteurs* like Villermé: while the former were able to reach a popular audience through sensational fictions, the latter had political influence and the power to shape policy. Indeed, the Académie des sciences morales et politiques was reinstituted in 1832 (it had been defunct since 1803) by the powerful historian-turned-politician François Guizot and quickly became one of France's most influential institutions. Under Guizot's watch, the Académie quickly began to promote research into topics that were dear to the Doctrinaires, the ruling political party of which he was the leader. Proponents of the *juste milieu*, a centrist political philosophy that sought to avoid the excesses of both absolutism and radical republicanism that had plagued France for fifty years, the Doctrinaires believed that it was necessary to reshape society in a way that would finally put an end to the age of revolutions. To do this, they sought to find a balance between theoretical ideals and empirical data. According to Aurelian Craiutu, "they paid attention to both rights and facts [and] combined experience and enlightened pragmatism with reason and philosophical investigation." In other words, "the Doctrinaires' method was animated by a spirit that carefully observed facts and only admitted generalizations slowly, progressively, concurrently with the ascertainment of facts. They maintained that no general idea could be of any real value unless founded upon—and supported by—the facts themselves."[16] Far removed from the dogmatic approach to governing that the label *Doctrinaire* implies, Guizot and his fellow travelers believed that evidence-based policymaking was the most effective way to ensure peace and stability. This was the motivation for the so-called Enquête Guizot of 1833, which sent inspectors out for "on-the-spot investigations" of primary schools across France in order to obtain statistical information about the system as well as insight into "the moral state of primary instruction and its results."[17] The survey was meant to compliment the Loi Guizot, enacted earlier that year, which sought to establish a centralized primary education system (for boys). The goal of having such a uniform educational program was not only to promote national unity across regions, but also to form a new generation of enlightened and cooperative citizens.

However empirically minded they claimed to be, the Doctrinaires were not without their own ideology. Guizot, like most liberals of his day, believed politics could not be carried out by just anyone, but that the political leader must possess some particular gifts, skills, or abilities. Haunted by the "spectre" (to borrow from Marx) of popular revolution, these liberals worried about the decisions that a truly democratic society would make, and argued that those in power must show proof of *capacité*, that is, "the faculty of acting according to reason."[18] The exact definition of *capacité* was somewhat ambiguous, but, as a "concept," it "allowed nineteenth-century liberals to legitimize a new economic, social, and political hierarchy based on a novel set of values and principles."[19] In Guizot's own words, the ruling class should represent "the true *legitimate aristocracy*, that which is freely accepted by the people over whom it should exercise its power." Far from espousing the traditional Republican ideals of equality and brotherhood, then, the ruling party of the July Monarchy argued for a modern version of elitism based on ability rather than birth.[20]

Like all branches of the Institut de France, the Académie had no lawmaking authority, but it was largely populated by members of the sitting government (including Guizot himself), and, unsurprisingly, its goals were closely aligned with the party in power. There was, as Corinne Delmas has demonstrated, "a necessary alliance between the scientist and the administrator," as the latter provided the former with the necessary financial means to carry out research, and, reciprocally, the researcher produced informational resources that could be used in the service of policy-making or even in order to shape public opinion.[21] Among its elected members were the nation's most respected political economists, scientists, mathematicians, and philosophers, most of whom were economic liberals with a keen interest in social reform; its founding members included Guizot, Antoine

Destutt de Tracy, Victor Cousin, Rene Villermé, and even Thomas Malthus, who acted as a foreign correspondent.[22] In keeping with these ideals, the Académie's activities tended to promote policies that would limit public disorder in a way that avoided authoritarianism or any undue appeal to religious faith. There was a strong agreement that the solution to social disorder would have to occur not through fervent patriotism nor through religious obedience, but through public morality. The role of the Académie was limited in terms of direct influence on law-making, but worked as something of a shadow institution, whose goal was, according to Pierre Rosanvallon, "to constitute an independent intellectual and scientific social space ... [and] to establish a moral voice that was freely allied with those in power." Finally, members of the Académie, composed of scientists, mathematicians, and other liberal professionals, were brought together by their belief that empiricist and rational methods must be applied to the upholding of a traditional hierarchical social organization.[23]

The liberals associated with the Académie tended to focus on the degraded, suffering bodies of the laboring classes, whose very existence, they believed, posed a threat to the delicate social order that had been established after years of revolutionary unrest. As Louis Chevalier famously demonstrated, the dominant bourgeois opinion of the time held that manual labor was closely linked to poverty, vice, and other forms of moral disorder. Tracing the long history of the term "proletarian" in modern French parlance, Chevalier remarks that "the bourgeois population's attitude to the laboring classes were borrowed from an older attitude to a population which had been regarded as not belonging to the city, as suspect of all the crimes, all the evils, all the epidemics and all the violence, not merely because of its own characteristics, but on account of its origins outside the city and of the immigration which had inconsistently been put down to a proliferation of beggars of old."[24] The growth in population and the increased visibility of the working poor within urban centers seemed to be bringing these "outsiders" into the social sphere, and the perceived disorder occasioned by these changes helped to feed a long-held and widespread view of laborers as potential criminals. In other words, public opinion and demographic and economic facts seemed to support one another.

Although many members of the Académie saw themselves as men of science rather than opinion, the close relationship between facts and perceptions at the time made it hard to distinguish when they were engaging with the former and when they were expressing the latter. A survey of the different contests and prizes that were offered during the years 1839–41 (a period of considerable social unrest in France) shows us that the Académie was intent on cultivating a docile and orderly workforce at home and abroad. For example, in 1839, one year after Britain had finally outlawed slavery in its colonies (the French would not take this step until 1848), the Académie solicited reports that would come up with "the best way, in the interest of both settlers and slaves, to put an end to slavery in the colonies."[25] In other words, they seemed to be asking, how can we peacefully transform an enslaved population into a productive working class? In 1841, in what was no doubt a nod to Louis Blanc's popular manifesto *L'Organisation du travail* (1840), the Académie sought research into "the influence of shared labor organization on the factory."[26] By 1843, a prompt called for information about "how progress and taste for material well-being impact the morality of a people."[27] Through these calls to research, members of the Académie were able to promote the values of industriousness, sobriety, and morality across the intellectual community, and the papers that they recognized as outstanding give us insight as to how they thought these values should be extended to the rest of the population.

Thus, the Académie was able to shape the public debate about social questions, not only as the arbiters of "good" research who could grant awards, but perhaps more fundamentally, as the framers of research questions. This was particularly true for the topic of labor. The prompts composed by the Académie guaranteed that labor would be studied using empirical methods and, perhaps more importantly, that it would be considered in terms of its value as a tool to promote moral order among the working classes. Indeed, the construct of the dangerous classes that was the focus of Antoine Frégier's *Dangerous Classes* was already present in the Académie's rather leading call for submissions: "According to the exact observation of facts, what are the elements in Paris or in any other large city, which make up that part of the population which forms a class deemed dangerous for its vices, its ignorance, or its abject poverty? What means might be employed by the administration, by rich men, or by intelligent and hard-working laborers to improve this depraved and unfortunate class?"[28] With this wording, the Académie assumes, and, in a sense, conjures, the existence of a "depraved and unfortunate" social class defined by its immorality, ignorance, and abject misery. The "dangerous classes" are the imaginary other to the upstanding members of society: government officials, the wealthy, and honest laborers. Frégier's paternalistic text is essentially, then, a further elaboration of a fictional social group invented by the Académie, offering an excellent example of how they determined how labor would be defined.

Buret, on the other hand, was responding to an excessively vague prompt: "Determine the nature and manifestations of pauperism [*misère*] in various countries. Research the causes which produce it."[29] To answer this call, the methodical Buret spends the first 200 pages of his report defining the quite ambiguous term *misère*. Concluding that *misère*, strictly understood, is "poverty that is experienced morally," he makes sure to distinguish it from it the physical depletion experienced by manual laborers living in economic poverty: "poverty works in the workshop, pauperism [*misère*] suffers in the hospital and the beggar's asylum."[30] Like Frégier, Buret believes it is important to distinguish between the material and the moral causes of poverty: while the former are associated with labor and are therefore inevitable in a modern economy, the latter are the result of social disorganization, and therefore can—and must—be remedied.

In both examples, we can see how the Académie's narrative of labor, situated at the intersection of morality and economic policy, is shaped by their prompts and then further emphasized through the award-giving process. In this way, they craft a narrative of cooperation between intellectual and manual workers, whereby the former, in studying the latter, come up with ways to organize and rationalize labor in a way that benefits not only the individual but society as a whole. In the end, the focus that the Académie des sciences morales et politiques placed on labor at the intersection of morality and political economy helped frame the terms of the dominant bourgeois narrative of cooperation between intellectual and manual labor.

A New Romantic Hero

While the reports of the Académie painted a sweeping portrait of the working classes as a whole, any portrayal of workers as actors in their own right remained largely absent from these texts. Instead, it was in the form of fiction that the figure of the individual laborer finally emerged, complete with subjectivity, emotions, and the will to act. In 1840, not one but two popular novels appeared, nearly simultaneously, depicting manual labor as the marker of a modern hero. George Sand's *Le Compagnon du Tour de France* (*The Journeyman Joiner; or, The Companion of the Tour of France*) and Etienne Cabet's *Voyage en Icarie* (*Travels in Icaria*) were quite different in terms of plot and style, but their shared use of working-class characters who act courageously and admirably invites comparison.³¹ Unlike Balzac's vision of the worker as "some kind of winch"—a tool of the machine age and victim of oppression—Sand and Cabet present workers who are fully realized in fiction. One might even argue that they represented a new iteration of the Romantic hero.

For decades, Johann von Goethe's eponymous bourgeois adolescent in *The Sufferings of Young Werther* (1774) had served as the model for the French Romantic hero in works from Chateaubriand's *René* (1802) to Vigny's *Chatterton* (1835). According to Lilian Furst's classic description, the Romantic hero is an object of both admiration and pity. On the one hand, she says, "Almost invariably he is a gentleman, a member of the leisured class at ease financially. Both his handsomeness and his freedom from mundane concerns raise him to the level of an idealized glamorous figure." These exceptional physical and psychological traits, she continues, come to him naturally and designate him as the focus of any space he occupies, but it is precisely this remarkability that leads to his inevitable downfall. Unlike the heroic type of legend and myth, who risked his own life in the service of some greater good (social, religious, etc.), the Romantic hero's focus was turned inward on himself: "The Romantic hero's dominance," she asserts, "stems not from his activity but from the interest in his psyche, since his heroic assertion is the egocentric one of his own personality, far indeed from the hero's traditional commitment to a cause outside himself."³² As we shall see, Sand and Cabet, each in their own way, adopt, undermine, and refashion many of the qualities of the Romantic hero in ways that help to establish a new type of socially aware heroism that is specific to the working classes.

In his *Travels in Icaria*, Etienne Cabet presents a typical Romantic hero as a passive and talentless individual in order to allow his working-class characters to shine. The novel, first published under the British-sounding pseudonym Francis Adams, is presented as the diary of an English nobleman named Lord William Carisdall, who, at first glance, fits the type of the Byronic hero quite nicely: "one of the wealthiest lords in the three kingdoms and one of the handsomest men that I have ever seen" (3). Like Byron, Carisdall leaves his native England to explore a faraway country (Icaria), meets interesting and courageous men, falls hopelessly in love with unattainable women, and suffers profoundly when the reality of these new relationships fails to meet his ideal. From the outset, however, it is apparent that this fairly simple love story is not the true focus of the text, nor is this hapless Romantic its real hero. Instead,

Lord Carisdall serves, first, as a pair of eyes through which to observe a wondrous new society and, second, as a mediocre foil to the exceptional people who live in it.

Indeed, the true hero of the novel is a young Icarian named Valmor, described by Carisdall in the most admiring of terms: "so natural and sincere that I was very moved ... so well educated, so good, and so kind that we began, then and there, an affectionate friendship that became stronger and more intimate every day" (16). Socially, Valmor is "one of the most distinguished and noble young Icarians," whose father and grandfather are high-ranking magistrates, so Carisdall is shocked to learn that despite the family's illustrious social status, they are all laborers. Although we never see them at work, we learn that Valmor is a locksmith and his sister Corilla is a seamstress (18).

By comparing the two men, Cabet plays with the stereotype of the Romantic hero in order to redefine heroism itself. Lord Carisdall, a handsome young man whose repeated experience of unrequited love paints him as a suffering, Werther-like character, is also quite boring and decidedly unimpressive. Rejected by a beautiful seamstress named Dinaïse, Carisdall retreats to his bed, surrendering quietly to his melancholy without any of the passionate outbursts or violent action that characterized Goethe's suicidal protagonist. In contrast, the locksmith Valmor—a man of great valor, as his name suggests—embodies true heroism in the *Travels*. Also spurned by Dinaïse, the valiant Icarian grieves for several days, but, unlike Carsdall, he quickly overcomes his emotions through reason and determination. Rather than avoiding Dinaïse, Valmor attends a party where she will be, an experience he compares to fighting in a war: "If only you knew how much I suffered and what battles I fought! I thought I was stronger! How weak is man! But it has been done, I have triumphed, and I am sure that I will continue to triumph" (143). Compared to Valmor's fortitude in the face of unrequited love, Carisdall's weakness is conspicuous.

Soon after Cabet's *Travels*, the well-established Romantic author George Sand published her own novel featuring a working-class hero. The story follows a young carpenter, Pierre Huguenin, who falls in love with his childhood playmate, the high-born Yseult de Villepreux. The two are drawn to one another because their political and social ideals match perfectly, even as they are put to the test by class loyalties: Yseult's Orleanist grandfather admires Pierre's handiwork but still considers him socially inferior, while the fraternal ties Pierre has with his fellow artisans make it impossible for him to imagine assuming the higher social rank that a marriage to Yseult would entail. The marriage plot ends inconclusively: the division between the laborer and the landed noblewoman proves impossible to bridge within the confines of Sand's narrative, and their reunion is delayed until some undetermined future date, when society will have changed. Nonetheless, the carpenter emerges heroic—empowered by his sentimental and social struggles.

Pierre Huguenin is the epitome of working-class virtue as envisioned by Sand: extremely skilled, extremely virtuous, and extremely handsome. His appearance is harmonious, as each of his physical traits is perfectly adapted to the type of labor he performs: his small delicate hands are especially suited to carving blocks of wood, and his large blue eyes allow him to envision geometrically sound blueprints. His physical beauty and aptitude for labor are inseparable aspects of his character, and, indeed, it is the labor he performs that *makes* him so attractive. Sand emphasizes this point from the very beginning of the novel when the young man is described as having taken on a new and attractive maturity after years of work on the road. "His bearing was noble and assured; his clear and pure complexion, which the sun had not tanned, was set off by a slight black beard. He was dressed as a mechanic, but with a scrupulous neatness" (19). Pierre's appearance combines delicate innocence ("his clear and pure complexion") with signs of virility ("a slight black beard") so that he embodies a distinct kind of working-class attractiveness that is both simple and powerful. He wears the modest uniform of a laborer, but in a "neat" way that signals care and intention. His profession as a carpenter is inextricably tied to his heroism, allowing his friend Amaury to see him as "more than a workman, more than a man perhaps," and going so far as to compare him to "the Christ, that son of a carpenter, poor, obscure, wandering upon the earth, and talking to wretched workmen like ourselves" (110).

Handsome, courageous, and even Christlike, the worker characters in Sand's and Cabet's novels are a far cry from Buret's miserable silk dyer, unable to feed his children and living in the London slums. Even if they are not quite the "idealized glamorous figure" of Furst's Romantic hero, they are noble and honorable. In this way, Sand and Cabet are redefining the heroic type, transforming him from a Romantic one to a working-class one.

Cabet's and Sand's respective iterations of the new worker-hero were well received by certain segments of the working-class reading public, although not exactly the same ones. While Sand's admirers were primarily highly skilled artisans and aspiring worker-intellectuals (whom we will discuss in the next chapter), Cabet's public was more diverse, and included illiterate workers who would gather to hear his writings read aloud.

The message in *Travels* was empowering for a broad swathe of working-class readers, and Cabet soon earned a faithful following. According to the mason-turned-politician Martin Nadaud, he and many other militants visited Cabet regularly at his home starting in 1839, the year he returned from exile. At around the same time, Cabet began to hold a weekly salon that was well-attended by a large contingent of Parisian workers, one of whom admits to being "greatly attached to this worthy champion of the people." By 1842, he had become so popular that groups of workers would go door-to-door, asking well-known writers like Eugène Sue and George Sand to invest in his newspaper *Le Populaire de 1841*.[33] Cabet's influence was not limited to a Parisian audience, thanks to the success of *Travels* and his newspaper. Joseph Benoît, a *canut* or silk weaver from Lyon, recalls evenings when twenty or thirty workers would come together in the poorly lit workshops to discuss the stories and ideas presented in the monthly. Indeed, it was common practice for Cabet's followers to read this paper collectively, both in the workshop and in social spaces.[34] His followers called themselves Icarians, eager to align themselves with the ideals embodied by the fictional Valmor and his countrymen.

The utopian context of Cabet's novel was a tactical choice, softening its radical thrust, and he was able to attract both moderate and radical socialists.[35] His pacifist version of communism spoke not only to disgruntled militants like Nadaud, but also to reformists like Louis Blanc, who described the questions raised in the *Travels* as those "most worthy of the attention of serious minds and people of good will. It is worth reading with care, even though one does not have to completely adopt its conclusions."[36] As communists with more conspiratorial and violent messages like Théodore Dézamy and Jean-Jacques Pillot were imprisoned or censured, Cabet was able to stay active, and his popularity remained untrammeled by censure or serious political criticism. Free to continue his political propaganda, Cabet disseminated his ideas widely among the working classes in political pamphlets as well as his newspaper, *Le Populaire de 1841*. *Travels in Icaria* was so successful that it went through five printings between 1842 and 1848.[37] Nonetheless, Cabet was unable to win support from the mainstream Left, and the leading moderate newspapers *Le National* and *La Réforme* completely snubbed him, refusing to "recognize him as having a place in the public debate" even though their offices were on the same street as the *Le Populaire*.[38]

Like Cabet, Sand's appeal to a working-class audience did not win her many fans in the mainstream bourgeois press. *The Journeyman Joiner* was even panned by Sand's erstwhile friend Marie d'Agoult, whose biting criticism of the novel's lengthy discussions of *compagnonnage* practices must have been painful to read. "A glacial chill extends across the narrative," she writes. "It is completely devoid of interest; one senses something unmistakably constrained and false."[39] Appearing in *La Presse*, one of the most popular daily papers of the day, d'Agoult's reflections were undoubtedly representative of a wider taste among the reading public. Nor was it a hit among Left-leaning journalists, whose political commitments might have made them more open to the subject matter. Louis Reybaud, a self-styled economist and specialist of social reform movements, scoffed at Sand's depiction of a working-class hero: "Seriously, an ideal such as this is inadmissible . . . a simple woodworker, no one could ever believe it!"[40] Writing in the Left-leaning *Le National*, Reybaud promoted a more radical agenda than that of the July Monarchy government, but, in hindsight, his classism was predictive of the conservative bourgeois policies that would ultimately win the day in 1848.

Despite this public critique, *The Journeyman Joiner* was a success. Illustrious figures such as Eugène Delacroix, Amable Tastu, François Rollinat, and even Jules Michelet spoke privately, in journals and correspondence, about their appreciation for the work. Flora Tristan, whose own "Tour de France" was inspired by Sand's novel, carried a copy of the novel with her and urged her supporters to read it. These quite well-known admirers must not have been alone, as the novel quickly went through several reprints, attesting to a large readership. By publishing with Charles Perrotin, an editor closely associated with the popular *chansonnier* Pierre-Jean de Béranger, Sand was aiming for a more popular audience than she had previously been able to reach, and the book's publication record proves that she accomplished this.[41] After Perrotin's first edition in December 1840, the novel was quickly reprinted by the Belgian publisher Hauman (in 1841 and then again in 1842), again by Perrotin in 1842, and then by Garnier Frères in 1847.[42]

It is difficult to know who exactly was reading Sand's work, but it must be assumed that a good number of them would have identified as working class. According to the artisan Agricol Perdiguier, who helped promote the work among his fellow *compagnons*, the working-class readers with whom he discussed the novel embraced it with enthusiasm: "The laborers [*les ouvriers*] begin to know you and to love you; I have placed so many copies of *The Journeyman Joiner* recently that I have almost become a book dealer, and as soon as they finish the first part, they want to read the sequel."[43] Perdiguier, it must be noted, had a stake in Sand's success. Her novel *The Journeyman Joiner* was inspired by his own *Le Livre de compagnonnage*, a firsthand account of the practices and traditions of the traveling craftsmen known as *compagnons*, published earlier in 1840. A journeyman joiner himself, Perdiguier served as one of the models for Sand's hero. Since the official guild system had been outlawed along with all other corporate bodies during the French Revolution, the journeymen's associations had taken on increased importance as spaces of working-class sociability, providing both material assistance (like mutual aid programs) and moral support (traveling workers lived together, sharing meals and performing fraternal rituals). The *compagnons* had long apprenticeships, during which time they traveled across the country, perfecting their craft in different towns. This Tour de France, as it was known, was a rite of passage that young artisans were expected to complete before settling down to start a family. Perdiguier's book recounted the rites and traditions of the Tour, but also had an edifying goal to promote worker solidarity. Not all *compagnons* were happy with Perdiguier's attempt to publicize and vulgarize their ancient customs, and, among those who did not mind, many were skeptical of the book's goal to cast them in a sympathetic light to a broader audience. These same readers, as Martine Watrelot has demonstrated, often found Sand's novel to be entertaining but were equally dubious of its ability to exert any social influence.[44]

When discussing the working-class heroism that emerges in these novels, it is important to note that the type of worker who would be able to embody such heroism was actually quite rare. Literate artisans like the joiner Pierre Huguenin and the locksmith Valmor represent an elite subgroup of French laborers who would have had very little in common with the industrial workers portrayed in Villermé's *enquête*. Indeed, these worker-heroes were not too different from novelists like Sand and Cabet themselves.

In both novels, one of the defining characteristics of the working-class hero is his ability to translate his thoughts and emotions into words—and eventually write those words down. In Cabet's text, this aspect of heroism is once again established through a comparison between the feeble Romantic Lord Carisdall and his socially inferior—but morally superior—friends. One morning, for example, Carisdall and Valmor observe a beautiful sunrise together, the perfect occasion for the decidedly Romantic practice of expressing one's awe in the face of nature's beauty. Carisdall is inspired to speak, but he is only able to pronounce a few platitudes, praising the sun as "the father, the benefactor, the god of nature." These banalities allow Valmor to showcase his superior poetic talent, interrupting his friend to propose a novel allegory of the sun as "a little lamp or a little stationary heater . . . next to the billions of other suns and other earths, each with its place and its function in the universal workshop" (135). Valmor's innovative—and pointedly productivist—depictions of nature as God's workshop are, we are to understand, more sophisticated and more compelling than Carisdall's silly and sentimental abstractions.

Carisdall's poor way with language also helps to point to the heroism of another working-class character, the French painter Eugène, whose linguistic genius is emphasized throughout the tale, and who serves, as Leslie Roberts has rightfully noted in the introduction to her translation, as Cabet's "mouthpiece" (lii). Eugène's explanation of the workings of Icarian society are essential to Carisdall's integration, and if the well-bred lord is initially taken aback by the militant painter, he soon comes to appreciate his sincerity: "Everything he had seen had made him so enthusiastic that he was feverish, delirious. At first, I thought him a madman. I soon discovered, however, that he was frank, warm in his feelings, and of noble heart and soul" (17). Carisdall's use of the term "noble" to describe his two new friends is both a reminder of the Englishman's old-fashioned conception of value and, as I will discuss further on, a gesture toward a new definition of nobility.

One evening, Eugène describes a walk through the city of Icaria, where he is passionately taken with what he sees as the rational beauty of the urban planning. Though overcome with emotion, Eugène manages to translate this fervor into words, writing them down in a letter to his brother. Carisdall finds the letter "so interesting and instructive" that he immediately asks to "copy" it into his own travel journal rather than formulate his own impressions. Later that day, he strikes up a friendship with some new acquaintances by reading them, word-for-word, the copied journal entry, exploiting Eugène's creative effort to achieve his own goals (36). Time and again, Carisdall fills his diary with the words of others rather than writing his own, claiming that he is "too upset" (172), too "ill at ease" (179), or simply that the others "took a more active role" in the event being described (225). In short, Carisdall recognizes that his own abilities for verbal expression pale in comparison to those of his working-class friends and has no qualms about appropriating them for his journal.

Like Valmor, Pierre Huguenin's superiority comes from his ability to perform both manual and intellectual labor. Just as his capacity for manual labor can be read on his body, his intellectual superiority is first detectible through aesthetic observation. Pierre's style of letter-writing is described by the town curate as "fine and flowing," noting that "there was in his style a measure, a nobleness, and even an eloquence that raised him above himself" (18). In contrast to Balzac's *grisette* Ida, whose hurried love notes, riddled with errors, give us insight into her frantic state of mind, Pierre's letters to his father reveal a steady and confident thoughtfulness. This formal excellence is actually a sign of a deeper intelligence, which is able to flourish when Pierre discovers Yseult's hidden library. Here, he quickly "devours . . . not the letter, but the substance of the greater part of these works" (37). His potential for intellectual reflection is limited only by his responsibility to labor: "What an extent of knowledge, what a superiority of ideas would he not have attained at that period, if he had had time and books at discretion! But he could not neglect his work" (37). To balance his desire to learn and his duty to work, Sand's carpenter hero carries out his physical tasks during the day and spends his nights in contemplation, a practice he shares with a growing number of so-called worker-poets (many of whom Sand supported and encouraged), whose writing had captured popular attention.[45] This lack of sleep—the renouncing of physical comfort in the pursuit of a higher calling—is a mark of Pierre's heroism, endowing him with a certain sense of nobility: "He felt in himself a nobility of nature more pure and more exquisite than all the titles acquired and consecrated by the laws of the world. He was every moment compelled to stifle the bursts of a nature in a manner princely, under the envelope of a mechanic. He resigned himself to it with a strength and serenity which so much more characterized this innate grandeur" (38). In fact, Sand often employs the term "noble" to describe Pierre's character. In the space of just a few pages, we learn that "his features had the nobleness and regularity of statuary," that he possesses "the noble ambition of acquiring talent in his profession," and that "his bearing is noble and assured" (15–19). Pierre's physical beauty, his confident gait, and his intellectual and moral capacities are all, in a sense, inherent to his "race," a term that Sand herself uses interchangeably with class.[46] This modern nobility of the working class, as defined in the novel, seems to be just as much a question of innate gifts as it is a willingness to work.

The working-class heroes in *Travels* are also described as noble. Carisdall praises Eugène for his "noble heart and soul" and Valmor is known as "one of the most distinguished and noble young Icarians" (17–18). However, when pushed to define the term, Cabet's mouthpiece Eugène elaborates: "there are many citizens who are noble, famous, and illustrious. They are mechanics, doctors, or any workers who distinguish themselves through some great discovery or service" (18). In other words, this nobility is not one of birth, but of action.

As the 1835 edition of the *Dictionnaire de l'Academie Française* states, the adjective "noble" was commonly used figuratively, designating that which embodies greatness, elevation, or superiority.[47] However, it does not seem that Cabet and Sand are using "noble" metaphorically, but, in fact, proposing a new definition that requires synthesis of both traditional and modern values. It is clear that Sand and Cabet were true progressives, promoting a decidedly modern form of social organization, where individuals were valued for the good they bring to society, notably through intellectual and physical labor, a clear break from the Old Regime system where a small but privileged group (a *caste*, as the Abbé Sieyès called it in 1789) held virtually all political power. At the same time, however, their use of the term "nobility" is quite conservative, depending as it does upon the existence of a certain form of natural superiority. In short, for Cabet and Sand, nobility is not *only* a question of action but of something more innate. The sources of Pierre's, Eugène's, and Valmor's noble "superiority" are at once quite new and quite old-fashioned. On the one hand, their nobility is closely connected to their labor, but, on the other hand, it seems to spring from their natural capacity for discernment—their ability to distinguish truth from falsehood, good from evil, virtue from vice—and from their sense of honor.

Above all, Pierre's nobility seems to stem from his innate ability to recognize the truth. Late at night, hidden away in Yseult's study, he works his way through her substantial library. With no guidance other than his own conscience, we learn, he is able to "admir[e] in the poets and philosophers only that which is truly great and eternally beautiful; believing in history only that which is in accordance consistent with divine logic and human dignity" (314). Pierre's understanding of the scientific, philosophical, and historical texts he encounters goes beyond what any instructor could teach. Time and again, his social "betters"—the Orleanist Count de Villepreux, the fiery Carbonaro Achille Lefort, and even the gentle Yseult—attempt to instruct or indoctrinate him into a way of thinking, only to find that his ability to sift truth from falsehood is superior to theirs. This is precisely thanks to his noble character, allowing him to distinguish right from wrong simply through an innate sensibility to morality and truth.

In a similar way, the working-class heroes of Icaria—the locksmith Valmor, the gruff and unrefined painter Eugène, and the lovely seamstresses, Corilla and Dinaïse—embody a form of nobility—to use Carsdall's own term—that comes from their ability to distinguish right from wrong simply through their innate sensibility and good judgment. Time and again, these workers prove themselves superior to highborn characters who are unable to recognize truth and goodness. A striking portrayal of this comes when the three friends, Valmor, Eugène, and Carisdall, go to a museum. They stop in front of a wax-figure of the beautiful Queen Cloramide, the last monarch of Icaria, who bears an uncanny resemblance to Dinaïse, the object of Valmore's and Carisdall's desire. Despite her beauty, however, the historian's account reveals her to be a wicked figure, who, by placing her trust in a corrupt prime minister, had led the nation to ruin. Icaria was saved only thanks to a popular revolution. The story of Cloramide exemplifies both the inability of high-born characters to recognize a falsehood and the heroism of the regular working-class people to find the truth. The portrayal of aristocratic characters as lacking judgment is further emphasized when Lord Carisdall—so struck by the resemblance between the statue and the living Dinaïse that he writes: "Only Dinaïse's voice was missing, and I listened, fully expecting it to slip out of the half-opened lips"—expresses pity for the duped monarch (157). He is immediately rebuked by Eugène who sagely points out that her downfall was caused by her position as queen, "a title that can pervert the best of hearts!" Like Cloramide, then, Carisdall has been tricked by appearances, and both these high-born characters serve as foolish foils to the innately noble and discerning working-class heroes of the tale.

Even more than this power of discernment, perhaps, what makes Sand's and Cabet's working-class protagonists so heroic is their sense of honor, or the fulfilment of family or social duty, a virtue that was traditionally associated with the nobility. For Cabet, labor itself is the mark of honor. Icaria is full of labor but free of suffering, thanks to the utopian powers of technology. Not only is work organized in a way that maximizes efficiency, but the laborers who perform that work are compared to a contingent of highly trained soldiers, subsuming their individual interests to some higher purpose, as in the following description of a clock-making shop. "On the bottom floor are enormous, heavy machines for cutting the metals and roughing out the pieces. On the top floor the workers, divided into as many groups as there are different pieces to make; each one always makes the same piece. You would think you were seeing an army regiment; such is the high degree of order and discipline there" (51). That working-class readers should find this depiction of piecework (*confection*) attractive is, at first glance, quite surprising. Many craftsmen saw the division of labor not only as a threat to their livelihood, leading to deskilling and lower wages, but also as a source of psychological suffering, caused by separating workers from one another. By casting these laborers as a corps of highly disciplined military men, however, Cabet reframes this labor as honorable and heroic. No longer a chore, labor becomes a joyous pastime through the processes of song, education, and attention to cleanliness. And most importantly, it is "the honor with which all forms of work are treated by public opinion, all equally" that helps to transform labor into a source of authentic pleasure (81–83). In this way, Cabet uses a modern understanding of honor to characterize labor as a noble and ennobling activity.

Sand also focuses on honor as a defining virtue of the noble working-class hero. The carpentry that Pierre Huguenin performs is not just a way to make money but a central element of his social and individual identity. One night, in a painful soliloquy that evokes the biblical scene of the Garden of Gethsemane, the Jesus-like Pierre experiences his own passion in the face of social injustice: "I must, from dawn of day till night, water with my sweat a soil which will grow green and flower for other eyes than mine. If I lose an hour each day in feeling my heart and thought live, I shall want bread in my old age; ... If I stop here an instant too long under the shade, I compromise my honor, bound by a contract to the incessant expenditure of my strength, and to the entire sacrifice of my intellectual life" (53–54). Using the economic language of spending and earning, Sand, through Pierre, adopts Balzac's logic of labor energy as a mysterious but quantifiable force: one lost hour of labor today means one less loaf of bread in his old age; the "expenditure" of his physical forces upon the objects of his labor means there is no energy left for contemplation. In this way, Pierre points up the proletarian nature of his labor. However, the alienation he experiences is not merely economic but psychological, as well. Indeed, the fact that Pierre's social/moral obligations are fulfilled only when he is performing physical labor, which, he knows, is damaging to his body, adds to the Christlike nature of his sacrifice.

The connection that Pierre establishes between honor and labor ("If I stop here . . . I compromise my honor") merits some discussion. Although honor had traditionally been the virtue of the Old Regime nobility, by the mid-nineteenth century, this link was necessarily transformed as the definition of nobility itself shifted. The first entry for "honor" in Pierre Larousse's *Grand Dictionnaire* (first published in the 1860s), for example, defines it as the "desire for others' esteem which leads us to noble and loyal actions," but makes no mention of Old Regime orders.[48] Thus, even if it no longer designates any particular social station determined by birth, honor remains closely connected to the modern definition of nobility as a matter of action and moral integrity. Even Pierre's reference to working land that belongs to someone else ("water with my sweat a soil . . . for other eyes than mine"), an allusion to traditional connections between land and nobility, is purely metaphorical: Pierre is no farmer, but a carpenter, a profession that was becoming ever more modern and threatened by industrialization. The Parc de Villepreux is the site of his wanderings and his dreams, not his labor. Still, the fact that the land belongs to someone else reminds Pierre of his solitude, and because of the caste-like social structure that still reigns in the countryside setting of the novel, Pierre is unable to marry the person he chooses, a future countess. Pierre's passion in the garden is therefore a concentrated form of the isolation that all Romantic heroes feel in the face of the individualist nature of modern society.

Sand's keen interest in the nature of honor in a postrevolutionary world brings her into dialogue with sentimental novelists from earlier in the century, such as Claire de Duras and Sophie Cottin, who, Margaret Cohen has demonstrated, explored the conflict between (outward-facing) honor and (individualistic) romantic love. In contrast to the novels written by her sentimental predecessors, however, Sand's *Journeyman Joiner* does not focus on aristocratic heroines, and, as a result, she cannot present the two moral imperatives of collective duty and individual freedom as equally good. Instead, Pierre's position brings to light the hardships caused by collective duty to those who are least able to enjoy the benefits of social order. These include, most notably, women and workers, who "experience the bonds of . . . society as oppressive rather than as a positively constructed ethical obligation."[49] In *The Journeyman Joiner*, the working-class hero is oppressed by his economic and moral obligation to labor, and yet, bound by a noble imperative to honor his duties, he refuses to cast them off to pursue his own happiness.

There are various ways to interpret the heroism of the working-class characters in Sand's and Cabet's texts. In what has perhaps become the canonical English-language reading of *The Journeyman Joiner*, Naomi Schor argues that Pierre Huguenin is an idealized character, an example of "the proletarian sublime" and that, according to the norms of the time, this idealization was a necessary condition for his appearing as the hero of the work: "Not only is idealization not incompatible with the representa-*tion of the worker, it is its very condition*. It is only by emphasizing Pierre's sublime sculptural beauty—through the novel, Michelangelo and Raphael are invoked as the guarantors of the proletarian sublime—the nobility of his traits and his style, in short, his difference from and superiority to the common worker that Sand affords him entry into the scene of representation. Aestheticized, asepticized, Pierre is a hybrid of the popular and the aristocratic" (emphasis in the original).[50] In Schor's eyes, Sand's depiction of Pierre as the embodiment of the modern nobility was a strategic choice. Writing at the edges—but still within the limits—of Romantic literature, she argues, Sand knows that the only way that Pierre can be heroic is through his transformation into someone who is the exact opposite of what a worker is usually thought to be: clean, handsome, intelligent, and honest. Although Schor does not discuss Cabet, we may infer that, because he was writing within the same context as Sand, she would have the same assessment of his decision to portray his working-class characters in such squeaky-clean terms as coming from the same motivation.

Another way to interpret the heroic nobility of Cabet and Sand's working-class heroes is to chalk it up to the utopian nature of their fictions. Indeed, it is not just these particular characters who are idealized, the very worlds in which they live suggest a level of perfection and purity that is hardly attainable. It was this utopianism that Marx and Engels, writing in 1847, found particularly problematic in their critique of French communism. According to them, the utopian way that Cabet and the other leading thinkers of his time envisioned a sublimation of class antagonism into true social equality and harmony without revolutionary violence was naïve at best: "They still dream of experimental realisation of their social Utopias, of founding isolated 'phalansteres,' of establishing 'Home Colonies,' or setting up a 'Little Icaria'—duodecimo editions of the New Jerusalem—and to realise all these castles in the air, they are compelled to appeal to the feelings and purses of the bourgeois."[51]

Their critique was not completely unfounded. Indeed, as Marx and Engels were writing their "Manifesto," class hatred was at an all-time high in France, even as utopian solutions to these problems proliferated. That same year, Cabet called for his followers to organize an expedition to North America to set up a colony according to the principles laid out in the *Travels*. Nor was Cabet's the only social movement of the time to entertain Arcadian solutions to real problems. Utopianism had a long history in France, and two of its major postrevolutionary manifestations still loomed large on the cultural landscape during the July Monarchy: the Saint-Simonians and the Fourierists. The latter were inspired by the writings and teachings of Charles Fourier (1772–1837), who, in his *Théorie des quatre mouvements et des destinées générales* (1808) and then in *Le Nouveau Monde industriel* (1829), established his theory of *attraction passionnée* (passionate attraction). Fourier believed that it was not reason (as the Enlightenment had established) but passion that guides how we understand and make choices in the world. He and his followers imagined a type of social organization that would make labor more attractive by allowing individuals to pursue their natural passions. The theory held that this harmony would lead not only to more happiness but to more efficiency. Although Cabet did not consider himself a Fourierist, the highly organized life of the workers in Icaria attests to the wide-reaching influence of Fourier's ideas, as did the Icarians' expeditions to found utopian societies in the United States, a move that Fourierists were making at the same time.

The other major utopian thinker of the postrevolutionary era whose influence was felt throughout the century was Henri Saint-Simon (1760–1825), whose ideas about literature have already been discussed in chapter 1. Unlike Fourier, Saint-Simon's followers included bankers and railroad managers, and went on to hold important posts in government throughout the nineteenth century. One such figure was Pierre Leroux, an influential philosopher who had left the Saint-Simonians in 1831, but who retained many of the group's spiritual and moral beliefs about the possibility of social renewal. He is best known for his conception of *humanité*, the idea that all humans—past, present, and future—are inherently connected with one another. "We gravitate spiritually toward God by the intermediary of humanity," he wrote in 1840.[52] George Sand was largely influenced by her close friendship with the philosopher, and *The Journeyman Joiner* features a dream sequence that is largely a realization of his theory. Like Leroux, Sand saw humankind as a unified force, moving along a single trajectory of progress and improvement.

Although they are known as utopians, both Saint-Simon and Fourier were intent upon establishing a scientific foundation for their social plans, pointing to the reality-based intentions of their writings. Indeed, as Paul Bénichou has demonstrated, the term "utopia" had a very specific meaning in postrevolutionary France. Whereas earlier utopians like Thomas More and Voltaire followed the etymological "no (U-) place (topos)," implying that their imagined spaces could never exist in the real world, the nineteenth-century utopians operated according to a different logic. "The Utopia of the early nineteenth century," says Paul Bénichou, "is not defined by its construction of an unrealistic level of social perfection; it lies above all in the intuition by which the scientific ordering of things is supposed to lead to the complete fulfillment of humanity as imagined by the philosopher."[53] Although these societies could only be conceived as imaginary spaces in the present, many people did believe that it was possible to make a utopia into a reality in the future. It was merely a question of promoting human progress, science, and reason in order to create the necessary public institutions needed to support them.[54] The utopian text was therefore a call to action, urging readers to engineer a shift in attitudes that would make change possible and, indeed, inevitable.

It is not surprising, then, that Cabet's *Travels* and Sand's *Journeyman Joiner* are in many ways quite realistic. The details of Icarian life are far from fantastic: its inhabitants dress and act very much like the citizens of contemporary France, and rational explanations are given for each aspect of the social structure. What's more, Cabet's characters grapple with unfulfilled desire: Carisdall's love for Corilla and then Dinaïse is unreturned, Valmor and Carisdall are unable to establish a true friendship, Eugène is frustrated that France is not more like Icaria. Each of these desires proves to be at least temporarily impossible, creating moments of tension that drive the narrative forward, leading Daniel Sipe to conclude that "Cabet's conception of society is anchored in the incitement and management of desire, not in its eradication."[55] In a similar way, although he could have eliminated labor completely in his utopia, Cabet maintains it—"manages" it—in order to present his readers with a society that is possible. In a sense, then, Icaria is not the perfect society but a perfectible one, a utopia in which people yearn and strive for utopia, and where desiring and laboring characters are depicted as fully human.

Sand also writes in a realistic mode, accepting that labor itself cannot be banished from the utopia but that the psychological anguish associated with it can be eradicated. *The Journeyman Joiner* includes scenes of real suffering, including Pierre's soliloquy in the garden (discussed above), where he elaborates his economic and social grievances caused by the very existence of private property and the social separation this entails (53–54). This separation is later healed in a utopian dream sequence, where the characters of the novel are seen "walking arm-in-arm ... conversing amicably," and Yseult, whose counsel Pierre has rejected in the waking-world, is now a trusted source of wisdom, calling him to "love, believe, work" (244). A slight alteration of the primary Christian virtues "faith, hope, love" extolled by Saint Paul in the New Testament (1 Corinthians), Yseult's dream-world prescription is not to *hope* for a better world, but to *work* toward it. In short, this is a dreamworld filled not only with perfect creatures, sublime works of art, and awe-inspiring landscapes, but also with labor: "beings which seemed more beautiful and more pure than the human race, all busy and joyous, animated [the garden] with their labors [*travaux*] and their concerts" (243). In the end, however, there is little that is truly marvelous or supernatural about Pierre's dream. It is not a pure invention of the carpenter's imagination but simply reality taken to its aesthetic ideal. The beautiful dreamscape is none other than the familiar parc de Villepreux, and its denizens are Pierre's own acquaintances and family members, reconciled from all earthly animosities. The dreamer, lying on a pile of wood shavings in the workshop, is aware of the real-live work-activities going on around him: "The plane and the chisel traveled victoriously as usual over the rebellious and plaintive wood. The workmen covered their muscular arms with sweat, and the consoling song circulated, regulating by its rhythm the action of their labor actions, evoking poetry in the midst of fatigue and contention of mind" (243). The juxtaposition of aesthetic beauty and physical pain in this passage is in perfect harmony with Pierre's (and Sand's) conception of manual labor. The rebellious protests of the "plaintive" wood are soothed over by the humming of the carpenters' tools, victoriously sanding and shaping the material to their will. Like the wood, the workers might like to complain about their mental and physical discomfort—their sweat-covered arms, their exhaustion, and the feeling of being intellectually constrained—but the aesthetic experience of singing brings a comforting rhythm to their suffering, the *chanson de compagnonnage* being a well-known practice of the time.[56] For Pierre, this buzzing of productivity is soothing and no doubt provides the soundtrack to his dream. Yseult's flowers, which Pierre tucked into his shirt, give off a lovely fragrance that hovers between the ideal and real of the dream. When he wakes up, his father tells him that he has been dreaming "with his eyes open" (244), hinting to the reader that the utopia is not some allegory or far-fetched fairy-tale, but a possible future, firmly rooted in reality.

In the end, then, the message in Cabet's and Sand's fictions is not so different from what we find in the *enquêtes* and essays promoted by the Académie des sciences morales et politiques. In both sets of texts, there is a hope, if not a belief, that society will be guided by a new group of elites whose legitimacy to rule comes not from the accident of their birth but from their capacity for intellectual and manual labor.

The bourgeois writers discussed in this chapter went about presenting the new reality of manual labor in different ways, but they all shared a single goal, to promote manual labor as the foundation of modern society. Indeed, even if socialists like Sand and Cabet hoped to use literature to establish a sense of unity between themselves and their working-class readers, the real solidarity that emerged at this time was not between literature and labor, but among bourgeois social thinkers. Idealist utopians like Sand and Cabet pointed up the intrinsically good and moral nature of the laborer, while empiricists like Villermé tried to define labor as a means of forming a more compliant and docile citizen. Despite these different methodologies and political beliefs, these writers come to the same conclusion about manual labor: that it is an ennobling and moralizing social force. They also put forth a shared narrative that manual labor and intellectual labor were two sides of the same coin, as two manifestations of the same fundamental act. Working-class writers had a more difficult needle to thread. To capitalize on the new popular interest in labor and those who performed it, without being subsumed into bourgeois conceptions of what their experiences were like, worker-writers had to walk a fine line between revolt and reconciliation, militancy and moderation. As many of the workers discussed in the next chapter would discover, literature provided a fertile medium through which to establish themselves as legitimate members of the social and political worlds of the July Monarchy, but it was also full of potential pitfalls.

4

A Literary Identity for the Worker-Writer

❧

As we saw in the previous chapter, a widespread bourgeois narrative in 1840 held that a new generation of heroes—defined not by their birth but by their accomplishments and their capacity to think and act with reason—must be tapped to lead France into a modern era of social stability and harmony. For middle-class thinkers as far apart on the political spectrum as the communist Etienne Cabet and the liberal René Villermé, these new heroes were imagined as laborers, with the understanding that writing down one's thoughts and working with one's hands were two manifestations of the same fundamental act of labor.

Among worker-writers, however, a counternarrative had emerged, based upon a clear distinction between the cerebral activity of literary creation (a moralizing, spiritual, transcendent activity) and the physical process of performing labor (perceived as merely an economic one). Working-class writers understood the importance of literature in the process of forming a working-class identity but wanted to emphasize that writing literature was not itself labor. Why, at a time when the political and social stakes were so high, did worker-writers invest so much time and energy into literary practice? In this chapter, we look at the role that literature played in the formation of a working-class identity in the 1840s.

Like the "bourgeoisie," the "working class" as a social category was constantly in the process of being redefined. At the time, the bottom portion of society was commonly referred to as *le peuple*, a vague category including individuals from a variety of economic situations, the master craftsman, the simple farmer, and the beggar on the street alike. The terms "*travailleurs*," "*ouvriers*," and "*classe laborieuse*" were more precise, imagining a group identity based on economic activity, and creating an aggregation of all those who performed manual labor to make a living, from the highly skilled artisan to lowly factory workers, from urban printing-press operators to agricultural laborers, needlewomen, and others. Such labels were crucial, then, for if a working-class identity was going to flourish, such different types of people, who wouldn't necessarily find themselves in the same social spaces, would have to cultivate alliances based on their common status as manual rather than intellectual laborers.

It is paradoxical, then, that the workers' movement of the July Monarchy—a movement that sought to establish an identity for manual laborers—should seek to define itself through literature. Figures as different as the monarchist Jean Reboul, the Saint-Simonian feminist Suzanne Voilquin, the Christian socialists of L'Atelier, and the *"ouvrière-coloriste"* Flora Tristan[1] all saw a relationship to literature to be a key element of who they were and where they fit into society. Jules Vinçard, the Saint-Simonian *chansonnier* (songwriter) and artisan, worked perhaps more than anyone else to establish the identity of the worker through literary expression in his worker-run papers, La Ruche populaire (1839–49) and L'Union (1843–46). Vinçard understood the stakes of establishing manual labor as the foundation of modern society, and of unifying all those who performed it, despite their different social conditions. He believed that literature was the most effective means through which a working-class identity could be expressed, but he also held that literary creation and physical labor must be considered as separate undertakings: one spiritual and the other economic.

Vinçard's writings give us insight into the evolution in the way worker-writers saw themselves as participants in the literary field and how they navigated a tenuous relationship with its dominant figures. On the one hand, Vinçard had to maintain a dialogue with the bourgeois media (both the elite *revues* and the inexpensive dailies) to get his ideas heard, but, on the other, he needed to distinguish his economically disinterested vision of literature from the commercial activities of publicists, journalists, and professional authors. Thanks in part to his efforts, a literary identity of the worker-writers that depends on a separation of literary and manual work would flourish in years leading up to 1841, but this soon turned into a complicity with the dominant bourgeois narrative that considered manual and literary labor as one and the same. Ironically, as we will see in the next chapter, just as worker-writers were accepting literary expression as a form of labor, popular bourgeois novelists—positioning themselves as allies—had begun to use narrative to evacuate manual labor of its importance.

A Polyphonic Field

The field of worker-writer productions of the July Monarchy was a diverse one, appearing in different genres and registers and focusing on a variety of topics. These laborers came from a wide range of backgrounds and political commitments, but they shared a belief that, by taking up the pen, they would improve their social situation. In the early 1830s, literature was seen by different groups—women workers and artisans in particular—as a way to claim distinct identities for themselves, celebrating their differences both from the dominant class and from one another. However, by 1840, a pan-proletarian class consciousness had begun to take root among some workers, and, in particular, among worker-writers.

One of the first examples of workers' use of writing to express a particular class identity appeared in the wake of the July Revolution in 1830. That year, thanks to a newly liberalized press regime, three worker-run papers began publication: *L'Artisan, journal de la classe ouvrière* (The artisan: Journal of the laboring class), *Le Journal des ouvriers* (The laborers' journal), and *Le Peuple, journal général des ouvriers rédigé par eux-mêmes* (The people: A common laborers' journal, written by themselves). Their titles identify these papers as speaking for the laborer ("*ouvrier*"), and, indeed, they all argued for labor organization, better wages, and other working-class interests. They were mostly run, however, by laborers and artisans in the printing trade who had little in common with the shoemakers and tailors who constituted the lower ranks of the working classes. Often literate, the press workers had long been known for revolutionary ideas, but their close proximity to bourgeois editors and publicists gave them an experience that was not typical of the working class. Already, in 1827, laborers and masters in the printing trade had worked together to block a hated censorship regime known as the "Law of Justice and Love," and relations between the different levels of the hierarchy were not as fraught as in other trades (although the spread of the steam-powered printing press was beginning to cause problems).[2] It should not be surprising, then, that the understanding of literature espoused in these papers is a bourgeois one. As Bettina Lerner has shown, the writers of the early worker press were focused establishing a dialogue with the Habermasian "bourgeois public sphere." They often praised "middlebrow" authors like Pierre-Jean de Béranger and Evariste de Parny, "stand[ing] here for the horizon of acculturation to which the editors of *L'Artisan* problematically aspire[d]."[3] In other words, the contributors to the early iterations of the worker press saw literature as a decidedly bourgeois form of expression upon which they would try to model their own compositions. Although laborers could appreciate popular bourgeois poems and fictions, an authentic working-class literary expression was not on their radar.

Another early example of the worker-run press appeared in 1832. Reacting against Prosper Enfantin's exclusion of women from the hierarchy of what had become the cult of Saint-Simonianism, several of the group's disaffected women members began publishing their own paper, first called *La Femme libre* (The free woman) then *La Femme de l'avenir* (The woman of the future), *La Femme nouvelle* (The new woman), and finally, *La Tribune des femmes* (The woman's tribune). The paper was unique in that it was completely run and written by women who called themselves "*prolétaires saint-simoniennes* [proletarian Saint-Simonian women]."[4] Most contributors worked as seamstresses or in other sectors of the garment industry, and they believed that the political emancipation of women would only be achieved through their economic independence. They provided what Siobhain McIlvanney has called "a particularly radical model of the working-class woman, who both worked and wrote."[5] To promote women's entry into the workforce (and, eventually, into the political sphere), the editors even set up schools and other training programs for working-class women.

While most pieces published in *La Femme libre* were explicitly political and economic, rather than poetic, feminist critics have found important literary value in the way they used language to formulate a new way of conceiving the world, one that departed from the rational masculine point of view. In the vein of Hélène Cixous's feminist theory of writing, as laid out in *The Laugh of the Medusa* (1975), Leslie Rabine has demonstrated that Suzanne Voilquin realized that she could not "act, write, organize, or create without inventing and identifying with a powerful maternal ego-ideal who epitomizes the nineteenth-century maternal qualities of love, nurture, and sentiment" and therefore sought to challenge the social, sexual, and symbolic orders of her time through literary expression.[6] Voilquin, a seamstress, was one of the most active women in the Saint-Simonian organization. She was particularly invested in bringing about both political change and a shift in the psychological paradigm of what it means to be a woman through literary expression.

Voilquin followed the Saint-Simonians to Egypt in 1834 and published her travel diaries in the literary section of the mainstream quotidian *Le Siècle* in 1837.[7] Through this interchange with the bourgeois public sphere, Voilquin uses literary expression to assert her particular identity as both a woman and a worker.

Not all worker-writers were radicals, socialists, or even republicans, however. Jean Reboul, a baker from Nîmes, was known for his Catholic and monarchist sympathies. His poetry expressed lofty Romantic themes such as love, death, and the sense of awe we experience in the presence of nature. His most famous poem, "L'Ange et L'Enfant" (The angel and the child) is told through the eyes of an angel who, in an act of heartbreaking mercy, decides to save a newborn from earthly suffering by taking its life. This and other works elicited strong emotional reactions and attracted praise from giants of the Romantic movement like Alphonse de Lamartine and René de Chateaubriand, as well as bestselling novelists like George Sand and Alexandre Dumas.[8]

In the eyes of many of his bourgeois readers, Reboul must have offered an exemplary model of what the *poète-ouvrier* (worker-poet) should be. His ability to compartmentalize, keeping his literary creation completely separate from the physical activities he performed to earn a living, was pointed out admiringly by Dumas, who agreed to write the preface to Reboul's first poetry collection, *Poésies*, in 1836. The preface takes the form of a narrative, as the successful playwright recounts the long journey from Paris to Nîmes to meet the talented baker-poet. Dumas is surprised when, instead of being met with adulation, he is told to come back after work hours: "You have come to see the poet and not the baker, have you not? Well, I am a baker from five o'clock in the morning until four in the evening. From four o'clock until midnight, I am a poet. If you want bread, stay. If you want lines of verse, come back at five o'clock."[9] Impressed by the worker's ability to separate so completely the two aspects of his daily activity, Dumas dutifully returns at the prescribed time and asks Reboul admiringly how he manages the "irreconcilable [*inconciliable*]" elements of his "double life." The worker-poet replies stoically that while his arms labor, his head rests; and when his arms are resting, his head is working, thus maintaining the clear separation between manual and intellectual labor (17–18). Reboul describes his poetry-writing as a sort of mixed blessing, an escape from the banalities of everyday life, but also a source of alienation from his fellow workers. Poetry is both the cause of and the solution to his emotional suffering. "These religious and solitary lamentations take on a poetic and exalted character that my words have never known. My thoughts come together in an idiom that is almost strange to me, and, as they are offered to heaven, and as they find no sympathy on Earth, the Lord gives them wings, and they float up to him." The Romantic theme of the artist's ability to connect with a higher power, and the poet's specific calling to carry out this spiritual practice through language, is clearly apparent here, and it is not surprising that Reboul was praised by Romantics like Chateaubriand and Lamartine. But, like all Romantic poets, Reboul also suffered greatly from this special gift. Addressing Dumas directly, he appeals to their common plight: "'You understand, don't you,' he asks, 'the need to unburden yourself of a great pain? Those with whom I have surrounded myself until now have been men of my own class, men of good but ordinary souls. Instead of saying, "cry and we will cry with you," they try to console me. My tears, which seek only to spill forth, are swallowed back into my heart, drowning it'" (19–20). Dumas, who was better known as a successful playwright than as a tormented Romantic hero, must have found Reboul's description of him as someone who needed to "unburden [himself] of a great pain" somewhat flattering. Reboul's aim here, however, was to show that the "compartmentalization" that Dumas so admired was also the source a strong sense of class alienation. It is as if, as soon as he begins to write poetry, he can no longer belong to the working class (they only try to dry his tears) but must find commonality with another group of people, whom we might describe as a writing class. Although Reboul and Dumas do not have the same social or economic concerns, Reboul is suggesting that their shared Romantic ideal of art as a form of expression that surpasses all earthly concerns brings them together under the umbrella of a new social category. At a moment when "authentic" forms of expression from lower-class and provincial poets were becoming increasingly popular, a savvy self-promoter such as Dumas could not help but enjoy being placed in the same category as Reboul.

In her 1838 novel *Mephis*, the colorist Flora Tristan promotes a similar Romantic philosophy about the role of art. The story focuses on the unlikely relationship between two artistic geniuses: a beautiful aristocratic *cantatrice* named Marequita and the eponymous hero who is identified as a "proletarian." Indeed, the longest chapter of the novel, which takes up about two-thirds of the first volume, is titled "Histoire d'un prolétaire" and is a first-person account of the hero's youth and young adulthood. Mephis, the son of an impoverished sailor, has through both hard work, and, it must be added, good luck, managed to become a brilliant painter. During his residence at the prestigious Académie des beaux arts, he accuses his fellow artists, supposedly the brightest in the nation, of a superficial understanding of art. His own aesthetic theory, by contrast, is quite spiritual. "In my eyes," he proclaims, "art is the means of communication between man and God; art is religion in all of its wholeness; the prophet, the poet, the sculptor, the painter, the musician are its priests! Their masterpieces are its revelation! For me, religion is a teaching. Anathema upon the priest who assembles his flock only to produce vain words."[10] Mephis stands out from the other artists in his elite circle as the only one who understands the true purpose of art as a spiritual and moral undertaking. Marequita finds herself drawn to him, both for his physical beauty and for his elevated aesthetic philosophy. However, in typical sentimental fashion, she is eventually forced to choose between her comfortable social position and her true love. She chooses the former. Overall, the plot is fairly banal, and the characters are rather unsympathetic. *Mephis* is best understood as a thinly veiled exposition of Tristan's social theory, inspired by the author's personal experiences, but the work gives us important insight as to why this proletarian woman was so drawn first to literature and then other forms of writing as means of self-expression.

With her long dark hair and dimpled arms, Tristan physically resembled the beautiful Marequita, but philosophically, she identified with Mephis and his idealist and exalted understanding of art.[11] Tristan, like her hero, had a complicated relationship to social class. The illegitimate daughter of a Peruvian aristocrat, she was thrust into poverty at the age of four, when her father died leaving the family nothing. At fifteen, she began to work as a low-level colorist in a lithographer's workshop, where her earnings were so meager that she was forced to take on supplementary work at night: "In her garret on the rue du Fouarre, she lacked even the wood to warm herself. She managed to earn a bit of money evenings by coloring perfume bottle labels, which allowed her to survive."[12] Out of economic necessity, she soon married her employer, an abusive man named André Chazal, who would try to murder her when she eventually sought a divorce.

Tristan's liberation from her husband marked the beginning of her writing career, one that was short but prolific. When *Mephis* received little public or critical enthusiasm, Tristan quickly gave up her literary ambitions, but she continued to write extensively about her social ideas. In the years preceding her untimely death in 1844, she tried out a variety of genres and modes of writing: a travel diary (*Pérégrinations d'une paria* [*Peregrinations of a Pariah*], 1837), a proto-sociological report on the working classes of London (*Promenades dans Londres* [*Promenades in London*], 1840), and finally, a direct organizing campaign (*L'Union ouvrière* [*The Workers' Union*], 1843). Stéphane Michaud blames her inability to write literature on her fraught relationship with language, what he calls "the obstacle of language [*l'obstacle du langage*]," no doubt a result of her intermittent education, and suggests that it was by focusing more on social and political discourse that she was able to come into her own writing style.[13] Tristan's shifts in genre—moving from literary expression to more direct forms of discourse—shows an evolution in her understanding of the relationship between labor and literature. If her 1838 novel *Mephis* presents literature—like art—as a higher calling and a moral activity that is best practiced by the "*prolétaires*" of this world, she soon gives up this ideal and takes up other generic forms in order to perform the social labor of uniting the working classes. In this later stage, fiction still plays an important role: for instance, she urges the workers she meets to read George Sand's *Journeyman Joiner*.[14] She now believes that it is through reading rather than writing—by exposing themselves to ideas of others rather than by engaging in self-expression—that workers will develop class consciousness.

La Ruche Populaire—Construction of a Literary Identity

Although Flora Tristan would give up literature as a form of working-class expression in 1838, the following year would mark the beginning of a new wave of working-class literary enthusiasm. In December 1839, the first issue of *La Ruche populaire* (The people's hive) was published. It was directed by Jules Vinçard, a Saint-Simonian artisan (a *fabricant de mesures linéaires*) who had achieved minor fame as a Parisian *chansonnier* (songwriter and performer). Like earlier iterations of the Parisian worker press that had emerged in the wake of the July Revolution, one of the goals of *La Ruche* was to promote a specific working-class identity. It was different, however, in that Vinçard saw this identity as being forged not through profession (as had been the case in *L'Artisan*) nor through gender (as the women of *La Tribune des femmes* had argued), but through literature itself. The first issue of *La Ruche populaire* offers an excellent example of how worker-writers saw their place in the media landscape in 1839. On the one hand, the paper was very much conceived of in literary terms, the founders announcing their contents to be "a mixture of items in prose and in verse [*un mélange de pièces en prose et en vers*]." On the other, the paper's prospectus makes it very clear that they do *not* intend to leave their jobs to become professional writers, whom they refer to as *littérateurs*: "They are not embarking on a literary speculation [*une speculation littéraire*]; they have no intention of passing for *littérateurs* or publicists; . . . the founders of *La Ruche* are committed not to profit from their undertaking; for them, it is a work of morality [*une œuvre morale*], and they are proud of it."[15] A key to understanding Vinçard's stance is his use of the epithet "*littérateur*." If, in 1819, Saint-Simon had employed the term positively, to highlight the productive nature of literary creation, Vinçard tries to distance himself from such productivist discourse. Defined by the Académie française, in 1835, as "Someone who is versed in literature, who has made it his profession," the term *littérateur* was clearly linked to the business side of writing as a money-making activity.[16] Indeed, the early nineteenth century saw a wave of literary speculators who sought to "master the marketplace" of popular tastes and trends in order to sell more books and newspapers.[17] By the early 1840s, this phenomenon had become so widespread that it was raised as a budget issue in parliament. Benoît-Marie Chapuys-Montlaville, a member of the Left opposition, accused modern literature of a "mercantile avidity" or "speculation" that left it "unconcerned by the lack of moral value of the merchandise it sells, so long as sales are up, and profits are good."[18] Accusing the sitting government of promoting this type of literary speculation, Chapuys-Montlaville refused to approve its budget.

The association between literature and commerce—or industry—was indeed a matter of debate. Some observers, like the newspapermen Emile de Girardin and Armand Dutacq, saw this commercialization as a path toward democratization, making education and the arts available to a wider swath of the population. According to others, like Chapuys-Montlaville and the critic Charles-Augustin Sainte-Beuve, the transformation of literary creation into an industry was nothing short of a cultural catastrophe. The editorial committee of *La Ruche* shared this more pessimistic vision; for them, the work of the professional writer was indissociable from the commercial practices of publicists and editors, looking for the next literary sensation. For them, then, it was imperative to cultivate a literary identity without promoting themselves in any commercial way. By refusing the term *littérateur*, Vinçard and his associates distinguished their literary practice from that of established writers who, working closely with financially-minded professionals, made a career of writing and evaluating literary texts.

Vinçard was also quite practical, however. He did not pretend to be a professional poet, but he knew from experience that it was much easier for uneducated workers to express themselves in easy-to-memorize verse and refrains than through rhetorical speechmaking. Indeed, singing, and by extension poetry, was a natural form of public speaking for the working classes.[19] Vinçard was himself a well-known *chansonnier*, or songwriter, and an active member of the popular singing clubs of Paris known as *goguettes*, but he turned to poetry as a more prudent way to express political ideas. Although singing had long been seen as a harmless feature of working-class life, certain events had begun to attract the attention of nervous authorities. Jules Michelet, in *Le Peuple* (1846), praised the melodious compositions of medieval weavers who used song as a simple way help pass the hours of labor more pleasurably, and the secret songs of *compagnonnage* were presented by Agricol Perdiguier (1840) as a picturesque reminder of the corporatist tradition, but suspicions about the subversive potential of music had been growing stronger. Thanks to the literary innovations and the republican fervor of Pierre-Jean de Béranger (1780–1857), whose *chansons* earned him the adoration of the popular classes, government officials could not ignore the revolutionary potential of this new craze. Authorities worried that the subversive messages in Béranger's and other songwriters' compositions could be spread among the illiterate working classes through music more easily than via printed material. As early as 1821, the prosecuting attorney in Béranger's first criminal trial noted: "Even the most outrageous political flyer is able to reach only a small circle of readers, while the *chanson*, a thousand times more contagious, can infect even the air we breathe."[20] By opting to publish poetry rather than songs, then, Vinçard chose a relatively apolitical and unthreatening medium.

Instead of taking up a political position, then, the prospectus of *La Ruche populaire* focuses on the nature of literary expression itself. By continuing to earn their living through manual labor, says Vinçard, the contributors to *La Ruche* can produce literature that remains separate from—and even stand above—the economic concerns of their daily lives. In this way, they maintain a disinterested and moral ideal of literature. Although Vinçard does not mention him by name, he is clearly aligning himself with the well-known critic Charles-Augustin Sainte-Beuve. In

1839, just months before the first issue of *La Ruche populaire* was published, Sainte-Beuve had penned a virulent attack on a phenomenon that he called "Industrial Literature," taking serial novelists and other contemporary authors to task for their opportunistic approach to literature as an economic activity and a way to make money. Sainte-Beuve bemoans the loss of the disinterested nature of literature, longing for a time when literary authors did not seek to profit from their work. "The thing we call literature [*la chose littéraire*; meaning in this case, the entirety of imaginary and artistic productions] seems increasingly compromised, and by its own fault. . . . sacrificing its generosity and talent to the gaping pits of egotism and cupidity which grow larger as their arrogance increases."[21] This Sainte-Beuvian conception of a sort of "good old days" of literature, when artistic creation was seen as a "generous" activity performed in the service of a higher power, is directly opposed to what he sees as the current state of the literary field, dominated as it is by commercialization, and, as a result, a lack of morality: "In a word, this literature which we are forced to name industrial, even though we know that this name is insufficient, has the will and the means, the capital and the talent, for innovation; but it has wasted them. To the critic, the idea of morality has completely disappeared; the selfish cupidity of the individual leads quickly to the ruin of us all."[22]

One of Sainte-Beuve's principal targets was the Société des gens de lettres, the writers' union that Balzac had helped to found in 1838. By focusing their efforts on obtaining higher wages, argued Sainte-Beuve, these authors were demeaning themselves and neglecting the artistic nature of their work. He also attacked the 40-franc press, pioneered by *La Presse* and *Le Siècle* in 1836, papers that had been conceived with the idea of using literature as a money-making activity. The idea was that, by selling advertising space and publishing a page-turning serial novel (the *roman-feuilleton*) on a day-by-day basis, costs would go down and sales would go up. In his prospectus for *Le Siècle*, Armand Dutacq justifies the need to prioritize economic interests by defining the cheap newspaper as a force for democracy.[23]

Sainte-Beuve, on the other hand, wrote for the elite *Revue des deux mondes*, considered, along with *La Revue de Paris*, to be one of only two journals of high art and culture in July Monarchy France. Both papers were founded in 1829 and prided themselves on publishing only the very best works of literature and criticism, serving as "a selective and elitist springboard for the man of letters, and especially for the novelist."[24] A critic writing in 1875 praises the *Revue des deux mondes* for aiming to "reconcile works of imagination and works of criticism at a time when literature and art, affected like everything else by the fallout of the political revolution, were about to go too far." By fostering such an "alliance," he continues, the *Revue* was "spared the mistakes of the great movement of 1830."[25] In other words, if the low-cost dailies like *La Presse* and *Le Siècle* seemed to be willing to allow literature and art to "go too far" into the realm of political engagement, says the commentator, the critics of *La Revue des deux mondes* took a stand, defending the special status of art as existing above everyday concerns.

The *Revues* were visually different from other periodicals of the time. Published in-octavo (book-sized pages in multiples of eight), each page contained one column of text with fairly large margins, resembling a novel or a brochure. Articles were long-form, and authors' names were included prominently at the end of each article, promoting the individual work of each writer. The format was intended for authors who "desired to be identified with their work and sought recognition for it."[26] The major dailies, on the other hand, including the *Le Siècle* and *La Presse*, had adopted an in-folio format, the multicolumned layout that we associate with the modern print newspaper. Each page was packed with articles and advertisements, and margins were tiny. The *roman-feuilleton* occupied the bottom-third of each page (called the *rez-de-chaussée*) and was cut off from the rest of the paper (the *premier étage*) by a thick black line. The areas below and above the line were meant to be quite separate, but the overlapping concerns of literature and politics meant the placement of an item often depended on an editor's personal belief system. The back page of the daily newspaper included advertisements, which helped subsidize the low price paid by the consumer. To save space, and perhaps because the emphasis was supposed to be on the facts being reported rather than the person reporting them, bylines were rare. In contrast to their importance within the pages of the prestigious *Revues*, the identity of the author was therefore quite diminished in the daily newspapers. This dynamic layout made for a somewhat chaotic read, where fact, fiction, and publicity competed for the reader's attention and where distinguishing one from the other was not always simple.

The continued success of the daily newspapers and the increasing pressure on writers meant that Sainte-Beuve's scorn would have little impact on the practices of mainstream authors (the Société des gens de lettres would continue its unionizing efforts and the writers of *romans-feuilletons* would only work harder to keep their readers at the edge of their seats). However, his ideal of an economically disinterested literature did seem to resonate with Vinçard, as we saw in the prospectus to the *Ruche populaire*. Visually, *La Ruche* looked more like a literary *Revue* than a daily paper, and the careful attention given to the identity of a piece's author (each article was signed with the author's name and profession) further emphasized their similarities. By adopting the layout of Sainte-Beuve's *La Revue des deux mondes* rather than that of the 40-franc papers like *Le Siècle*, Vinçard was implicitly aligning himself with their literary philosophy.

This desire to distinguish his paper from the money-making ventures of the 40-franc press did not stop Vinçard from communicating with them, however. Seeing *La Ruche* as an important voice on the literary scene, the managing editor (the *directeur-gérant*, as he calls himself), shows his desire to intervene in major literary events from the paper's very first installment. In December 1839, he prints a letter addressed to Armand Dutacq of *Le Siècle* (a fellow *directeur-gérant*). Vinçard is upset by a series of articles written by Honoré de Balzac, published by the former, on September 27, 28, and 29, 1839. In these pieces, the novelist argues for the release of a man named Sébastien Peytel, who had been sentenced to death for murdering his wife, Félicie, and their servant Louis Rey. The trial, known as the Peytel Affair, had caught the attention of the Parisian literary world because Peytel, a country attorney in the Ain region at the time of the crime, had formerly been a successful journalist, best-known as the author of the satirical *Physiology of the Pear* (*Physiologie de la poire*) (1832), the pear being a well-known and thinly veiled symbol of Louis-Philippe's shortcomings, from his bottom-heavy figure and large nose to his inability to govern.[27] Balzac, who was just beginning his literary career when Peytel's *Physiologie* created a stir in political and literary circles, was a great admirer of the illicit text and even owned a signed copy of it.[28]

In his *plaidoirie*, published in *Le Siècle*, Balzac tries to tap into what he assumes will be a strong sense of class and regional identification among his readers. In the first place, he claims, Peytel was from a well-off family from a different part of the country and did not hold the same petty bourgeois values of his neighbors in the Ain. He had trained as a notary and settled down in his wife's country town only recently, and his former life as a Parisian journalist made him the subject of local rumors. If he mocked his neighbors, says Balzac, it was only in self-defense. "He indulged in the dangerous pleasure of composing several epigrams and songs at the expense of his enemies. The Parisian finding himself pitted against the Provincial, the *littérateur* reappeared, and he was wittier than his adversaries: yet another crime!"[29]

These petty provincial attitudes, Balzac argues, become serious matters when they influence judicial decisions. Indeed, he claims, the local prosecutor, judge, and jury in charge of deciding Peytel's fate were all biased against the defendant because of their bourgeois wariness of anything that was not useful or industrious. Again, then, Balzac takes up the theme of class antagonism between the misunderstood artist from the city and the narrow-minded provincial bourgeois, representative of "*la classe maîtresse des institutions de Juillet.*"[30] Indeed, in taking up the *cause célèbre* of the Peytel Affair, Balzac transforms a legal matter into an occasion to argue for a reevaluation of literature within bourgeois society. To the modern reader, Balzac's framing of Peytel—who works as a notary, a rather lucrative and staid profession—as a suffering artist is somewhat awkward, but for his contemporaries, Peytel's memorable caricature of Louis-Philippe was enough to align him with the literary avant-garde of the day.

Upon reading Balzac's *plaidoirie*, Jules Vinçard was in his turn compelled to write a letter to Dutacq.[31] At trial, the defense team's strategy had been, essentially, to accuse Louis Rey of killing Félicie, and admitting that if Peytel killed Rey, this was only out of self-defense. There was little evidence to support such a theory, but Balzac's articles—carefully composed and based on his own on-site investigation of the crime scene—say nothing to contradict it. This silence leads Vinçard to conclude that the novelist was just as guilty of class prejudice as he had accused the provincial justice system of being. His letter, dripping with irony, mocks the sense of class superiority that Balzac ascribes, first to Peytel and then, by association, to himself: "I wouldn't dare to address myself directly to the author of the article. Perched upon the summit of the high classes, he might, if he were to open up his gaping beak to respond, accidentally allow some crumbs of intellectual nourishment fall to the rest of us, the crafty foxes that we are."[32] The allusion to the famous fable figures Balzac as a pompous crow, while painting the worker-writers as clever and ingenious foxes (but more ethical, in that they choose not to humiliate their ridiculous interlocutor). The fable, with its moral—"The flatterer, my good sir, / Aye liveth on his listener"—thus serves as a warning to the self-important literary class, reminding them that they are only as grand as their (working-class) public allows them to be.[33] But even more than Balzac, the lesson is directed at Armand Dutacq, who, like Vinçard, is the managing editor of his paper, and, therefore has a moral responsibility to his readers: "It is you, sir, that this artisan, this man of the lower classes, holds to account for the sacred office [*sacerdoce*] you hold; ... your responsibility is great, serious, and deep; you must answer, at least morally, for everything that appears in your tribune."[34] By portraying himself as both an artisan and as Dutacq's peer, Vinçard elaborates what he sees as his literary identity. No longer the simple writer of poems and songs for which he is best known, he is also, as the director of a newspaper, the guarantor of its moral content. Unlike Dutacq and his peers, commercially-minded entrepreneurs of the 40-cent dailies, Vinçard has a noble and disinterested understanding of his role as a literary figure, one that resembles Sainte-Beuve's literary ideal.

It should be noted that the aspiring worker-journalist was probably eager to participate in such a controversial public discussion because of the publicity it would bring to himself and his paper. Addressing his missive from one "managing editor [*directeur-gérant*]" to another, Vinçard was undoubtedly hoping that his piece would appear on the pages of the bestselling *Siècle*, implicating himself—and the working classes more generally—in the literary event. Although Dutacq never printed Vinçard's letter in *Le Siècle*, the contributors to *La Ruche* continued to seek out correspondence with major bourgeois writers, and sometimes their overtures were answered. In 1841, they even engaged in several interchanges with Victor Hugo, widely recognized as the *chef d'école* of the French Romantic movement of the day. For example, when the shoemaker Savinien Lapointe dedicates his poem "Une voix d'en bas" to Hugo, the author responds promptly. "Continue your doubled function: your task as a worker and your calling as a thinker. You speak to the people from close up, others speak to them from high above; Your word is compelling. You do well to divide yourself in this way [*Vous êtes bien partagé*], believe me."[35] Hugo's designation of Lapointe as a split personality recalls Dumas's praise of Reboul the baker, and it was typical of the way he and other bourgeois patrons approached their worker-writer mentees. Several years earlier, Hugo had encouraged the Saint-Simonian woodworker-turned-philosopher Gabriel Gauny in a similar way: "Always be what you are ... so that we can remain what we are [*Soyez toujours ce que vous êtes ... afin que nous puissions demeurer ce que nous sommes*]."[36] Thus, Hugo's support for worker-writers relied upon a clear distinction between his own art and the more rustic compositions of his protégés. This type of advice to compartmentalize the activities of manual and intellectual or creative labor was common in exchanges between worker-poets and bourgeois writers during the July Monarchy.

The writers of *La Ruche* had their own limits, however, as to how much direction they would accept from bourgeois outsiders. Several months after Lapointe had basked in Victor Hugo's praise, Vinçard published a lengthy and strongly worded letter condemning Hugo's use of the terms *peuple* (meaning the "good" members of the lower classes) and *populace* (meaning the vicious or lazy ones).[37] Hugo's reply, also published in *La Ruche*, is somewhat dismissive, but the very fact that he was compelled to respond to Vinçard is indicative of the cultural weight the worker-writer movement had taken on. Later on, Vinçard would characterize the printed exchange between Victor Hugo and Savinien Lapointe as: "the correspondence between the two greatest poets of our era, ... a precious monument to the holy equality and fraternity of men." Looking back on this moment of literary exchange, he continues, one finds a "religious and sacred archive" of how true equality and fraternity can be achieved through art.[38]

Hugo's relationships with the worker-writers in his orbit were, much like the friendship between George Sand and Agricol Perdiguier, symptomatic of the more general phenomenon that Carol E. Harrison has called "bourgeois emulation." Throughout the nineteenth century, enlightened bourgeois thinkers across the country and in a variety of professions tried to impart the values of "harmony and peaceful competition" to their working-class compatriots, all while maintaining a position of influence and authority over them. A typical example of this was the founding of mutual aid societies, a type of pension fund, which were meant to encourage thrift and help workers provide for their families in difficult times. To promote participation in these societies, bourgeois industrialists would match worker contributions to the fund. However, as Harrison's research shows, workers were often wary of these societies, and either refused to contribute or used the money for purposes that were more in line with their own values and immediate needs.[39] Rightly suspicious of their bourgeois patrons' motives, workers would often accept financial and other material assistance without integrating the moral teachings that they were meant to absorb. For a short time, it seemed that the harmonious relations between worker-writers and Romantic literary figures could escape this type of mistrust. In 1840s, both workers and their literary bourgeois patrons seemed to agree that artisans who took up the pen were following a calling, engaging in an activity that Dinah Ribard has compared to "missionary work." Nonetheless, as Ribard reminds us, this period also represented a moment when worker-writer publications and publicity were quite in fashion, so that both working-class and professional writers had a vested interest in keeping this narrative alive.[40]

Crystallization of the Working-Class Identity

As mentioned earlier, *La Ruche populaire* was different from earlier iterations of the worker press in the way it assembled worker-writers from a variety of social and professional contexts. This heterogeneity could be seen quite clearly in the first two issues, where we find, unsurprisingly, many contributions from workers in the print trade (Henri Fugère signs his name as a *graveur*, Duquenne is an *ouvrier imprimeur*, Gustave Biard is a *correcteur*, Vannostal is a *typographe*). However, they also included writers from a variety of other professions and social contexts: a watchmaker (*horloger*) named Benoist gives an economic argument for association in a piece called "Du salaire" (On the question of salary), Vinçard himself is a woodworker, and Savinien Lapointe is a humble shoemaker.

La Ruche was also unique in the emphasis that was placed on literary expression from workers of different regional backgrounds. For instance, one of the first issues featured a poem written by a cabinetmaker (*ébéniste*) named Boissy and another included one written by a farmer (*cultivateur*) named Dufoux. It is hard to overstate the contrast that reigned between city and country life in France at this time, and, while both pieces express Romantic themes and follow the same classical structure (alexandrine couplets), they attest to very different social experiences. The farmer Dufoux's "Le Songe" (The dream) is a lyrical piece that focuses on natural imagery. Beginning with a complaint that, unlike the simple insect, the agricultural worker does not know his place in society, the piece ends on a hopeful note, when a God-figure reassures the farmer that he is destined for bigger things than the insect. In contrast, the artisan Boissy expresses a more socially conscious message in "Aux philosophes" (To the philosophers). The poem starts out with a condemnation of liberal individualism, a system that creates a society of "Shameful parasites, bane of the nation, / bringing only hate and revolution." Over the course of the piece, however, the mood shifts as the speaker adopts a more hopeful and harmonious tone: "Let us work together, charmed by our labors, / Rivals, friends, united, connected; / Through our great industry let us complete our conquest; / Let's go, new soldiers, masters, music in our ears."[41] The difference between the pastoral setting of the "Le Songe" and the industrial one of "Aux philosophes" is indicative of the various social situations of the individual contributors to *La Ruche*, who nonetheless felt united in their desire to write poetry.

Along with their different social environments, the contributors to *La Ruche populaire* express a range of political positions. Monarchists like Jean Reboul were rare, but even within the socialist-republican majority, ideas varied widely. For example, in the paper's first issue, a chemical products worker (*un chef d'atelier de produits chimiques*) named Emile Varin declares the goal of the paper to be political rights through nonviolent means: "We aim to ... compensate for a lack of education and understanding of our rights and social duties: rights which they refuse us, duties which they impose on us. Slaves of yesterday, only just recently liberated, we want to conquer peacefully our right of citizenship. The bourgeois may sleep peacefully: fighting and war are weapons which we reject openly."[42] Varin, who would have been among the more educated contributors to *La Ruche*, makes a political claim for the right to vote using a discourse that is evacuated of any hint of revolutionary violence. In the same issue, however, a tailor named Desplanche offers a very different political stance. Desplanche, who in December 1843 would join Vinçard in founding a new paper, *L'Union*, argues that politics is *not* the solution to the problem of bad social organization, because those in power are completely ignorant, and they "confirm their incompetence daily." Instead of political reform, then, he calls for revolt, "upending the natural order of things by turning the governed into governors, and the governors into the governed."[43] Thus, while we see that Varin and Desplanches share the ideal of social harmony, they disagree about how such harmony will come about.

In the second issue, a typographer named L. J. Vannostal, who would also join Vinçard at *L'Union*, expresses a similar argument about the uselessness of politics without education. He tempers his revolutionary message with a positive portrayal of bourgeois reformers, calling them "the most generous portion of the new aristocracy [who] want to give the people political rights." However, he adds, if nothing is done to teach the working classes how best to use their political rights, then "these rights will lead to nothing more than what has happened so many times before: the working class will become the steppingstones of political exploiters."[44] Desplanches, a lowly tailor, and Vannostal, a well-respected typographer, come from very different backgrounds, but they share a belief that social change must take place not as the result of political discussion but through a complete rethinking of how society itself is organized.

As a foreman in a chemical production workshop, Varin occupies a slightly more prestigious position in the social hierarchy than the other two writers mentioned. In contrast to Desplanches and Vannostal, he argues that better social organization must happen through political means such as universal suffrage and acts of class solidarity. It is perhaps not surprising that Varin would soon leave *La Ruche* to join the followers of the Catholic-socialist Philippe Buchez in founding another worker-run paper, *L'Atelier*, in September 1840.

Literature

Although the contributors to *La Ruche* were far from monolithic in their political ideals, one area where most of them seemed to agree, at least for a brief period, was the importance of literature in forming a working-class identity. This belief seemed to reach a high point in 1841, when poetic representations of labor and the laborer as exalted objects of contemplation and moral goodness filled up the pages of *La Ruche populaire* and other publications. In March, for example, a joiner named Michel Roly published a poem titled "L'Amour de la gloire" (The love of glory). In it, he compares his own humble labor to that of Jesus, reminding his readers that Jesus, too, had been an artisan. This evocation of the figure of Jesus as the poor carpenter allows the worker to claim the exalted and heroic qualities of God. He furthers the comparison by evoking the scene in the desert when the devil tempts Jesus with riches in exchange for his adoration. Just as Jesus surmounts this temptation, so will Roly spurn all those who try to stop him from writing poetry:

> And if those great men who are inconvenienced by my work
> Come offer, in order to stifle my voice,
> rank, honor and fortune,
> or even threaten me with the strictness of their laws.
> [I will remember that] When the devil, that horrible tempter,
> Came to offer Jesus all the kingdoms of this world
> If he would just worship him, Jesus chose the cross.[45]

Like Jesus, the worker should not trade his honest work for the temptations of the devil. Roly was one of many worker-poets to draw parallels between his own situation and that of Jesus Christ. George Sand, for example, used the trope in her depictions of her suffering joiner, Pierre

Huguenin. As Frank Paul Bowman has demonstrated, the figure of Christ had, throughout the postrevolutionary period, been recuperated from Old Regime clericalism and transformed into a socialist hero by writers, political figures, and even members of the clergy. Worker-poets were especially keen to establish an identification between themselves and their Lord, endowing their manual labor with a sacred sense of vocation, as a type of spiritual work that benefits all of humanity, and even justifying their eventual revolt against unfair working conditions.[46]

The triumphant tone of *La Ruche* continued in May, when a porcelain painter (who by 1841 had been promoted as an assistant merchant, *un commis negotiant*) named Francis Tourte published a versed dialogue between an allegorical Sword (*L'Épée*) and a Hammer (*Le Marteau*), the former representing the nobility and the latter the working class. The piece opens with the Sword scolding the Hammer for making too much noise during his nap, and the two begin to dispute their respective places in the social hierarchy. The Sword claims to be chosen by God, stating boastfully: "I come from the heavens / I am their creation! / I am the heir / of our heroes and our gods!" The Hammer endures this bluster for several pages, but he will have the last word, closing the poem with this final retort: "It matters not the laurels with which you are crowned! / Do not disdain me, for whether sword or scythe, / You would be ungrateful to deny your father! / Steel! It is I, the hammer, it is I who forged you!"[47] The moral of this allegory is clear: claims to any sort of nobility or social privilege that do not recognize the debt we all owe to physical labor are weak and unfounded. One might even read it as a poetic argument for the labor theory of value.

The year 1841 was also when Olinde Rodrigues published his compilation of worker poetry in a collection entitled *Poésies sociales*. A Saint-Simonian banker, Rodrigues wanted to assemble what he deemed to be the best pieces by the worker-poets associated with the Saint-Simonian movement. Vinçard is featured prominently, as are Michel Roly (the carpenter), Savinien Lapointe (the shoemaker), and even a woman, an embroiderer named Elisa Fleury. Coming from different professions and various social statuses, the contributors are brought together through their ability to write poetry. In his introduction to the volume, Rodrigues emphasizes that poetry is the best way to "characterize the progress of the moral sentiments of the working class," thus promoting the idea of a worker-writer identity.[48]

At the same time, the idea of solidarity among worker-writers was weaponized by the movement's detractors. In December 1841, Eugène

Lerminier published a virulent attack on what he called *la littéature des ouvriers*, using the label "workers' literature" pejoratively. Lerminier's new category lumped together not only the various worker-poets in Olinde Rodrigues's *Poésies sociales*, but also the joiner Agricol Perdiguier, the typographer-turned-social theorist Adolphe Boyer, and, indeed, all contributors to the worker press. Lerminier flattened the differences between their very different works (many of which were not at all literary), diminishing the value that each individual text had to offer. He ascribes to them a sort of identity politics, defining this "workers' literature" as expressing their writers' "aware[ness] of their suffering and of society's obligation to relieve them of this." But, he adds, this expression of social identity is not enough to make them good writers: "It is not the case that they have suddenly been illuminated by marvelous intelligibility and are suddenly gifted with philosophical and literary genius. The writing in prose and verse which has recently been published by authors who belong to the working classes lacks all originality: it is characterized by imitation. This is not to say that individual genius may not ever spring from the popular classes, but it has yet to happen."[49] In other words, according to Lerminier, proletarian writers have neither the natural genius nor the education to allow them to create great works. When bourgeois promoters (and here, although he does not name names, he is targeting authors like George Sand and Eugène Sue) encourage them, he adds, they do so for selfish reasons, precisely because proletarian literature had become such a popular phenomenon. Lerminier's article was unsurprisingly not well received by the figures he attacked. Sand, for example, dedicated two articles, a first and second "Dialogue familier sur la poésie des prolétaires," in her own paper, *La Revue indépendante*, in defense of both the value of proletarian literature and her own motives. The worker-writers Lerminier targeted were not so well situated to defend themselves, but they tried.

For the Saint-Simonian contributors to *La Ruche populaire*, these attacks were particularly painful, in that they came from Lerminier, himself a former Saint-Simonian. One of the critic's principal critiques was that worker-writers did not respect "the division of labor, which assigns action to some and thought to others." In fact, by characterizing the writing practices of *La Ruche*'s contributors as an infringement upon the "division of labor" between manual and intellectual labor, Lerminier was completely misunderstanding them. The accusation was in direct contrast to what Vinçard and his collaborators had been arguing for in the paper's prospectus, where they declared their intention to avoid any "literary speculation" that would bring the professional and the poetic together. What's more, his article appeared in *La Revue des deux mondes*, the paper that had published Sainte-Beuve's attack on industrial literature and served as a model for Vinçard's own literary position (and formatting choices). Worse still, Lerminier, who was critical of the worker press in general, did manage to find some positive words for *L'Atelier*, the only other major worker-run paper on the scene, and, therefore, the direct competitor of *La Ruche*. In contrast to Vinçard and his collaborators, the founders of *L'Atelier* had positioned themselves as the antiliterary publication, declaring, in the first issue, a policy against publishing articles by "*hommes de lettres* [lettered men]," or accomplished literary authors, whose works (especially melodramas), they saw to be a corrupting force. Indeed, the stated goal of *L'Atelier* was "to expose the odious intentions of these corrupted writers who, in pretending to educate us, are actually depraving us."[50] In a similar way, *La Ruche* was focused on publishing pieces by authentic workers rather than professional writers, but this did not mean they had to eschew all literary writing. Indeed, by calling itself "a mixture of articles in prose and in verse," Vincard's paper showcased its literary ambitions as a major feature of the publication. Thus, Lerminier's praise for *L'Atelier*'s absence of "literary pretention" amounts to a complete rejection of *La Ruche* and its mission.

A New Literary Identity

If 1841 marks the apex of the literary identity of the worker-writer, it also represents a turning point. It was soon after Lerminier's attack, in December 1841, that Vinçard decided to hand over the direction of the paper to a colleague. In order to remain "disinterested" in the Sainte-Beuvienne sense, he believed he had to give up the commercial activity required for running a solvent newspaper. Taking stock of how well the journal had been able to live up to the ideals set up in the prospectus, Vinçard insists: "No, we did not wish to become *littérateurs* and to disdain [*prendre en mépris*] our manual labor! ... We wanted to be taught and to teach ourselves to reward equally with love, glory, and joy the laborer who carries out the tasks of a project, the architect who plans them, the scientist who invents them, and the poet who sings them."[51] Despite giving up his role at *La Ruche*, Vinçard maintains that he has not lost his ideals. He still believes that the objective of literature is not to make money but to express something sacred. In the case of the worker-writer, this sacred idea is "the cry of our independence and our dignity." And yet, he admits, "let us be honest, we dared to practice what is called journalism." Here, however, journalism is described as "dar[ing] to take an audacious initiative of formulating and transmitting our thoughts publicly by means of the press."[52] In a sense, it seems that Vinçard has found a positively coded way of saying that he and his collaborators have indeed become *littérateurs*.

Recognizing the publicity-focused nature of the press, and admitting, finally, the journalistic ambitions of his own work, Vinçard also asserts that, all along, the goal of *La Ruche* had been to communicate not only with fellow workers but also the bourgeoisie: "For, truly, to whom could we address our grievances, if not those who, alone, have the power to fix them?" With this in mind, Vinçard hands over the direction to Jules Paton, identified as a *commis* (a vague term designating various types of assistants or clerks, usually associated with banking or sales of some sort). Vinçard calls Paton a "son of the bourgeoisie, whose childhood was nourished with the fruits of instruction and science," further emphasizing his willingness to cooperate with—and even recruit the help of—bourgeois allies.[53] Vinçard's attitude toward mainstream journalism shifts even more drastically in December 1842. He writes, "So, who better to embrace this sainted cause best and with ardor and courage, if it is not the journalistic press? Who alone can and must make the greatest strides in the progressive march toward the people's happiness, if it is not the great voice of journalism?"[54] In these articles, we can see Vinçard's evolving attitude toward the *littérateurs*, a shift that involves not only an opening up to bourgeois values but also a sophisticated working-out of the function and value of literature in society typical of the cultural moment, and true for both workers and bourgeois readers and writers. These trends will become even more apparent in his new journalistic venture, *L'Union*.

Vinçard's abandonment of the direction of *La Ruche populaire* in December 1841 marked the beginning of the end for the paper in its original state. Due to a lack of funds, *La Ruche* stopped production in January, February, and March 1842. It ran for two months under Paton's direction in April and May 1842 and then passed through several different hands until March 1845. At this point, the journal took a new direction. Rather than allowing working-class writers to express themselves on the pages of the press, the new iteration of *La Ruche* intended to "bring hidden sufferings to the attention of rich benefactors."[55] The paper sought subscriptions from important literary and political figures who would, it was hoped, offer assistance to the most unfortunate members of the working class, either through publicity or monetary aid.[56]

Vinçard's departure from *La Ruche* did not, however, mark the end of his literary ambitions. For about a year, he continued to work with the new director, Paton, and to contribute poems and other pieces to *La Ruche*. By 1843, however, Vinçard had joined forces with worker-poets Michel Roly and Savinien Lapointe to found a new paper, *L'Union*, which saw its first issue in December of that year. Here, Vinçard and his colleagues seemed to have changed tactics, but not in the way that Lerminier would have them do. Instead of focusing strictly on practical questions, the founders of *L'Union* seemed more committed than ever to taking an active part in producing and commenting on contemporary literature and participating in the wider discussions surrounding mainstream literary production. In other words, Vinçard was ready to embrace quite fully the profession of the *littérateur*.

The directors of *L'Union* made two important formatting changes, signaling a new literary identity. By opting for an in-folio design rather than an in-octavo one, the founders aligned themselves with the major popular dailies of the time such as *Le Journal des débats*, *La Presse*, and *Le Siècle*, rather than the *La Revue des deux mondes*, where Sainte-Beuve and Lerminier had published their critiques of modern literary practices. In a similar fashion, they began to include the thick black line of the *feuilleton*. Precisely because of the close proximity between the *roman-feuilleton* and the columns of news items, as we saw above, the modern papers were contributing to a new way of conceiving of literature as an accessible form of entertainment that was separate from, but keenly attentive to, the events of the day.

Jules Paton, who had taken over *La Ruche populaire* in December 1841, also joined Vinçard, Roly, and Lapointe at *L'Union* in 1843. Interestingly, while, in 1841, he was presented as a *commis*, or clerk (a bourgeois ally to Vinçard and the other working-class writers), two years later he had adopted a more working-class persona, signing off as an *"ouvrier de Chemins de fer"* or a railroad laborer. Speaking in this persona, he explains at length why it was important to split the page into a below-the-line *feuilleton* and an above-the-line factual section: "The founders of *L'Union* have agreed to consecrate the superior columns of the paper to the *methodical recording of all of the facts* which may be interesting to the new idea of labor organization.... But, in order to allow for the different penchants of the human spirit, we have reserved a space for the elucubrations of our friends—philosophers and poets, publicists and economists—a feuilleton where they will give an account of their *impressions* and of the signification of their writings" (emphasis added).[57] Paton's exposé serves not only as a belated response to Lerminier's call for a division of labor in literary production, then, but also as a gesture of solidarity with the mainstream press. He shows a sophisticated understanding of the role of the *feuilleton* as a space where various aspects of culture—including literature—could be explored without taking away from the "methodical" or "factual" nature of the articles appearing above the line. In the early days of the *roman-feuilleton*, the thick black line that separated the *rez-de-chaussée* from the *premier étage* was supposed to signal a clear distinction between poetry and politics, or entertainment and information. The *premier étage* was supposed to represent a paper's political opinions and could be linked to the deeply held beliefs of the paper's editors, whereas the *rez-de-chaussée* concentrated on art and fiction. This distinctive repartition of space allowed a progovernment paper such as *Le Constitutionnel* to print Eugène Sue's subversive novel *The Wandering Jew* (1844–45) even as the government was officially opposed to socialist ideas espoused in the novel.

However, as the *roman-feuilleton* gained in popularity, it soon became clear that people were buying issues of papers for the single purpose of reading the fictions contained therein. The Left-leaning deputy Benoît-Marie Chapuys-Montlaville bemoaned this lack of interest in above-the-line content, which, according to him, included "in-depth articles written dutifully by a paper's most illustrious writers in the name of general education and to promote public discussion." The fact that the *premier étage*—both spatially and qualitatively superior to the *rez-de-chaussée*—had lost prestige compared to the latter, is what he calls an "anormal situation . . . which proves the simultaneous breakdown in morality and weakening of the public spirit."[58] From a modern standpoint, we can see that the thick black line was little more than symbolic. Indeed, the porosity of subject matter between the spaces above and below the line was one of the defining elements of nineteenth-century journalism and a major aspect of literary style specific to the period.[59] However, what is important here is that the editors and critics of nineteenth-century papers *believed* that the *premier étage* and the *rez-de-chaussée* represented different ways of seeing the world: one factual and political; the other affective and impressionistic.

In Paton's description of what types of pieces should appear "below the line," he groups philosophers, poets, publicists, and economists all in the same category of cultural thinkers who write about their impressions, but it is doubtful that such different writers would see themselves as having much in common with one another. This aggregation was symptomatic of the difficulty that many papers encountered in deciding how to classify their articles. Indeed, Paton, in the very next issue, would break his own rules by printing a literary review in the *premier étage* (above the line). At first glance, everything seems to be in order. The *rez-de-chaussée* contains two "literary" items: one is a song in honor of Béranger written by a lithographer named Barillot, the other is a review of Savinien Lapointe's poetry collection *Une Voix d'en bas* (signed, simply "C.B."). Both pieces—an original literary production and a piece of literary criticism—fit with Paton's definition of what belongs in the *feuilleton*. Most of the articles above the line also seem to be in the right place, such as an in-depth analysis of a plan to establish a national pension fund for workers. However, among these is a review of Charles Poncy's latest poetry collection, written by Paton, the very same Paton who had laid out the rules about separating the more practical business of organizing labor from the "elucubrations of philosophers and poets." How could Paton justify this inconsistency? Why does his review of Poncy belong above the line while C.B.'s review of Lapointe belongs below it? One explanation may be that Paton's article moves beyond literary analysis to make a more general statement about worker-poets as the future of literature: "A new alliance is forming between the oldest and the newest literary celebrities, between the likes of Lamennais, Chateaubriand, Lamartine, Béranger, and George Sand and the worker-poets Roly, Savinien Lapointe, Poncy, Magu, and a crowd of others."

Paton believes that the "alliance" between worker-poets and bourgeois writers is more than a cultural issue. It is also one of survival. The literary sterility (*l'impuissance poétique*), that he identifies among bourgeois artists will lead to their fall from power: "You cannot see the future if you have no poetry; you live from day to day, you sacrifice everything to the status quo, you become petrified, immobilized, blind."[60] Poetry is, in other words, an integral part of politics, and therefore Paton believes that this analysis belongs above the line.

In this way, Paton is announcing a new era in the worker-writers' position regarding the nature of literature: a confirmed acceptance of the importance of economic, political, and other worldly concerns in literary expression as well as the close relationship between journalism and literature. While signaling, through the use of the *feuilleton*, a sophisticated understanding of the difference between fact and fiction, between news and art, he nonetheless maintains the Saint-Simonian principle expressed by Barrault in 1830 that artistic expression must play an integral role in how we understand the world and try to change it. It is not a matter of giving up their understanding of the power of literature—in fact, it is a digging-in of their identity as literary producers, by proving that, if they amalgamate literature and politics, this is an intentional move on their part.

Indeed, although *L'Union* claimed to be a vessel for working-class expression, its contributors were quite willing to collaborate with bourgeois *littérateurs*. If, in the prospectus to *La Ruche populaire* (December 1839), worker-writers had argued for a disinterested ideal of literature *à la* Sainte-Beuve, the paradigm has clearly shifted in *L'Union*. For example, Vinçard uses the "Chronique" of March 1844 both to publicize forthcoming poetry collections by the worker-poets Charles Poncy and Savinien Lapointe, and to laud the participation of George Sand and Eugène Sue in their publications: "How happy for us all that to see that these wonderful literary authorities hold out their hands and pull the most intelligent men of our class up to their level. The man who is able through his work and genius to attract the gaze of these grand authors is glorified; but so are those who patronize with such love the first efforts of our popular intelligence."[61] Vinçard makes a point to congratulate both the worker-writers for capturing the attention of the "literary authorities" and the "authorities" themselves for being able to recognize the talent of the poets. Thus, as worker-writers and bourgeois patrons continued to work more closely together, the working-class literary identity as one of disinterestedness and generosity became less important and a more enterprising understanding of literary publicity as a way to further political, social, and even economic goals took over. The narrative that worker-writers had been promoting since the early days of the July Monarchy—namely, that their literary practices were fundamentally separate from their professional activities—had peaked in 1841 and given way to a more pragmatic understanding of what it meant to be a writer. Rejected by the illustrious critics Lerminier and Sainte-Beuve, Vinçard and his collaborators found willing allies in best-selling novelists like George Sand, Eugène Sue, Alexandre Dumas, and even Victor Hugo. In a political sense, the relationship was natural, as both groups were committed to social change, and they were also sentimentally aligned, as Dumas's depiction of Reboul's melancholy illustrates. Workers and writers shared many experiences, including that of being seen as different from and often rejected by the people around them. What's more, the popular interest in worker-writers seemed to indicate that their cooperation would be financially beneficial to all those who participated in bringing their texts to print.

As we shall see in the next chapter, however, the process of growing solidarity between bourgeois and working-class writers that played out on the pages of *La Ruche populaire* and *L'Union* was woefully one-sided. While the bourgeois authors mentioned above continued to ask their working-class protégés to espouse a belletrist and disinterested literary ideal, they themselves profited from their writing, presenting it as a form of productive labor. In the end, these divergent narratives of literary labor would both help to stoke the enthusiasm driving the February Revolution of 1848 and contribute to the misunderstandings that emerged in the weeks and months that followed.

5

Building Character

A Formula for Success

If, in the previous chapter, we looked at popular literature as a form of cultural production originating from "the people," here we will focus on a different form of popularity, understood in terms of how many people were reading the work. This type of popular literature can be difficult to study, since it is, by its nature, composed of many texts that have not withstood the test of time, a problem that is heightened with the press revolution of the 1830s and 1840s. The main interest in reading these works, according to Martyn Lyons, is to gain an understanding of "the consensus of a society," based not on which ideas would pass the test of academic scrutiny, but rather on "those tastes that were most widespread tastes among French readers" of a given moment.[1] According to Lyons's calculations, based on numbers of books printed, most of the bestsellers of the 1840s were reprints of seventeenth-century classics such as Jean de La Fontaine's *Fables* (1668) or François Fénelon's *Télémaque* (1699), sentimental works from the eighteenth century like *Paul et Virginie* (1788), and educational texts like Madame de Saint-Ouen's *Histoire de France* (1832). By focusing on official book sales and publication announcements, Lyons limits the society whose "consensus" we are measuring here to that of the literate working classes and petite bourgeoisie in major cities. This misses the large part of the population living in rural areas, where the practice of colportage continued to thrive well into the Second Republic.[2] Even if it does not take into account that the public may have been *reading* works that were quite different from the ones they were buying, Lyons's data is quite useful for the insight it gives us about normative attitudes toward literature at the time, namely, that this was a society that, at least on the surface, valued books more as sources of moral or intellectual improvement than as forms of entertainment.

Because old classics dominated book sales, it is hard to measure the reach of contemporary novelists who often published serially in newspapers rather than in book form. And yet, starting in the 1840s, the *roman-feuilleton*, or serial novel, was *the* most important way that most readers consumed literature. The practice of publishing novels incrementally had been in place since the seventeenth century, and Honoré de Balzac's *La Vieille Fille* (1836) is often considered to be the first "official" *roman-feuilleton*, but the genre did not truly come into its own as such until the early 1840s. Indeed, many of the classics from the mid-nineteenth century that we now call novels were originally published in daily installments. Alexandre Dumas's *Les Trois Mousquetaires* appeared over the course of a year in *Le Siècle* (1844) and his *Comte de Monte Cristo* was published chapter by chapter in the *Journal des débats* (1844–46). Both were later released as bound books, and appear on Lyons's list. Others, like Paul Féval's *Les Mystères de Londres*, published in *Le Courrier français* (1843–44), have since fallen into oblivion but were intensely popular in their time. Dealing with the demands of daily output, serial novelists were always in search of newness: new developments, new situations, and new characters with which to fill their pages and keep their public's attention. At the same time, the format imposed constraints: descriptions of people and places could last only a few pages (the length of the daily installment) and had to be straightforward enough so that the reader could recall them easily, should they reappear weeks, months, or even years later. Simplicity was key, and, as we shall see in this chapter, flat or typical characters, with their legibility, and their memorability, were perfect for the format.

One author stands out among all others as the master of the early *roman-feuilleton*: Eugène Sue. His ability to capture popular attention by capitalizing on the constraints and freedoms of the genre was unequalled by any of his contemporaries, except, perhaps, Alexandre Dumas. Unlike Dumas, however, who first earned a name as a dramatist, Sue's success was born of the *roman-feuilleton*. His *Les Mystères de Paris* (*The Mysteries of Paris*), which first ran in the *Journal des débats* (1842–43), was an immediate sensation.[3] It was quickly published as an illustrated volume and translated into multiple languages, representing one of the first instances of an international literary phenomenon that Berry Chevasco has fittingly called "Mysterymania."[4] Riding on this success, Sue quickly produced *Le Juif errant* (*The Wandering Jew*) for another popular daily newspaper, *Le*

Constitutionel (1844–45).[5] Its success helped boost subscriptions to the paper from 3,600 in June 1844 to 25,000 in July 1845 and confirmed Sue's title as the king of the *roman-feuilleton*.[6] The similarities between the two works can help us identify what may be seen as a sort of formula for success at this moment.

The *Mysteries* focuses on the adventures of Rodolphe de Gerolstein, a German prince who has assumed the identity of a laborer in order to infiltrate the Paris underworld and rescue his kidnapped daughter from a life of prostitution. In his pursuits, Rodolphe encounters a cast of characters with varying moral natures, and, in detective-like fashion, he quickly determines which of them are good and which of them are evil, rewarding or punishing them as he sees fit. The Stabber (*Le Chourineur*), for example, is a murderous butcher who nonetheless counters his bloodthirsty impulses with a tender heart and a strong sense of fairness; he soon becomes Rodolphe's faithful sidekick. The Schoolmaster (*Le Maître d'école*), on the other hand, uses his cunning intelligence to dupe those less powerful than he, and the German prince punishes him fittingly, by blinding him with a toxic concoction. Ever the gentleman, Rodolphe does not kill but merely incapacitates his enemies.

In *The Wandering Jew*, Sue once again makes use of a sprawling cast of characters of varying moral fortitude. They are all connected to one another through a noble but tragic character, the titular Wandering Jew, an apocryphal shoemaker condemned to walk the Earth for eternity as punishment for refusing to help Jesus carry his cross. In Sue's reversal of the antisemitic legend, the titular artisan plays a chastened, benevolent figure, watching over his remaining descendants, the Rennepont family. Scattered across France, the members of the family are destined to assemble in Paris on February 13, 1832, to fulfill a mysterious prophecy and claim their family treasure. At the same time, a group of wealthy and power-hungry Jesuits conspire to prevent this meeting and confiscate the riches. Like Rodolphe, the eponymous wanderer intervenes to protect the flawed but basically good members of society (here, the Renneponts and their allies), ensuring that righteousness triumphs over evil.

Unlike many other bestsellers of the time (which were, as we saw above, old classics, moralistic texts, or historical novels), Sue's popular fictions were set, quite intentionally, in times and places that would have been quite familiar to his readers. The *Mysteries* opens on the rainy night of December 13, 1838 (*MP* 1:1), and *The Wandering Jew*, although it is based on a centuries-old trope, begins as "the month of October 1831 draws to its close" (*WJ* 1:1). These contemporary settings allowed Sue to address what he saw as some of the most pressing social problems of the time, namely criminal justice reform and labor organization. In *Mysteries*, for example, Sue sets his tale of crime and poverty just steps away from the imposing Palais de Justice (city courthouse), spelling out the irony of the situation in no uncertain terms: "Is it not strange, or even fatal," interjects the narrator, "that an irresistible attraction always makes these criminals gravitate toward that formidable tribunal which condemns them to prison, to the penal colony, or to the scaffold?" (my translation).[7] This remarkable irony points to a failure of the status quo and indicates serious social disorder, making room for Rodolphe's particular form of vigilante justice. Unwilling to leave anything open to interpretation, Sue allows the prince to lay out the details of his philosophy in a passionate monologue:

> To succor those unfortunate beings who solicit you is well; to seek out those who uncomplainingly struggle against adversity with energy and honor, and to assist them—sometimes without their knowledge—to prevent, in time, misery, and temptation to crime, is better; to reinstate in self-respect—to send back to honesty those who have preserved some generous and ennobling sentiments in the midst of the contempt that withers them, and for the sake of doing this, to brave in person contact with this misery, this corruption, the infection of this moral position—this, this is the best of all! To pursue, with untiring hatred, with implacable vengeance, vice, infamy, and crime, whether groveling in mud, or enthroned on velvet, is justice; but inconsiderately to give help to merited degradation, to prostitute charity and commiseration by bestowing one's wealth and sympathy on base and unworthy wretches, is horrible, impious, sacrilegious! (1:89)

Real justice, says Sue/Rodolphe, must take into consideration the economic and moral realities of society, a task that the current system is unable to fulfill. Indeed, the legal system is so corrupt that the only solution to the problem would have to come from outside the law. Rodolphe's mission, therefore, is to bypass the current legal structure so that society's victims can be compensated for their undeservedly disadvantaged stations in life, and so that its bullies—those who profit from an unfair system—can face punishment.

Like *Mysteries*, *The Wandering Jew* also includes a latent critique of the criminal justice system, as all official channels of law and order seem to have been corrupted in one way or another by the Jesuits. However, Sue reserves most of his moralizing here for what he calls the "Inorganization of Labor" and the associated problem of the "Insufficiency of Wages," terms that Sue, in the original French, sets off in italics (the English translator chose to highlight them with capitalization). In fact, the narrator inserts several lengthy tirades into this section of the story, blaming the lack of labor organization for the inability of ordinary workers to earn a living wage, and making the link between moral disorder and poor labor conditions quite explicit (*WJ* 2:4). Just as he did in the *Mysteries*, the narrator here knows how to ameliorate the situation, and he believes that this solution must happen in a way that goes beyond official institutional channels. Not only must wages go up, he declares, but the workingman must be given public recognition: "Why do we not see in France, a single workman wearing a medal as the reward of his skill, his courageous industry, his long and laborious career?" Without this type of sign of public gratitude, he warns, "they have no defence against the reductions of indolence; and if, by chance, they find the means of living awhile in repose, they give way by degrees to habits of laziness and debauchery" (*WJ* 2:4). In this way, Sue condemns society's inability to recognize the social and economic value of manual labor.

In both *Mysteries* and *The Wandering Jew*, then, the solutions to society's problems—whether they take the form of an unfair criminal justice system or an unregulated labor market—must come from outside of those broken systems. In fact, one may argue that Sue believed that literature—and, more specifically, the pages of his own immensely popular *roman-feuilleton*—would be the perfect place for such solutions to emerge. He used his public platform not only to criticize existing systems, but also to promote various socialist ideas. For example, already, in 1843, as *Mysteries* was coming to a close, he had begun to include an increasing number of direct appeals to his massive middle-class and lower-middle-class readership. In July of that year, for example, he incorporated the proposition of a philanthropic bank for unemployed workers into the lines of his narrative. He also promoted the cause of proletarian self-expression by reprinting workers' letters within the columns of his popular *feuilleton*. These included some from Jules Vinçard, the former director of *La Ruche populaire*, and the worker-run periodical was even mentioned by name, giving the Saint-Simonian *chansonnier* a real bump in publicity. In short,

Sue used his popularity to extoll the social value of labor and act as a champion of the working classes.

There is some evidence that Sue's attempts to influence popular opinion were successful. Many of his readers saw his writing as a call to act, thrilling at the possible real-life solutions to social problems that his fictional narratives seemed to suggest. For example, a fan named Ernestine Dumont, introducing herself as a real-life Rigolette (the *grisette* character in *Mysteries*), addresses the author as if he were his character. "Let's pretend that you are Rodolphe," she says, asking him to help her neighbors, describing them a real-life version of the destitute Morel family from the novel.[8] It was around the same time that the new editors of *La Ruche populaire* (Vinçard had left to start a new paper, *L'Union*) began to feature a quote from Rodolphe in the header of each issue, recognizing the authority that this fictional character held over a broad swathe of the reading public.

Indeed, Sue was remarkable for his ability to espouse radically socialist ideas that aligned with working-class demands and, at the same time, maintain the mainstream bourgeois readership that propelled him to star status. How did he manage to situate himself as both the champion of the little guy and darling of the dominant class? Sue's *romans-feuilletons* contain a variety of elements that were appealing to a broad audience, but it was perhaps his expert use of character development that contributed most to his ability to walk this line. In particular, his depictions of working-class characters not as flat or clichéd types but as interesting and even heroic individuals seems to point to an affirmation of labor not only as a social value but also as an important element of personal identity. Sue uses manual labor as a building block of character, showing that productive effort was both the marker of a particular social type and an important element in the construction of a complex and even heroic individual.

From Type to Hero

In addition to taking up the causes that were crucial to the working classes (criminal justice and labor organization), Sue also appealed to this audience, no doubt adherents of the bourgeois value of productivism, by including labor as a positive force in character development. In other words, hard work was portrayed not only as determinant of social class or type, but also as a marker of an exceptional and exemplary individual. Both works discussed here use descriptions of manual labor to endow otherwise typical or unchanging characters with a psychological complexity and even a heroic element.

As we have already seen, the July Monarchy was a time when the study of character and personality was of great interest to both scientists and artists. Opposing tendencies toward generalization on the one hand and exceptionalism on the other entered into conflict. The theory among physiognomists and physiologists that the specific characteristics of individuals could be determined simply by looking at their physical features had dominated popular opinion since the previous century; however, the concept of *l'homme moyen* (the average man), elaborated by Quetelet in 1835, posited that studying humanity must take place at the level of population, not the individual. Balzac had already tapped into this intuition in 1830, by describing the laborer as "a means [*un moyen*]," a term that carries—in English as well as in French—a double signification, as both a tool (a winch, an instrument providing assistance) and an average (that is, a figure of mediocrity). Indeed, the Romantic hero who broke out of the mold as an exceptional and often exemplary character was becoming increasingly rare. Misunderstood dreamers like in Chateaubriand's *René* (1802) and exceptional geniuses like the heroine of Madame de Staël's *Corinne* (1807) were disappearing from the literary landscape. As realist techniques became the norm, narrators increasingly engaged in the project of deciphering the social makeup of their imaginary worlds by reading the cues of dress and manners in a way that corresponded with contemporary society. The 1830 generation of Romantics like Honoré de Balzac and Stendhal had to weigh the impulse to portray their characters as singular individuals against a sociological desire to classify those same individuals as types. For example, Stendhal's ambitious Julien de Sorel, the Romantic protagonist of *Le Rouge et le Noir*, can only be understood within the context of his social class, as the son of a factory owner. In the *Human Comedy*, the Balzacian understanding of the worker as either a "winch" or a mere type essentially rejects the importance of individual virtue, bravery, and modern nobility. And yet, Sand's and Cabet's social utopias offer a counterexample to this trend, representing a return to such values in the form of the working-class hero.

This tension between individuals and their social group, the singular and typical, is why literary and visual representations of the 1830s and 1840s tend to represent characters who fall into one of two "types," which Amélie de Chaisemartin has identified as "fictional [*le type romanesque*]" and "sociological [*le type sociologique*]." The former, she argues, was conceived as "a hyperbolic and exceptional individuality" meant to stand out from the norms and expectations of their social situation, while the latter was more of a "synthetic average of the characteristics of a particular social class."[9] Of course, these two types represent two extremes, and most fictional characters can be situated somewhere along a continuum between them.

Chaisemartin's classification—the romanticized individual and the social type—brings a new social dimension to E. M. Forster's classic distinction between "roundness" and "flatness" of character. According to Forster, a round character is one who "waxes and wanes and has facets like a human being," whereas a flat one is "constructed around a single idea or quality" outside of which it has "no existence."[10] Writing from the heights of British Modernism, Forster focuses on flatness and roundness as a measure of psychological complexity and largely ignores the social content of the narratives under consideration. Additionally, pulling his examples mainly from British eighteenth- and nineteenth-century novels, Forster's analysis is less applicable to our corpus than is Chaisemartin's. The terms "round" and "flat" are useful shorthand, however, for the two types of characters that we examine here.

Poor and working-class characters had long played minor roles throughout literary history. The sentimental novels of the eighteenth century, for example, contained their share of virtuous peasants, nurses, servants, and the like; the seventeenth-century picaresque novel was full of poor people (working and not), and even Chaucer and Boccaccio did not shun the working man or woman. However, the growing tendency toward democratization and the expansion of the middle classes of the eighteenth and nineteenth centuries meant that individuals who had, in the past, remained in the background were now appearing in more important roles and in greater numbers in fictional representations of real life. By including a large number of middling, working class, and poor characters in their works, and by assigning them important functions in the narrative, serial novelists like Charles Dickens, Sue, and Balzac were taking part in a larger phenomenon in the nineteenth-century European novel that Alex Woloch has referred to as a redistributing of "character space," whereby a growing attention to "minor" or "marginal" characters corresponds with the shrinking significance of the singular and heroic protagonist, whose space becomes increasingly "endangered."[11] For Woloch, this shift in characterization is closely linked to the growing importance of labor and the laboring classes in society, as, even if many marginal characters are superficially cast as criminals, a closer look at the way they function in the narrative "reveals [the source of their marginality to be] more fundamentally, modern labor: which is to say, the production of wealth through the same process that fragments the worker in relation to what he produces."[12]

The tension between the exceptional Romantic individual and the sociological type was especially visible in the French context. On the one hand, the "frenetic Romanticism" of the previous decades still influenced the literary world, and readers expected literature to provide intense emotions and sensations.[13] On the other hand, these same readers seemed to want to identify with the characters and situations that appeared on the pages of fiction. As we saw in chapter 1, the rise of the serial novel in France was contemporaneous with the vogue of "panoramic" literature, so named by Walter Benjamin because of its aim to represent all levels of society simultaneously. Sue's *Mysteries* coincided almost directly with the rise of the literary *physiologie*, those "small illustrated books" that "inundated the shelves of booksellers" in 1841–42.[14] The two genres seemed to play off one another, with the authors of the *physiologies* and other panoramic texts finding inspiration in novels and the *romans-feuilletons* of the mid-1840s borrowing from the social types found in panoramic literature. Indeed, there was often a good deal of cross-over between the characters who populated the *romans-feuilletons* and the typical figures of Parisian society studied in *physiologies'* brief proto-sociological sketches.

One of the keys to Sue's success was his ability to create characters who were at once "flat" or "typical" enough to be easily read and remembered and yet "round" or "exemplary" enough to move his readers to strong feelings. A notable example of how this takes place can be found in his character Madame Piplelet, a stereotypical example—or "type"—of *la portière*, the (female) concierge, or porter. Appearing as a stock character in numerous novels by Paul de Kock (*Le Barbier de Paris*, 1827; *Le Cocu*, 1831; and *La Pucelle de Belleville*, 1834, to name just a few) and other popular authors, the ubiquitous *portière* was given her first treatment as a sociological type in James Rousseau's *La Physiologie de la portière*, published with caricatural vignettes by Daumier in 1841. It was not until September 1842, however, that Sue begins to develop the complexity of the *portière* through the character of Madame Pipelet in *Mysteries*. There are of course many details of her character that recall the comedic figure in

Kock's work or the sociological type of the *physiologie*, but Madame Pipelet captures the reader's emotions in a way that the typical *portière* cannot.

The introduction of the Pipelets to the narrative marks a new focus in the *Mysteries*. Previous chapters had focused on the clash of Rodolphe's aristocratic values with the criminal underworld of the Ile de la Cité neighborhood, but this one, "A House on Temple Street," shows Sue's increasing interest in the laboring classes. It is in this titular boarding house that the reader meets, for the first time, characters who work for their living. The house is Sue's idea of what a microcosm of popular Paris would look like, and Rodolphe's investigation of the space helps him (and the reader) to better understand the dynamics of the city's working classes. Its residents include a bootlegger, an abortionist, a shady pawnbroker, a *grisette*, and, in the attic, the poorest of spaces, a family of working-poor *misérables*, the Morels. Significantly, labor will prove to be the most important character trait by which Rodolphe can distinguish between those inhabitants of the underworld he can trust and those he cannot. The working poor are at first represented as just one social type among many, but it soon becomes clear that the nature of the labor performed by a character—whether it is productive or not—will play an outsized role in determining whether they are moral or immoral. While the bootlegger, the abortionist, and the pawnbroker (who pursue criminal activities rather than doing or creating anything real) remain shadowy and rather flat figures, the hardworking manual laborers such as Morel and the Pipelets take on more fully developed (round or individualized) personalities.

When Rodolphe arrives at the porter's lodge, it is empty, allowing him to investigate the couple's living space. Monsieur and Madame Pipelet will prove to be reliable interlocutors, acting as Rodolphe's guides through the labyrinth of the boarding house, but their virtuous nature is only apparent after some deciphering. Their living space is decorated with an eclectic variety of objects, including a remarkable quilt, a wax statue of Saint John (patron saint of authors), and a pair of decorative boxes, crafted in the nearby prison. Among this hodgepodge of visual signs, the narrator finally homes in on a curious sight:

> And lastly, between the two boxes, and under a glass clock-cover, a pretty pair of red morocco boots—a veritable pair of doll's boots, but most artistically and carefully worked and ornamented. This masterpiece, as

the artisans of old would have called it, combined with the abominable odor of old shoeshine, and certain fantastic designs sketched on the walls, with an innumerable quantity of old shoes and boots, sufficiently announced that the porter of this house had been an expert craftsman before he was forced to take up the humble occupation of mending old footwear. (*MP* 1:186; translation slightly altered to follow more closely the original)

These two types of footwear—the miniature ornamental leather boots and the smelly old shoes in need of repair—are not only signs of the Pipelets' financial difficulties, as the narrator points out, but also proof of the couple's industrious nature, and, consequently, their trustworthiness. This judgment is borne out as they helpfully provide Rodolphe with all the information he needs to understand the social structure of the boarding house, notably by revealing the line of work practiced by each tenant. Through these descriptions alone, it becomes easy to distinguish the good characters from the bad ones. Some lodgers, such as the abortionist Bradamanti and the pawnbroker Madame Burette, are condemned by their dubious occupations. In contrast to these former, who make a living by, respectively, performing illegal abortions and duping the financially desperate, a *grisette* named Rigolette, who spends her days making women's clothing, is instantly tagged as a saintly creature. Madame Pipelet describes her as "a jewel of a lodger..., Industrious, too; always fagging away, like a little beaver; sometimes earning as much as two francs a day—but that's by going it hammer and tongs.... She gets up at five or six o'clock in the morning and works till ten, and sometimes even eleven" (*MP* 1:204–5). Despite the long hours required to eke out a living as an honest seamstress, Rigolette manages to be "kind and charitable" to her neighbors and is "worthy of confidence," so that, in Madame Pipelet's eyes, the girl's propensity for hard work goes hand in hand with her moral goodness.

The porter-led tour of the house follows an ascending path (a familiar trope in realist depictions of Parisian living spaces that we also find in Balzac's "Physionomies parisiennes"), until we arrive at the attic, where the suffering Morel family serves as an object of both pity and fascination for the other tenants. Monsieur Morel, a jewel-cutter forced into the business of diamond counterfeiting, works tirelessly to support his family, and, even then, they often go hungry, unless a kind neighbor such as Rigolette offers them her own dinner. The other members of the family spend all day in bed, suffering from some undefined illness, and their attic room is so cold that their water bucket is covered in a layer of ice. Meanwhile, Morel labors day and night, hunched over his worktable. Just as Madame Pipelet fits the type of the *portière* to a tee, Morel is the perfect model of the proletarian. Sue makes sure to stress that the jeweler's physical and moral condition is common to men of his class. "One of those constrained positions, but too common among such weakly constitutions among the working classes as are compelled by their occupation to remain nearly all day in the same attitude, had distorted his meager figure. Constantly stooping over his board . . . his naturally feeble frame had become, as it were, petrified, ossified in that position . . . he was completely bent and twisted on one side" (*MP* 1:424). In this way, Morel first appears as a sociological type or flat character, "constructed" around the "single quality" (Forster) of laboriousness. Even his body is stuck in place: it has been "petrified" and "ossified" by the constant repetition of a few physical movements. The social type of the low-skilled worker whose body was completely malformed by his intense physical labor was not new. Indeed, the power of low-skilled manual labor to mangle and petrify the body into a particular shape was already something of a social *topos* by the time Sue wrote *Mysteries*. Just a few years prior, René Villermé had described the *filtiers* (thread-twisters) of Lille as having "knock-knees [*les genoux cagneux ou rapprochés l'un de l'autre*]" as a result of their "habitual stance while working," supporting his own observations with the work of fellow medical doctor Jean-Baptiste Monfalcon, who, in 1834, had recorded that the legs of the Lyonnais silk workers were often "deformed at an early age" and pointed out the "irregular development of their bodies."[15] Work-related disfigurement was not seen as a uniquely industrial or urban phenomenon, as Balzac demonstrates in his 1833 novel *The Country Doctor*. Here, the eponymous doctor introduces his guest (and the reader) to an itinerant fieldworker who "had worked till he was almost past work," so much that he is "a piece of humanity in ruins" difficult to recognize as human from afar. "His legs seemed to be warped, as it were; his back was bent by continual toil; he stooped so much as we walked that he leaned on a long stick to steady himself."[16] In all these cases, the physicality of the laborer is all that matters—there is little or no psychological depth or capacity to change or evolve.

Later on, however, Sue's novel includes a scene that presents Morel as a complete, and even exceptional, individual, thereby surpassing his social *type*. Pushed to his limits by a particularly difficult interaction with his senile mother-in-law, the stonecutter lashes out at his family, leaving them shaking, howling, and crying in terror (*MP* 1:426). Immediately following this outburst, however, he begs for their forgiveness, showing a level of psychological complexity that is not present in the representations of the working poor found in Villermé's *enquête* or Balzac's novel. "Pray do not add reproach to my misery; it will be all right if I retain sufficient strength and reason to work," he explains, adding with surprising tenderness: "Thanks to my love for you all, I find I have sufficient strength to work sometimes twenty hours a day, though it has made me crooked and lame" (*MP* 1:427–28). These raw expressions of violence, anger, and sadness, brought about by the difficulty and the long hours of his labor, bring out the psychological complexity of his character, and his ability to transform his negative emotions into the energy needed to support his family mark him as exemplary and even heroic. Full of surprises, then, Morel is an exceptional character whose complexity heightens the pathos of his situation. Readers were so moved and expressed so much sympathy for Morel that he and his family would be given a central role in the theatrical adaptation of the novel.

We see a similar move from flat type to rounded character in Sue's depictions of La Mayeux, one of the central characters in *The Wandering Jew*, a needleworker whose precarious economic situation is worsened by a physical disability. Born with a hunched back, says Sue, she will never find love or the conjugal security of marriage. Due to her lack of physical charm, she is worse off than Balzac's *grisette* Ida, and her own beautiful sister, who has chosen the life of a debauched courtesan, serves as her foil. Despite these exceedingly unfortunate circumstances, Sue asserts that La Mayeux's lamentable situation represents not the exception but the rule for women workers in Paris: "This is not private wretchedness, but the wretchedness which afflicts whole classes, the type of which we endeavor to develop in [La Mayeux]. It exhibits the moral and physical condition of thousands of human creatures in Paris" (*WJ* 1:28). In Sue's own words, then, his pathetic character represents the "type" of the underpaid woman-worker; her suffering is just another instance of the hardships suffered by women of her class. And yet, the long descriptions of her remarkable qualities, particularly her industriousness and her frugality, reveal a real interest in her individual character. The narrator highlights the meticulous nature of her labors, for instance, by enumerating the specific tasks that go into each shirt produced: "They had to be hemmed, their collars scooped-out and adjusted, buttonholes had to be made and buttons sewn on" (my translation).[17] The numerous steps which go into such painstaking work contrast with the scant pay she receives, four francs per week. La Mayeux only manages to eke by through extraordinary measures of frugality, which Sue highlights by listing her weekly expenditures: "eighty-four cents for three kg of second-rate bread, twenty cents on water, fifty cents on lard (butter being too expensive), and other ingredients for a vegetable soup that she eats cold, seven days per week" (*WJ* 1:28). Sue reveals La Mayeux's individuality through a detailed account of her exceptional industriousness and frugality, and it is through these descriptions that she begins to take on the qualities of a "round" and even exemplary character.

In the examples that we have discussed so far, Sue's portrayal of working-class characters as admirable individuals seems to elevate the importance of an entire class as worthy of heroic treatment. However, as the moralist criticisms of the criminal justice system and labor organization that he interjects throughout the novels indicate, and as a closer reading of the texts demonstrate, the experiences undergone by his laboring characters tell a more pessimistic tale: namely that manual labor—poorly compensated and incapable of bettering a worker's station in life—was economically and socially fruitless. This mechanism of giving high importance to manual labor in the construction of character while, over the course of the narrative, portraying that same labor as virtually useless, leaves us to wonder if Sue might have quietly nurtured a completely different attitude about the status of manual labor in the modern economy.

As the moralist interjections found in Sue's texts indicate, the author's pathetic depictions of unrewarded manual labor were meant in part to serve as social critique and may support the theory that he expressed a largely positive attitude toward the social value of manual labor. However, there is an ambiguity in his depictions of the working classes that muddles such an interpretation. While it is true that labor is a powerful element in character construction, it is also the case that this labor is essentially useless and that those same characters earn more pity than admiration.

Simultaneously, the pathos of his works could also be a tool to convince readers of the utility of literary labor, and perhaps, even of its superiority over manual labor. In a productivist society such as nineteenth-century France (one where the Left and the Right agreed that the creation of wealth was an important public virtue that should be promoted by society and government), one could assert the value of one's labor by proving that it had achieved its social purpose. Thus, a shoemaker could prove himself productive by making footwear that someone actually wears, and a joiner does the same by building a cabinet that can hold dishes. As a *feuilletoniste*, Sue could claim his literary labor to be useful only by *producing* precisely what it was supposed to: strong emotions. If he could manage to move his readers to tears, laughter, indignation, or any other feeling, then he could consider his literary labor to be a success. Pathos—the literary device meant to evoke of feelings of sadness, pity, and sympathy—was, therefore, an important tool for the author of the *roman-feuilleton*. The pathetic descriptions of working-class characters were therefore a way of highlighting the productivity of the author, whose "job" we might say, was to stir up the emotions of the public.

The Pathos of Manual Labor

As a consequence of this productivist focus, Sue's "social" goals risked getting lost behind his need to affirm his own personal social utility. Indeed, although Sue portrays manual labor as an important element of personality, the living conditions of these characters tell us that this labor builds little else *besides* character. More precisely, the manual labor performed by Sue's characters does not produce social wealth nor is it even very useful. Instead, it serves a source of pathos. The effect of opposing the workers' laudable industry and craftsmanship to their pitiful living conditions is not only sociopolitical, but also aesthetic: arousing strong feelings of pity, sympathy, and sadness in his readers. By doing so, Sue highlights his own literary genius, his ability, through description, to evoke such feelings. Indeed, in this section, we will see that, according to Sue, the craft of storytelling outperforms all other forms of labor in terms of both social utility and economic compensation.

As we saw above, Sue spends a good deal of energy describing his working-class characters and the products of their labor, which is part of what makes them round and interesting rather than flat and typical. In an economic sense, however, the artisanal labor they perform is worthless. Pipelet's masterfully crafted boots, Morel's perfectly cut diamonds, and La Mayeux's meticulously assembled shirts are each rewarded in a similar way: that is to say, poorly. The sharp contrast between the laborers' exceptional skill and their abject state of poverty shows that manual labor is not compensated by modern society. First, take the case of Pipelet. Even if the fine craftsmanship of the proudly displayed miniature boots in his front room helps Rodolphe to peg him and his wife as potential allies, the chaotic state of the rest of the room complicates that impression. The shining masterpieces are surrounded by rows of old shoes, a sign that Monsieur Pipelet has been forced to take on the low-skill work of shoe repair, described as "the last of the trades ... the one chosen out of necessity or bad luck."[18] Proof of this social malaise is expressed in Pipelet's smile, which is "quite bitter and where one could detect a profound melancholy" (my translation).[19] This mixture of admiration for the highly skilled work of the master *cordonnier* and pity for the struggling boot repairman forced to spend his days surrounded by stinking shoes establishes a high level of pathos in this scene.

The *misérabiliste* depictions of the Morel family play out in a similar way: like Pipelet, Morel's craftsmanship is very fine, and yet, despite working day and night, he is unable to provide the basic necessities for his family. The contrast between the brilliance of Morel's handicraft and the somber misery of the home workshop is spectacular in its own way. "This depressing picture," says Sue, "is lighted by a candle whose flame, agitated by the freezing north wind that whistles through the tiles, casts fitfully its pale and flickering light on the wretched scene; then darting a ray across the bench where sleeps the wearied lapidary, calls into existence a thousand brilliant gleams, a thousand prismatic sparkles, from the dazzling cluster of diamonds and rubies which lie uncovered before him" (*MP* 1:423). This tableau of abject misery framed by glittering luxury is crafted to pull at the heartstrings all while presenting a visually appealing spectacle. Just as Monsieur Pipelet sometimes watches the Morel family's suffering through a hole in the wall "as one goes to see a melodrama" (1:2, 11; my translation), Sue's readers may be compelled to continue reading by the strong emotions brought forth by his descriptions. Morel's profession as a jeweler also seems to point to an aesthetic rather than a social reading of the scene. Because of the steady demand (at home and abroad) for French luxury goods throughout the nineteenth century, it seems unlikely that a skilled diamond-cutter would find himself in such a dire economic situation. A more realistic choice for Sue's suffering laborer would have been a tailor or a shoemaker, professions that were the worst hit by the changes in production of the early nineteenth century. However, the diamond offers a more aesthetic object of representation, supporting the argument that Sue's main concern is not to denounce the inadequate remuneration of manual laborers but rather to bring a heightened sense of pathos to Morel's situation.

In *The Wandering Jew*, La Mayeux's situation is no less pathetic. As we saw above, her plight offers Sue an opportunity to denounce the unfairness of the current system of work organization, especially for women. In another scene, however, Sue invites his reader to go beyond a purely social reading of the situation, by portraying La Mayeux as a worker-poet. Her capacity to translate her emotional experience into touching verse and moving prose is a detail of her character that frames her as someone who is more endearing, more complex, than descriptions of her labor could do. Indeed, this trifecta of personal attributes—poverty, physical disability, and poetic sensibility—work together to heighten the pathos of any scene where she appears. "This soul must have been great and beautiful, for in all her unlettered strains there was not a word of murmuring respecting her hard lot: her note was sad, but gentle—desponding, but resigned; it was especially the language of deep tenderness—of mournful sympathy—of angelic charity for all poor creatures consigned, like her, to bear the double burden of poverty and deformity. Yet she often expressed a sincere free-spoken admiration of beauty, free from all envy or bitterness; she admired beauty as she admired the sun" (*WJ* 1:28). Sue is particularly keen to show that La Mayeux, in the face of such misfortune, exhibits no envy. She doesn't aspire to become beautiful, he adds, she simply admires it from afar. This purity of heart—a lack of jealousy and, perhaps, of ambition—compounds with her emotional suffering to portray her as an angelic but pathetic character.

As moving as Sue's descriptions of his proletarian characters may be, however, they also contain a latent criticism of the working classes' failure to grasp the true stakes of the productivist economy. Morel, for example, participates in the important but largely useless luxury market, and the suspicion that the jewels he is producing may be (unbeknownst to him) counterfeit further questions his status as a useful contributor to the productivist economy. Similarly, Pipelet's masterpiece, the boots that are proudly displayed in his front room, are for decorative purposes only and will never be worn. La Mayeux's shirts are antiproductive in a different way, for, while they are themselves quite useful, she (like all women workers it seems) manufactures them in an inefficient way. "They are paid not half as much as men who are employed at the needle: such as tailors, and makers of gloves, or waistcoats, etc.—no doubt because women cannot work as well as men—because they are weaker and more delicate—and because their need may be twofold as great when they become mothers"

(*WJ* 2:4). There is a mixed message here, for while Sue deplores what he calls the "revolting injustice" and the "savage barbarism" of the low wages women receive in comparison to men, he explains this inequality by pointing to the inefficiency of women's work: their physical weakness, their reproductive responsibilities, and, quite simply, their inability to produce as many goods as a male worker would in a given amount of time. Thus, as psychologically complex or "round," as the working-class characters in Sue's narratives may be, the manual labor they perform is essentially unrewarded and unproductive. These scenes are, above all, pretexts for evoking strong feelings of sadness, pity, and sympathy in their readers. In this second, more cynical, reading of Sue's pathetic depictions of workers, the utility of manual labor is shown to be tenuous, if not inexistent. By contrast, Sue's own literary labor is highly productive, doing exactly what it is supposed to, that is, moving his readers to strong emotions.

To further the point, it seems that the only truly productive work that La Mayeux performs is her literary labor. Like Sue himself, La Mayeux is a writer who produces strong emotional reactions in her readers, or in one reader, at least. A flighty servant named Florine, who has been paid to steal the seamstress's personal diary and to blackmail its author, finds herself so moved after reading its contents that she decides not to go through with her mission. "These lines, expressing so simply the sincere gratitude of the hunchback, gave the last blow to Florine's hesitations. She could no longer resist the generous temptation she felt. . . . Electrified by all that was warm, noble, and magnanimous in the pages she had just read, Florine bathed her failing virtue in that pure and vivifying source, and yield[ed], at last to one of those good impulses which sometimes carried her away" (*WJ* 2:47). Unlike her sewing abilities, which are praiseworthy but unproductive in a modern industrial context, La Mayeux's literary skills are effective and efficient: her writing produces the desired aesthetic effect on her reader. Sue's estimation for La Mayeux's literary skills has its limits, of course. The narrator is thus quick to assure the reader that her verses, although surprisingly good, are inferior to those of her friend, the manly artisan Agricola (*WJ* 2:4). Like many men of his day, including the worker-poets with whom he had begun to cultivate relationships, Sue appears to believe that women writers were naturally less talented than men. What's more, as a female reader, Florine's opinion was considered less valid than a man's (although we should note that Sue's readership was dominated by lower-middle-class women much like Florine). Still, the contrast between the essentially uncompensated work of making shirts and the "purifying" (to use Florine's own term) effect of poetry demonstrates the superiority of the latter over the former.

Upon closer examination, then, Sue's use of manual labor in character development is less about promoting the social value or utility of manual labor and more about bringing attention to his own literary labor. Indeed, in the scenes where labor is described, Sue manages not only to signal a problem in the remuneration of manual labor, but also to showcase his literary abilities of crafting a fine description. These are opportunities for intensifying the reader's feelings of sadness, pity, and sympathy. In other words, a vivid description of an admirable work of craftsmanship serves not to glorify its creator but to glorify the describer, the writer who is able to capture in words an extreme contrast between what that laborer is capable of, and how he or she is compensated for his work.

Sue knew firsthand the labor that was required to write literature. Before the dizzying success of *Mysteries* and *The Wandering Jew*, he had been crippled by debts and was working himself sick in order to find a way to reconcile his desire to make money with his drive to create literature, two pursuits which had been, to this point, incompatible. He describes this struggle in a letter to a friend in October 1841: "I thought it necessary [to take a rest] after such strenuous labor [*un travail si forcé*], and now I find that there is nothing more unbearable; what the devil does God do throughout eternity if he has no more worlds to make? undo his creation? These are my ruminations since I am no longer *creating*" (emphasis in original).[20]

Thus, the feelings of sadness, pity, and sympathy for the working classes that Sue tried (and, most will agree, succeeded) to provoke in his readers were perhaps inspired by his own struggles to make ends meet as an author. This sense of suffering, if not grievance, that he believed he shared with the working classes allowed him to present himself as supportive of the plight of the working classes. Ironically, it was these very descriptions of manual labor that helped to propel him to bestseller status, solidifying his position as a valuable contributor to the economy. The heartbreaking depictions of manual labor therefore served a double purpose in Sue's novels. In the following pages, we will see that, even as Sue claimed to be critical of the liberal economic system of ruthless competition for market share that characterized modern French society, he had thoroughly internalized that system and used it to his advantage.

The extensive use of pathos by Sue must have been, at least in part, deliberately crowd-pleasing. The literary market, as Sue well knew, was composed of limited resources: even as readership was expanding, so were the numbers of newspapers and authors hoping to appeal to those readers, making for a competitive environment. Much to the chagrin of cultural conservatives like Sainte-Beuve, literature had begun to resemble the manufacturing industry in more than one way. Critics, it seemed, were losing their clout, and literary success was increasingly measured by who could attract the largest numbers of "customers" (readers in the case of the fiction writer), rather than artistic merit. Sue thrived in this environment precisely because of his ability to adapt his production to consumer preferences. In the modern era of cheap daily newspapers and heightened awareness of social problems, populated by a generation of readers who had been raised on the sensational experiences of Romantic and sentimental novels, Sue's pathetic depictions of the working classes were a surefire way to dominate the marketplace.

In a competitive system such as the one France was quickly becoming, however, it was not enough to affirm the productive value of one's *own* labor; one also had to prove that their rival's labor was less valuable. According to a free market understanding of society, writers, as economic actors, would have to outperform their competition, both in the field of literature and across the wider labor economy. Therefore, the portrayal of manual labor as a largely futile activity could serve not only to arouse pity and sympathy for the working classes, but also, by comparison, strengthen Sue's position as a productive member of the laboring society. By denying the productivity of manual labor and, simultaneously, pointing up his own ability to provoke strong emotions in his readers, Sue was positioning himself as a competitive player in the overall labor economy.

In short, the fact that Sue uses pathos to devalue manual labor shows that he had his sights on something larger than the literary market, and that he was competing not only with other writers, but with all working members of society. To present manual laborers as unproductive or "bad" workers and, simultaneously, to present himself as an effective or "good" one, was to position himself—the literary laborer—as superior. In other words, Sue considered himself an active player in the labor market, in direct competition with the shoemakers, stonecutters, and seamstresses depicted in his fictions. In a system of finite resources such as the market, more recognition for the labor performed by the latter—be they fictional characters or real-world individuals—would lead to a greater allocation of resources to manual labor, and less resources for the literary laborer. This logic of competition (while not openly avowed by Sue), was emulated and expanded by Honoré de Balzac in his desire to achieve financial success.

Balzac and the Zero-Sum Game

If Sue concealed the competitive nature of his literary ambitions behind personal gestures of solidarity with the working poor and heartbreaking depictions of their heroic labors, Balzac, on the contrary, barely bothered to hide his cutthroat intentions in *La Cousine Bette* and *Le Cousin Pons* in 1846 and 1847. As we shall see, these two novels—the last ones Balzac would write—are monuments to the author's determination to prove himself as the most important author of his time and as a legitimate contributor to the broader labor economy. By examining his narrative choices, we can observe his astute understanding of the fundamentally market-driven logic of the serial novel as an economic dynamo. Adopting the formula for success developed by Sue, Balzac brings attention to his own literary labor by using his excellent descriptive skills to depict working-class characters who are what Forster and Chaisemartin might call "round," or "individual." However, he "flips" this process, in a sense, by presenting not labor but an avoidance of labor as the determining element of their roundness.

As we know from a letter to Madame Hanska dated June 16, 1846, the titular characters of the novels *La Cousine Bette* and *Le Cousin Pons* were conceived by the author as a pair of "poor relations."[21] These "cousins" are nevertheless quite different from one another: Bette is hard-working former peasant, still bitter about the wrongs she suffered as a child; Pons is an urbane and self-indulgent art collector, possessing (unbeknownst to him) millions in rare works, but barely able to put food on his table. Their stories, too, are very different. While Bette lies and schemes her way to obtaining the riches of those closest to her, Pons is a victim, the object of several conspiracies to rob him of his treasures. Indeed, there is really only one element that seems to bring these two characters in parallel: both cousins, in their old age, must pander to their wealthy "rentier" relations in the hopes of securing a comfortable retirement. That this similarity is economic is not without significance. Balzac clearly had financial concerns on his mind when writing the pair of *feuilletons*. He had just learned Madame Hanska was pregnant and was determined to accumulate enough money to marry her and buy a house for their growing family. After listing off a number of things he has done to put his finances in order—including meeting with his finance advisor Auguste Fessart, ensuring his investments in the Chemin du Nord railroad company, and selling off a Holbein painting—he mentions, for the first time, *The Poor Relations*, which, he imagines will be an instant success.²²

Balzac had never had much success with money—wheedling cash advances from friends and editors in his most desperate moments; investing in large ventures, from a railway corporation to a Parisian pineapple farm, in happier times—and his literary endeavors were no exception to this rule. He had been trying for quite some time to dominate the literary market, and, despite a short period of solidarity in the founding of the Société des gens de lettres in 1838, Balzac and his fellow writers usually saw one another as rivals rather than colleagues. Successful authors often "borrowed" themes, character types, and even entire scenes from other writers as well as from their own previous works, making minor changes that they believed would attract a larger audience. This practice of modifying existing "tropes for new texts and for the new readers the serialized form engendered" was not seen as dishonest but savvy, "demonstrat[ing] an in-depth understanding of the market."²³ These were merely the rules of the game. Balzac admits, for example, that his *La Fausse Maitresse* (1841) was really an attempt to improve upon what he called Sue's "rocambalesque" *Mathilde*, published that same year.²⁴ His competitive spirit was stoked in 1844 when, following unfavorable reader reactions to his *Modeste Mignon*, the *Journal des débats* decided to cut its publication in order to start running Alexandre Dumas's *Comte de Monte Cristo* instead.²⁵ His jealousy only increased over time, and by 1846, the goal of "killing off" Sand, Dumas, Féval, and Sue "on their own turf [*sur son propre terrain*]" had become something of an obsession for him.²⁶

Balzac was convinced that his work was, quite simply, of better quality than that of his fellow *feuilletonistes*, and he was especially disdainful of Sue. Nonetheless, the author of *The Human Comedy* was not above making use of his rival's stylistic innovations. The sprawling *Splendeurs et misères des courtisans* (1838–47, most of which was published between 1843 and 1847), featuring a virtuous prostitute and other underworld characters, was an important example of this. A Balzac biographer has remarked that the "surprising mix of romantic themes, melodramatic absurdities, and various observations" found in *Splendeurs* can be read as proof of the author's determination to rival Dumas and Sue.[27] Still, when Madame Hanska confessed to reading *Mysteries* with great pleasure, a jealous Balzac urged her to read his own exploration of the Paris underworld, which was even more realistic, more tragic, and therefore more enjoyable than Sue's. "You will find in my *Esther* [the original title of *Splendeurs*]," he assures her, "a Paris that was and always will be unknown to you, quite different from the Paris in *The Mysteries*, which is false and comical."[28] Thus, even if he admitted to borrowing from the style of his rivals, Balzac would always insist that the content of his works was far superior.

Interestingly, by the time he begins to work in earnest on *The Poor Relations*, the author of *The Human Comedy* seems to change his tone a bit. Rather than seeing his relationship with the other popular novelists in his orbit as one of pure rivalry, he expresses a sense of shared suffering, and even complicity: "I will work like a Dumas in December, January, February, March, and April," he writes in October 1846, adding, one month later: "If anyone told Dumas about my project, he would laugh, because only he could understand the temerity of my undertaking."[29] The image of Dumas and Balzac laughing bitterly together implies that, if the latter had once imagined himself to stand above the fray, he was now very much down in it. What's more, rather than limiting his emulation of other serial novels to setting and theme, as he did in *Splendeurs et misères des courtisanes*, Balzac now seemed to want to follow Sue's model at a more substantial level: notably by addressing problems of social justice and including manual labor as a major character trait in his own works.

The fact that Balzac, in his two final *romans-feuilletons*, speaks directly to issues of social justice—and especially to the sufferings of the working classes, even perhaps as their champion—is remarkably uncharacteristic of him. In his earlier texts, society was seen as something to be observed, described, and even judged, but he never saw the author's calling as interventionist, a position he reiterated as late as 1842, calling himself the mere "secretary" of French society in the "Avant-Propos" to *The Human Comedy*. A series of narrational interjections in *The Poor Relations*, however, seem to indicate a change in approach. In *Le Cousin Pons*, for example, he features a *portière* named Madame Cibot, who in many ways resembles the Madame Pipelet of *Mysteries*. Like the Pipelets, Madame and Monsieur Cibot work so hard and with so little to show for it that, the narrator assures us: "The day will come when, after thirty years of such a life, a doorman will accuse the government of injustice, demanding a medal for the Legion of Honor!" (*CH* 7:522). If the astute Balzacian observes a hint of irony, a similar sentiment is expressed with sincerity later on, when Pons passes away in apparent penury. Because his wealthier relatives are nowhere to be found, the art collector's funeral arrangements are left to his only friend in the world, the equally clueless and equally penniless Schmucke. The injustice of the situation becomes an opportunity for the narrator to inveigh against the system more broadly: "Everywhere and in every way, inequality is overtaking Paris, a country drunk with equality. In rich families, mourners are spared the details [of organizing a burial], but in this, as in the paying of taxes, the people—the helpless proletariat—suffer under the weight of their own pain" (CH 7:723). Together, these two moralist intrusions from the narrator paint Balzac as someone who is much more indignant about social injustice, more sympathetic to the plight of the *concierges* and the *"prolétaires"* of the world than he had been in the past. An eager reader may even reason that he would be apt to participate in a social revolution, and, indeed, some did, as we shall see in the epilogue.

The narrator expresses a similar concern for social injustice in *La Cousine Bette*, where the crafty spinster embodies the problems of social inequality in her person and her personal history. Growing up under the same roof, Bette and her cousin Adeline, we learn, were treated quite differently. At an early age, Bette was deemed too unattractive for marriage and so was forced to work the fields, while the pretty Adeline was kept inside and given lovely dresses to wear (CH 7:80). From this experience, Bette retains both a propensity for hard work and an acute sense of injustice. Even when Adeline and her wealthy husband Baron Hulot secure her a good job and provide opportunities for marriage, Cousin Bette still seethes. Aware that her future economic comfort depends upon her securing a pension from these wealthy relatives, Bette cannot voice this grievance aloud, but she continues to mutter under her breath: "Adeline and I are of the same blood, our fathers were brothers, yet she has her beautiful apartments while I am in the garret" (CH 7:82). Even as her shrewd character combined with her hardworking nature opens up other possibilities to Bette (beneficial marriages to wealthy men, an extortion conspiracy with the beautiful Valérie Marneffe, for example), she prefers to nurture a secret passion for revenge.

The close attention paid to the unfairness of a socioeconomic structure that does not reward laboriousness is clearly an attempt to tap into the popularity of *Mysteries* and *The Wandering Jew*. However, the way that Balzac resolves these problems is quite different from Sue's. That is, they are not resolved at all. If Sue relies on characters who take justice into their own hands, punishing the exploiters and rewarding the hardworking innocents within the confines of the narrative, there is, on the contrary, no justice in *The Poor Relations*. True to his calling as the "secretary" of society, the author of *The Human Comedy* allows for no godlike hero who can put things right. "Careful to preserve the current order of things as they are, he approaches them as a novelist who desires to shed light on the many aspects of a contemporary history. He offers no propaganda for any solutions that may appear good to him."[30] In fact, while the distinction between the "good" and the "bad" actor plays a fundamental role in Sue's works, such classifications are much more difficult to pick out in *The Poor Relations*.

This point about character judgment brings us to the second important way that Balzac borrows from Sue's formula for success: the use of manual labor to transform "flat" types into "round" individuals in scenes that simultaneously arouse strong feelings of pity, sadness, and sympathy and bring attention to his own literary labor. Some of the working-class characters in Balzac's works are clear pastiches of those found in Sue's and Dumas's works. For example, when we first meet the Cibots, the porters in *Le Cousin Pons*, they possess many of the same characteristics of Sue's Pipelets: a shrewd, hardworking couple doing their best to construct a comfortable retirement for themselves. It is only later, when Madame Cibot becomes obsessed with her mission to obtain Pons's inheritance, that she becomes truly repulsive. Bette, too, starts out as a somewhat sympathetic character. Her unjust treatment as an innocent child is similar, in a way, to the unjust persecution of Rodolphe's long-suffering daughter Fleur de Marie in Sue's *Mysteries*, who was kidnapped and sold into prostitution by her own mother in order to punish her father. Whereas the angelic Fleur never seeks to retaliate, Bette's initial desire for vengeance is quite human. Why should she be forced to labor in the fields while her cousin is protected and coddled? Had the novel been written differently, Bette's lifelong quest for justice might have mirrored that of Alexandre Dumas's beloved Count of Monte Cristo, who, after years of false imprisonment, heroically escapes to seek retribution for himself and the people he loves.

This is not the Count of Monte Cristo, however, and Bette's desire for revenge—revenge for being forced to work—goes beyond the limits of justice. Indeed, the angry spinster will only be satisfied when she has managed to shed completely her identity as a working-class woman. In this way, labor serves a function in Balzac's texts that is quite the opposite of what it does in Sue's: it is an enemy to be conquered, an evil to be avoided. In other words, the "rounded" working-class character of a Balzac tale—far from being "constructed by labor" as they are for Sue—avoids work altogether. For instance, while the industrious Pipelets seem willing to perform any number of occupations to make ends meet, Madame Cibot, over the course of the novel, gradually sets aside her many odd jobs to focus on the social machinations that will assure her a comfortable *rente*, namely, but convincing Pons to put her in his will. When not conspiring with art dealers, lawyers, and unscrupulous physicians, she spends her time chatting with the bedridden Pons, reminding him pointedly to keep his friends in mind when apportioning his estate. "Don't forget," she warns, "otherwise God will never receive you in Heaven; he only admits those who show their gratitude to their friends by leaving them an inheritance" (CH 7:608).

Bette, too, really only becomes an interesting and "rounded" character once we see how she *avoids* performing work. At first, her deeply ingrained laboriousness is useful to her, both economically (her fine needlework earns her a decent living) and as a means of obtaining affection, such as in her relationship with Wenceslas, the brilliant but indolent Polish sculptor. Bette maintains his devotion by supporting him financially and giving him lessons in household economics: "make a fortune," she advises, "and then, when you have money in the funds, you may amuse yourself, child" (CH 7:108). Laboriousness also plays a role in her marriage plans with the wealthy Marshal Hulot. She first enters his orbit working as a housekeeper: "and from there, my dear, you are practically his wife," says Adeline (CH 7:300). And yet, despite the proven utility of such laboriousness, Bette surprises the reader by focusing most of her efforts on carrying out vengeance against her cousin. Indeed, it is by avoiding work that both La Cibot and Bette are most interesting, transforming them from typical working-class women into surprising and complex individuals. In short, if Balzac "borrows" from Sue's formula for success by depicting manual laborers as major characters, he does so in a way that flips the value of labor on its head. For Balzac, it is not hard work and skillful production that help construct a rounded or unique character, it is a working-class character's ability to avoid work that makes him or her compelling.

Allegory

An important difference between Sue and Balzac is the way they view the relationship between fiction and social change. While both authors feature social (in)justice as an important theme in a way that communicates sympathy and perhaps even a level of solidarity with those seen as social victims, Balzac, unlike Sue, does not offer any solutions to the problems raised in his novels. This very stark difference can be explained in part by the fact that the two were writing in radically different modes. While Sue aroused his readers' sentimental and sensational excitement through a certain Romantic realism, Balzac, on the other hand, chose to write *The Poor Relations* as allegories, stories that were meant to reveal a deeper or more general truth about the world. Sue's depictions of the suffering working classes bring out the sentimental experience of what is before our eyes, but Balzac's crafty labor-shirkers are meant to help us perceive truths not visible to the naked eye.

Balzac was a master practitioner of allegory, especially in his earlier works. *The Wild Ass's Skin* (1831), where Raphael de Valentin feeds his worldly desires for sexual and material satisfaction to such excess that his body simply disappears, is the classic example: one man's insatiable drive to material consumption translates easily into a critique of society at large. At a certain level, the allegories of *The Poor Relations* are not all that different from the one he had written fifteen years prior: the tales feature a succession of characters who, like Raphael de Valentin, are driven to destruction in their respective quests for satisfaction—for revenge in Bette's case, for beautiful things in Pons's, for money in Madame Cibot's, and for sex in the Baron Hulot's. However, while the earlier text focuses on one man's individual struggles, *The Poor Relations* feature many different characters, each one striving to fulfill his or her own desires, a task that often places them in conflict with other self-seeking characters. In this way, Balzac expands upon what he now sees as a fundamental truth of modern life: the competitive nature of human relations as a simultaneously productive and destructive force. *Cousin Bette* in particular represents a new stage in Balzac's understanding of the purpose of character: he is no longer interested in the individual but in the system in which the individual exists. The effacement of the individual by the idea or drive that they represent is indicative of this shift.[31]

As we saw in our analysis of *The Wild Ass's Skin*, Balzac's universe was one of competition, where the vying for limited resources and limited shares of the market implied an imperative to draw from someone else's hoard in order to satisfy one's own insatiable desires. Characters take steps to fulfill their own desires, which are often fueled by comparisons with—or a fear of losing ground to—others. For example, Madame Cibot targets Pons because she has heard of other servants being left generous inheritances by their masters and does not want to find herself without a benefactor (CH 7:522); the miserly Célestin Crevel desires Adeline Hulot (and, later, Valérie Marneffe), simply because she "belongs" to his rival Hulot; Bette's ambition it not merely to gain a fortune, but to do so in a way that robs Adeline of hers. The form of the allegory allows Balzac to demonstrate that this cutthroat battle for limited resources is not only evidence of an individual character's weakness, a particular case of uncontrollable desire, but rather a feature of the very social structure in which they live. In other words, the nature of social relations is one of a zero-sum game, where one person's gain necessitates another's loss.

In *The Poor Relations*, then, Balzac allows each character, driven by a specific compulsion, to live out his or her excesses, taking them to their logical conclusions. Pons's love for art, for example, leads to a mania for collecting, an inability to part with any of his works, and, finally to a penniless death. Bette's obsession, vengeance, has a similar outcome. Seeing that, despite all her machinations and efforts to the contrary, the Baroness Adeline will live out her days in relative comfort and happiness, Bette becomes ill. "Lisbeth, made already quite miserable by the happiness which seems to shine out from this family, could not stand this happy event. She grew so ill that Bianchon predicted she would die just one week later, finally vanquished at the end of a long struggle which had been previously marked by so many victories" (CH 7:448). Neither the vengeful Bette, nor the greedy Madame Cibot, nor the sex-crazed Hulot is completely unlikeable when we understand their drives and histories. Indeed, the very interest in these texts is the way that Balzac, seeming to anticipate the Naturalist determinism that would dominate literature decades later, allows these manias to play themselves out to their logical and most extreme conclusions.

The use of allegory helps Balzac to bring attention to the laboriousness of his creative practice in a more explicit way than the pathos-laden depictions of social injustice found in Sue's works. Much of the narration in *Mysteries* and *The Wandering Jew* are given through direct dialogue and realist descriptions of settings and character. Aside from Sue's direct moralist interjections, which are clearly delineated from the rest of the text, the narrator strives to keep a low profile, offering the audience what is meant to seem like an unfiltered reading of the events. In the scene where Morel loses patience with his family, for example, the readers are meant to put themselves in the place of Pipelet, observing the events directly through a crack in the wall.

In allegory, however, the focus is not on giving readers the impression that they are observing a real scene of pathos, but rather on bringing to light social problems that may not be readily observable if one adheres to the rules of *vraisemblance*. By breaking these rules, writers of allegory make themselves known, calling attention to the distance between the banality of real life and the artificiality of the literary creation. In this way, the allegory is an emphatically craft-like and self-conscious form of literature.

As Cindy Weinstein has demonstrated in her study of antebellum American literature (roughly contemporary with Sue's and Balzac's *romans-feuilletons*), the allegory was a problematic genre for a society that was quite worried about the possible negative consequences of industrialization. Allegories were often criticized precisely because they foregrounded the author's literary effort, bringing attention to the laboriousness of artistic creation. As many members of society were reaping the benefits of economic modernity (cheaper goods, greater technology, more leisure time), reports of poor working conditions and factory accidents were unwelcome reminders of the perils of industrialization. As such, cultural commentators tended to focus on the benefits of a modern work ethic, and discussing in detail what that work actually involved became almost taboo. "Erasing the visible signs of labor," Weinstein explains, "became a cultural imperative, whether in factories, in landscapes, or in fictions.... All labor, whether performed by men or women, becomes potentially damaging as anxieties about the role of industrialization in the production of individual character are reproduced in texts that not only have little to do with mechanical labor but explicitly aim to celebrate work."[32] Weinstein demonstrates that allegorical works published at this time, such as Edgar Allan Poe's "The Man That Was Used Up" (1839) and Nathaniel Hawthorne's "The Birth Mark" (1843), made transparent the labor-intensive process of writing literature. Constructing characters who resembled absolutely no one in the real world, these authors hoped to make visible some truth about the world that would not be readily apparent in a natural or sentimental account of events, but the artifice of such representations brought attention to the fact that writing literature requires more effort than a mere transposition of things into words, and the harsh criticism they received points to society's desire to separate labor from leisure, literature belonging to the latter and not the former.

Balzac, like Poe and Hawthorne, bucks the trend of pro-industry cultural production that was also present in France by leaning into the allegorical genre. Like Sue, Balzac knew that, to carve a spot in the modern productivist economy, he would need to communicate his utility, that is, his ability to *produce* something valuable in society. However, unlike Sue, who saw the utility of literature to be its ability to produce feelings of sadness, pity, and sympathy, Balzac envisioned its utility as revealing those elements of society that are imperceptible to the casual observer. His goal was to produce a work of true craftsmanship, an allegory that was both aesthetically compelling and socially significant and which called attention to his role as creator. By bringing attention to the laborious nature of writing stories, Balzac could strengthen his claim to a legitimate position in the modern workforce to assert himself as a major contributor to the labor economy more generally. Indeed, instead of hiding behind dialogue or what is meant to be objective description, as Sue often does (i.e., when the reader observes the Morel family's emotional and material suffering through the eyes of Monsieur Pipelet at the peephole), Balzac brings attention to himself as a worker, as the creator of a narrative.

In the end then, Balzac's *Poor Relations* includes many elements that had helped make Sue's *romans-feuilletons* wildly successful. Like Sue, Balzac focuses on themes of social injustice, even going so far as to make statements that are almost sympathetic to the plight of the working classes. And like Sue he depicts working-class characters as "rounded" individuals rather than flat social types. Unlike Sue, however, he does all of this in the form of a well-crafted allegory, which brings attention to his own literary labor and reveals the competitive nature of society. In Balzac's hands, the goal of the serial novelist is made transparent: to compete not only in the literary market but in the labor economy more generally.

Balzac never did make it as a bestseller, at least according to Lyons's calculations. Based on what we know of his personal impetus to gain financial stability and to knock out his competitors, the author of *The Human Comedy* must have been trying to appeal to a popular audience with *The Poor Relations* but, as his contemporaries knew, the artist in Balzac was unwilling to stray too far from his ideals to suit popular tastes.[33] Because of this, the works were seen by both Balzac and his contemporary literary critics as successes, despite their modest sales. More importantly, the similarities that can be found in *The Poor Relations*, *Mysteries*, and *The*

Wandering Jew can tell us something about the status of the solidarity between manual and literary laborers on the eve of the February Revolution. Namely, that, while there was a popular appetite for such a solidarity, serial novelists such as Sue and Balzac were operating according to a system of intense competition, not only within the literary market, but also across the labor economy.

If we believe that it is possible to determine the values of a society in part by the stories they choose to read, then we can conclude that July Monarchy France was a turning point in the way the French viewed labor. In addition to purchasing old classics, which reinforced traditional and religious morality, readers were devouring Eugène Sue's *Mysteries of Paris* and *The Wandering Jew*, contemporary tales addressing questions of social justice such as criminality and labor organization. The success of these stories indicates that the public believed that working-class people were important social actors, capable of evoking strong emotions in the reader. However, a closer look at Sue's depiction of these characters reveals that their function was not only to inspire social change but also to highlight his own efforts as an author, therefore placing him at the same level with other types of workers.

In his quest to conquer the literary market, Balzac borrowed these elements from Sue, and his two final works, *The Poor Relations*, focus on working-class characters who suffer social injustice. However, unlike Sue's Romantic realism, which attempts to move his readers by placing them in his characters' place, Balzac's tales are allegorical, meant to bring attention to his work as a literary creator. These allegories reveal the true nature of the social system in which his characters live: a system of unadulterated competition. Balzac's vision of the modern economy as a zero-sum game of energy spending and saving (discussed in chapter 2) followed the very same logic of the market that drove Sue to devalue manual labor in his serial novels.

Balzac's transparent adoption of Sue's model allows us to come quite firmly to the conclusion that both authors wrote their *feuilletons* not in the spirit of solidarity or cooperation with the working classes but in accordance with the rules of the market, driving them to undercut their competitors, both within the literary market and across the laboring part of society. Sue, just as much as Balzac, understood the need, on the one hand, to appeal to a working-class audience and, on the other, to discount the manual labor performed by that group as essentially worthless to promote the value of their own productive labor in the modern economy.

In hindsight, the growing presence of manual labor as a marker of exceptional character and, more generally, as a central theme in popular literature was *not* an affirmation of growing solidarity between writers and workers as many readers seemed to assume, but rather an opportunity for misunderstanding and false hope. Authors had internalized the importance afforded to economic productivity as a determinant of social value and this, ultimately, helps explain why workers misjudged the level of solidarity that existed between them and bourgeois fiction writers in the years leading up to 1848. If we may understand the beliefs of a society, at least in part, through their literary preferences, then the great commercial success of these texts shows that, on the eve of the revolution of 1848, the bourgeois public considered manual labor to be a source of emotional and aesthetic spectacle but not as a basis for political rights.

Epilogue
THE WRITERS' REPUBLIC, FEBRUARY–JUNE 1848

ON FEBRUARY 26, 1848, just one day after the Second Republic was declared, the directors of the Porte-Saint-Martin Theater opened their doors to the public for a free performance of Félix Pyat's melodrama *Le Chiffonnier de Paris* (*The Ragpicker of Paris*). In 1847, *Le Chiffonnier*, starring the famous actor Frédérick Lemaître, had been one of the best-selling shows in the theater's history, but for its return to the stage in February 1848, some significant changes were made to the script. The most notable of these appeared the scene where the ragpicker-hero Old Jean (or Père-Jean) sifts through the rubbish he has gathered during the night: "Love, glory, power, riches—into the rag-sack! Into the sack all of the scraps. Everything comes, everything stays, everything falls in... what a melting pot! Everything is rags, tatters, shards, apple-cores, rubbish... [*He finds*] *a velvet crown decorated with fleur de lys.* Look at this! It was worth twelve million when it was fashionable, nothing but garbage now! *He tries it on.* Old Jean, king of France! Maybe it would be a nice sleeping cap. No, I would only dream of blood. Into the sack! Into the sack, with all the rest!"[1] Among the rags and other bits of trash that were originally in his sack, the 1848 version has him pull out two additional objects: a copy of the law abolishing banquets (the final act of government repression that had set off the uprisings) and a crown. The affable ragpicker places the crown on his head, symbolizing, perhaps, a new era of the people as king, but then quickly tosses it into the pile, along with the legal document and the rest of the rubbish. The daring, irreverent gesture, carried out for all to see by the well-loved Lemaître, was a sign to the people that they had finally triumphed. As one reviewer put it, "The way the actor marked out and accentuated the purpose of his role served to heighten the effect upon this popular audience, still warm with victory, who were welcomed, doors wide open, to this celebration of joyous accession."[2] Indeed, the jubilant crowds who flocked to the Théâtre de la Porte-Saint-Martin were delighted to find their revolutionary enthusiasm mirrored back to them in this scene and in others. Before the play had even begun, actors paraded across the stage carrying tricolor flags. They were dressed in National Guard uniforms, a nod to the Guard's decision not to defend the government, which had been decisive to the people's victory. The stage manager led the crowd in singing "La Marseillaise" and other patriotic songs. As one observer, writing in *La Réforme* (February 27, 1848) put it, "the enthusiasm of the crowd cannot be described."[3]

Pyat's melodrama follows the events in the life of a rag-picker named Père-Jean, who, despite his own difficult circumstances, spends his time helping others. The *chiffonnier*, or rag-picker, so called because he collected discarded cloth, glass, paper, and other articles to sell, was a ubiquitous figure in nineteenth-century literature, often serving as a moral commentator for the society whose trash he collected. Pyat's Père-Jean incarnated this type so fully that in his *Dictionnaire universel*, published twenty years later (1866–76), Pierre Larousse dedicated several pages to the melodrama *Le Chiffonnier de Paris* in addition to the long entry on the common noun *chiffonnier*.[4] The play reused many of the tropes and themes that had made Eugène Sue's *romans-feuilletons* so successful: a lost child, secret identities, Carnival balls, and social justice. As discussed in the previous chapter, it was typical for popular authors to "borrow" from one another, and Sue had also been quite influenced by Pyat. The pathos-ridden scenes in the Morel family's garret are quite similar to some scenes in Pyat's *Les Deux Serruriers* (1841), performed a year before *Mysteries* began running in *Le Journal des débats*, and, apparently, it was over the course of a dinner with Pyat and a worker named Fugères that Sue was converted to socialism in May 1841.[5]

Already a favorite of the literary world, Pyat was quickly propelled to political fame after the February staging of *Le Chiffonnier*. He was especially praised for the regicidal gesture of inserting the crown into Old Jean's bag of trash, and the Provisional Government appointed him as a *commissaire général*, entrusted with representing the Republican government in his local department, the Cher. When elections took place two months later, he was chosen by his fellow Cher natives to represent them in the Assemblée Constituante and then again, several months on, in the

Assemblée Nationale. As a politician, he fought hard for the rights of authors and artists and argued for an aid package to help them through the financial difficulties that the economic instability caused by the Revolution had brought upon the culture industry.[6] The theater had been hit especially hard, and many actors and managers found themselves forced to enlist in the doomed *ateliers nationaux*, digging ditches and performing other hard labors to which they were little suited. Pyat was also a staunch supporter of the working classes long after the fervor of February was over, and his passionate defense of the "right to work" was lampooned in the satirical paper *Le Charivari*. "Imagine the state of the audience just before the curtain rose! Then, little old Marrast [president of the Assembly] struck his gavel three times and Félix Pyat came onstage with his manuscript. He was actor, director, and scenery all in one—he was the entire theater really. Nevertheless, it was an utter illusion."[7] The writer of the article seems at once bemused by the playwright's conviction and scornful of his dramatic methods, but his description can give us important insight as to the tenor and content of the Assembly's debates. Through his performance, Pyat embodied the idea that the "right to work" was as important to the writer as it was to the manual laborer, and the riotous reaction to his speech was proof of its strength. According to *Le Charivari*, the members of parliament were "stamping their feet," "smashing benches," and, "because they had no bouquets, they were going to throw [the communist deputy Louis] Greppo onto the stage." Even if it did not translate into serious votes (the very next day, the constitution was ratified, guaranteeing only the "right to assistance," basically a form of unemployment insurance), then, Pyat's appeal for the "right to work" demonstrates that this socialist ideal was still tightly intertwined with its literary origins.

Pyat was not the only literary figure to find himself in the halls of power. The vaudevillist Étienne Arago, whose *27, 28, 29 juillet* had glorified class solidarity in 1830, was appointed as minister of the post office (*directeur général des Postes*) and was later successful in his first run to represent his native Pyrénées-Orientales department. By far the most popular politician of the moment, the poet Alphonse de Lamartine, was nominated in ten separate departments and won in all of them, including the Seine (where Paris is located), where he received more votes than any other candidate.[8] Lamartine had been an early proponent of the "right to work," calling it "the right to live" in a speech from 1844, and this helped him to maintain credibility among a working-class public.

George Sand famously chose not to run for any public office, explaining to the disappointed Saint-Simonian feminists who had nominated her that a woman's place was not in the public sphere but at home, where she could influence her husband, father, and sons.[9] However, she managed to keep her hand in politics in another way, composing many of the *Bulletins de la République* between March 13 and May 6. These large official sheets were posted by the Ministry of the Interior (headed by Sand's good friend Alexandre Ledru-Rollin) in prominent public spaces every two days, so that the public could follow the goings-on of the Provisional Government.[10] Told in Sand's voice (although she did not sign them), these events took on a decidedly Romantic tone. See her description of the events of April 20, for example: "The morning was rainy and somber, and yet, despite the sky's inclemency, the entire city, animated with patriotic energy, had been armed and at attention since seven o'clock. . . . 300,000 men were there, all quivering with love for France, all devoted, all hailing with emotion the dawn of a new government, imperishable because it will have been made by all for all."[11]

On this comparatively uneventful day, Sand transforms the streets of Paris into a scene of high emotion: a mix of ebullience and gravity. The cold and stormy weather contrasts with the warm enthusiasm of the people, united in their excitement and devotion for the new Republic, painting a striking tableau of a nation on edge but united. From this description, one would hardly guess that, just days earlier, a confused mix of protesters and counterprotesters had gathered in front of the Hôtel de Ville and that, just one month later (on May 15), crowds of workers would invade the Chamber and (unsuccessfully) declare a new government.

Not all *littérateurs* were able to translate their literary success into political power, however. Despite their reputations as popular authors concerned with questions of social justice, neither Eugène Sue nor Honoré de Balzac was elected to office in 1848, for example. Even though conservatives had blamed Sue's socialist bestsellers for inciting the *peuple* to revolt, these same people were not, it seemed, inclined to grant him their votes.[12] Over time, Sue had become a true believer in the revolutionary cause, but, despite his active campaigns in Paris and in the Loiret region, his election results in both April and June were quite disappointing. It was not until April 1850 that Sue finally made it to elected office.

Balzac's attitude was more ambivalent. In an unpublished "Lettre sur le travail" (undated, although it is thought to have been written sometime between February and June 1848), for example, he shows quite clearly his disdain for what he sees as an ignorant and dangerous working-class movement. He characterizes Louis Blanc's "labor organization [*organisation du travail*]" as nothing short of "an attack on liberty and on private and public prosperity [*un attentat à la liberté individuelle, à la richesse privée et à la richesse publique*]."[13] Still, he holds on to the very same belief, expressed fourteen years earlier, that *all* types of workers—manual and intellectual alike—are indeed workers and must be valued as such. The crux of his argument in 1848 is not that manual workers are less valuable than intellectual ones, but that they have claimed special privileges for themselves and therefore obtained an unfair advantage in the zero-sum game of society described in the previous chapter. He complains that literary authors like himself have been left out of the discourse on labor rights: "The words 'labor organization [*organisation du travail*]' signify a coalition of laborers [*travailleurs*], and the term laborer [*travailleur*], really means manual laborer [*ouvrier*]. It's as if, like magic, we have erased all other forms of work: that of intelligence, leadership, invention, travel, science, et cetera."[14] In this way, Balzac accuses the working-class militants and their allies—most of whom adhered to republican and communistic ideals—of disrespecting the values of equality and fairness, which should, he reasons, form the basis of their political programs. Whether or not Balzac believed his own rhetoric is up for debate. In the same "Letter" he mentions the restoration of the Bourbons to the throne or the arrival of an "Industrial Bonaparte" as being preferable to the workers' republic that was currently in place.

Simultaneously, in his private letters to Madame Hanska, Balzac offered a more bemused assessment of the Revolution. True to his *flâneur* nature, he observed the revolutionary fervor firsthand by walking the streets of Paris, interpreting the political events taking place in literary terms. On February 25, he took a catastrophizing tone, predicting the end of the newspaper, the end of the *roman-feuilleton*, the end of the bookstore, and therefore "indigence in our profession for the foreseeable future."[15] In a letter written several days later, he called the Revolution a veritable "Shakespearian drama," even as he complained that "the establishment of a republic is incompatible with literature and the theater."[16] Nonetheless, in what was undoubtedly a strategic move, Balzac publicly affirmed his desire to govern in a "letter of candidature" on March 18 and a "profession of political faith" on April 19 (both in the *Journal des débats* and *Le Constitutionnel*, two of the most widely circulating papers of the day), but he confided privately to Madame Hanska that he hoped *not* to win. His wish was granted, and he was soon free to return to Ukraine to be with her.[17]

Another best-selling author, Alexandre Dumas, tried and failed to get elected, basing his political philosophy on a belief that it was through literature and staging (*mise en scène*) that the people would learn to be good citizens and that, as a playwright and *feuilletoniste*, he was best suited to do this.[18] He began his campaign on March 15, by publishing an open letter addressed to "the workers," fashioning himself as an entrepreneur and a laborer. In the short text, he makes a decidedly productivist argument, claiming that, in addition to having worked ten hours per day for twenty years (for a total of 73,000 hours by his calculations), the production and distribution of his plays and novels have provided employment for 2,160 workers.[19] Who better than a job creator and a hard worker like himself to fight for the interests of the laboring classes? Apparently, his argument was not convincing, for he lost in both April and then again in June, but the passion with which he threw himself into politics, and, as we shall see, in defending his legitimacy as a voice of the people, speaks to the widespread belief in literature's political role at this time.

Pierre-Joseph Proudhon, the moderately well-known author of *What Is Property?* (1840) who would soon become the leader of the workers' movement, observed the events of the early days of the Republic in silence.[20] "Cold, skeptical, and even bitter" at the political rather than economic turn that the Revolution had taken, Proudhon had remained largely absent from public discourse for several months. It was not until April that he decided to speak, declaring his candidacy.[21] In an open letter to his constituents in the Doubs, dated April 3, he attacks "with severity" the Provisional Government's promotion of symbolic acts such as planting Liberty trees and singing patriotic songs. These gestures, he asserts, might lead one to think that "this revolution took place only so that comedies could be performed on the street: Paris is nothing but a theater where the old revolutionary drama is played out." Instead of these spectacles of Republican spirit, he argues, the government should be focusing on producing something: namely, radical economic reform. Armed with both experience as a worker "in the workshop and at the counter" and with "ten years" of studying economics under his belt, Proudhon argues that he, more than anyone else, is best prepared to do this job.[22]

Around the same time, Proudhon began disseminating his ideas in *Le Représentant du peuple*, a radical paper run by a group of militant typographers.[23] In most of his pieces, Proudhon's rhetorical style was persuasive and logical, and he proposed concrete solutions, such as a *banque d'échange*, where workers would be able to gain access to credit, guaranteed by their work rather than capital.²⁴ On May 28, however, he published a different type of article, "Ce que la révolution doit à la littérature" (What the revolution owes to literature), which took not politics but literature as its main target. Just as he had done in his famous essay *What Is Property?*, Proudhon uses a rhetorical question to evoke a polemical answer. The revolution, he responds, owes "absolutely nothing" to literature. Instead, he declares, "the man of style [the *littérateur*] must cede his place to the man of action [the politician]."

Calling out several authors by name, but targeting most directly Victor Hugo and Alexandre Dumas, Proudhon affirms that the revolution did not take place *because* of them but *"in spite of* them" (emphasis added).²⁵ He attacks from several angles, first of all denying that literature—the product of imagination—could have any epistemological value in today's world, rightly understood through facts and logic, where "reason subjugates imagination [and] content prevails over form." Such a positivist stance puts him in line with the young Auguste Comte, whose *First Course on Positive Philosophy* (1830) figured among Proudhon's many readings. In the second place, Proudhon points to the ethical problem of modern literary production. Like Sainte-Beuve, he posits a nostalgic view of literature, contrasting the classical and moralist works of the past with the modern concerns of literary writers who seek glory and wealth. Finally, he attacks the economic value of literature. Perhaps thinking of Dumas's productivist appeal to working-class electors in his "Aux Travailleurs," Proudhon defines literature as nothing more than "the art of arranging words and periods … an instrument that is itself incapable of producing anything at all." Within this definition is an implicit contrast with what he considers to be the real productive work of artisans and laborers, among whose number Proudhon counts himself, even as he pursues a career as a writer. Indeed, the distinction that he needed to establish between himself and literary writers like Dumas was something that he had been grappling with for twenty years. In 1838, he had written, "Born and raised in the working class, belonging to it still through love and affection, my greatest joy … would be … to work tirelessly, using science and philosophy, and with all of the strength of my will and the power of my mind, to bring about the moral and intellectual improvement of my brothers and my companions."²⁶

This statement, written in application for a scholarship that would allow him to complete his studies in Paris after working for ten years as a printworker, was an early manifestation of Proudhon's determination to identify himself as a worker-writer whose identity was, unlike the one promoted by Vinçard, decidedly *un*literary. He would continue this stance for most of his career, focusing on what he saw as a scientific study of political and economic questions, therefore affirming his writing as real labor.

No doubt feeling attacked, and with good reason, Dumas responded to Proudhon, in an article published in his own paper, *La France Nouvelle*, one week later.[27] Borrowing Proudhon's title, "Ce que la révolution doit à la littérature," Dumas arrives at an entirely different conclusion: the Revolution owes to literature "what the Autumn owes to Spring, what the harvest owes to sowing; she owes it everything." Dumas uses several different modes of literary expression to support his position. First, he adopts a metaphor, comparing Proudhon to an ass who must "bray" in the midst of "nightingales' songs." Next, he assumes a lyrical voice, bemoaning the modern world's inability to appreciate art, wondering if we have "really gotten to this point of savagery that we dare to blaspheme art eternal." However, the bulk of his article is rhetorical, using all his powers of persuasion to convince his readers of the productive value of literature. His evidence of this are the writers themselves, poets and novelists whose works were crucial to the formation of a revolutionary spirit. They are, in other words, the producers of the Revolution. Lamartine, he says, "put into the air those ardent and fruitful ideas that we still breathe today," while he himself can boast of "one or two hundred volumes that have brought the past to life for the people and given them a vivid awareness of who they are." The chasm between Proudhon and Dumas is therefore based on the nature of production: for Proudhon, literature creates nothing, does nothing, and adds nothing, while, for Dumas, literature produces ideas, thoughts, and emotions.

On the surface, the exchange between Proudhon and Dumas seems simply to reinforce the dominant narrative of the February Revolution as a tragic one whose failure can be linked directly to the literary—and therefore illusory or imaginary—nature of its goals. If, as historical hindsight allows us to do, we choose to look at the February Revolution from the point of view of its failures, then Proudhon (along with Marx, Flaubert, and countless others) saw correctly: the early days of the Second Republic were a "lyrical illusion," founded on abstract ideas and beautiful words, but lacking any concrete staying power. If, however, we pause to contemplate the very existence of this debate, then we can recognize the real power that literary expression wielded at this moment. The fact is, a revolution took place, a king was dethroned, and the nature of writing (as Roland Barthes has argued) changed forever. Literature—a form of expression that today has been relegated to the university lecture halls and the culture and leisure pages of newspapers—played an outsized role in a historical event that had social, political, and economic consequences. Although there are various cultural aspects that could explain the weight literature carried (related to the media landscape and the structure of the literary market, for example), part of this must be because there was also a recognition that the individual's imagination and their emotional life were just as important as their physical and economic well-being.

As the battle raged on between *littérateurs*, philosophers, politicians, scientists, romantics, and realists, it is worth taking a moment to reflect on what the workers themselves—those who had participated in the Revolution and called for the right to work—thought about the role that literature had played in events. Some workers assumed that the new government would assure them not only political rights but also access to culture. Amid the overarching political and social changes demanded by the crowds, a painter named Pouillaude reports writing a letter to the Provisional Government, asking for the establishment of a system of municipal libraries. "A few days after the February Revolution, I . . . asked that Libraries be established in each Paris neighborhood, where workers could meet and spend their moments of leisure . . . the worker would go to these meeting spaces with pleasure, sure to find good company and good books and spend three or four careless hours [*sans ennui*]."[28] The writer couches his pitch not only in terms of utility (new citizens will need to be educated to perform their civic duties), but also in terms of pleasure and of sociability: the leisure time that would come from better labor organization would require new spaces. The library could fulfill both these needs. And who could blame Pouillaude for thinking that the new government would grant him such a request? With countless authors in positions of power and a great deal of talk of worker-writer solidarity, it was reasonable to think that the new government would support institutions that developed the individual's emotional and imaginary life as well as physical and economic well-being.

The Second Republic's failure to do any of those things is well recorded, but that doesn't mean it was meaningless or that the events that led up to its establishment were unimportant. The power of literature to inspire workers of all different stripes to fight together for a common cause showed itself in February 1848, and if this solidarity was fleeting, it was nonetheless formidable. Nor was literature rid of labor in the postrevolutionary years, despite attempts by Second Empire authors to cultivate a purely aesthetic—or at least politically uncontroversial—literary field. Even Charles Baudelaire, the poet who claimed to be completely "depoliticized" by the coup d'état of Napoleon III in December 1851,[29] could not deny the presence of labor as an all-encompassing force in modern Paris:

> Once nearby was displayed a great menagerie,
> And there I saw one day—the time when under skies
> Cold and newly bright, *Labour* stirs awake
> And sweepers push their storms into the silent air—
>
> A swan, who had escaped from his captivity,
> And scuffing his splayed feet along the paving stones,
> He trailed white array of feathers in the dirt. (emphasis added)[30]

Published in 1861, the titular swan in "Le Cygne" escapes from his cage and is enveloped in the world of modern labor, cold, dirty, and impersonal as it is. The shock created by this a clash of realities—a nostalgic and playful past that evokes feelings of home and belonging confronted with the harsh reality of the impersonal and overwhelming modern urban landscape—causes an intense emotional reaction in the poet. Here, the working classes are neither a political entity, nor a productive motor. Instead, Labour is allegorized, depicted as a waking monster that heightens the poet's trauma: a symbol of modernity and progress that, it seems, will not be put back to bed.

NOTES

Introduction

1. Balzac, "Lettre adressée aux écrivains français du XIXe siècle," 63. All translations are my own unless otherwise indicated.
2. Spary, *Feeding France: New Sciences of Food, 1760–1815*, 312. See also Kaplan, *Bread, Politics, and Political Economy in the Reign of Louis XV*.
3. Stearns, "Patterns of Industrial Strike Activity in France during the July Monarchy," 375, 390.
4. Jarrige, "The Contested Productivity of the Baker's Body," 94–97.
5. Lichtlé, "Balzac à l'école du droit," 137–56.
6. For an exploration of how different groups adopted the "association" model, see Christen, Fayolle, and Hayat, *S'Unir, travailler, résister: Les Associations ouvrières au XIX siècle*.
7. Balzac's calls for solidarity here anticipate his future role as president of the Société des gens de lettres (Society of Men of Letters), an association of writers focused on protecting the right to "literary property." See Le Hir, "The *Société des Gens de Lettres* and French Socialism," 306–8.
8. Proudhon, "Aux électeurs du Doubs," in *Correspondance de P.-J. Proudhon*, ed. Langlois, 2:302.
9. Marx, "The June Revolution," *Neue Rheinische Zeitung* (New Rhenish daily), June 29, 1848, cited in *The Class Struggles in France (1848–1850)*, 57.
10. Flaubert, *Sentimental Education*, trans. Constantine, 23.
11. This is the title of Duveau's chapter, "L'Illusion lyrique," in the edited volume *1848: Le livre du centenaire*. The term was adopted by Philippe Vigier in his short introduction to the topic in *La Seconde République* (*Que sais-je?*), first published in 1967, with eight editions, the last in 2001.
12. Duveau, *1848, the Making of a Revolution*, trans. Carter, 61.
13. Vigier, *La Seconde République*, 26.
14. Barthes, *Le Degré zéro de l'écriture*, 31–33.
15. Duchet and Amossy, "Entretien avec Claude Duchet," 127–28.
16. Quoted in Bourdieu, *The Rules of Art*, trans. Emanuel, 45. Bourdieu does not give the original reference.
17. This is the chronology followed by the French national education system, for example. See, e.g., Marie-Ève Thérenty, *Les Mouvements littéraires du Xixe au Xxe siècle* (Paris: Hatier, 2001).

18. Oehler, *Juin 1848, Le Spleen contre L'Oubli: Baudelaire, Flaubert, Heine, Herzen, Marx*, 19.
19. See, most recently, Samson and Roger-Lacan, *1848 et la littérature* (2021); Deluermoz and Glinoer, *L'Insurrection entre histoire et littérature, 1789–1914* (2015); and Millot and Saminadayar-Perrin, eds., *1848, une révolution du discours* (2001).
20. Rancière, *Mute Speech: Literature, Critical Theory, and Politics*, trans. Swenson, 50.
21. Lerner, *Inventing the Popular*, xi.
22. Locke, "The Second Treatise on Civil Government" (1689), 118.
23. Garnier, Introduction to *Le Droit au travail à l'Assemblée nationale*, x–xi.
24. *Le Dictionnaire de l'Académie française* (1694, 1762, 1798, 1835, 1878, 1932), s.v. "travail," https://artflsrv04.uchicago.edu/philologic4.7/publicdicos/bibliography?head=travail.
25. Quoted in Vila, *Suffering Scholars*, 156, 172.
26. Lamartine, "Du droit au travail et de l'organisation du travail," in *La France Parlementaire (1834–1851)*, 4:110.
27. Duveau, "L'Illusion lyrique," 207.
28. Alphonse de Lamartine was a popular poet. Other members of the Provisional Government included Louis Blanc, a journalist and the author of the famous pamphlet *Organisation du travail*; Ferdinand Flocon, journalist and newspaper editor; and Alexandre Ledru-Rollin, who was not a writer, but had founded a newspaper and was a close friend of the novelist George Sand who penned several of his public decrees as minister of the interior.
29. Lamartine, "Du droit au travail," February 25, 1848.
30. Article 7 of the first draft of the Constitution, June 20, 1848.
31. Rosanvallon, *The New Social Question: Rethinking the Welfare State*, trans. Harshav, 77.
32. Cole, *The Power of Large Numbers: Population, Politics, and Gender in Nineteenth-Century France*, 72–74.
33. Perrot, *Enquêtes sur la condition ouvrière en France au 19e siècle*, 25.
34. Rabinbach, *The Human Motor: Energy, Fatigue, and the Origins of Modernity*, 3.
35. Saint-Simon, "Prospectus," in *Œuvres complètes*, 2:1449.
36. Saint-Simon, "Premier extrait de *L'Organisateur*," in *Œuvres complètes*, 3:2119–24.
37. Voltaire, *Dictionnaire philosophique*, 175. Cited in Ranciere, *Mute Speech*, 33.
38. Barrault, *Aux artistes: Du passé et de l'avenir des beaux-arts (Doctrine de Saint-Simon)*, 83–84.

1. Between Two Revolutions

1. Agulhon, *The Republican Experiment*, trans. Lloyd, 23–24.
2. Hayat, *Quand la République était révolutionnaire*, 120–25.

3. Quoted in Chevalier, *Laboring Classes and Dangerous Classes in Paris during the First Half of the Nineteenth Century*, trans. Jellinek, 372.
4. Quoted in Démier, "Droit au travail et organisation du travail en 1848," 161.
5. *Le Moniteur universel*, February 26, 1848. Cited in Bouchet, "Le Droit au travail sous le 'masque des mots': Les Économistes français au combat en 1848," 596.
6. Anon., *La Voix des femmes*, April 24–25, 1848, 2. Cited in McIlvanney, *Figurations of the Feminine in the Early French Women's Press, 1758–1848*, 230.
7. Jeanne-Désirée [Gay], [untitled article], *La Femme libre*, [n.d.],1832, 3.
8. Sewell, *Work and Revolution in France*, 252, 264.
9. Bouchet, *Un jeudi à l'assemblée*, 73–83.
10. Verley, "Annexe statistique," *La Révolution industrielle*, 504.
11. Horn, *The Path Not Taken: French Industrialization in the Age of Revolution*, 209.
12. Verley, "Annexe statistique," 507.
13. Verley, "Annexe statistique," 219–23.
14. Jarrige and Le Roux, *La Contamination du monde*, 117.
15. Sewell, *Work and Revolution in France*, 157–58.
16. Rancière, "The Myth of the Artisan," trans. Lake, 2–3.
17. Offen, *The Woman Question in France*, 193.
18. Tilly and Scott, "Women in the Family Wage Economy," in *Women, Work, and Family*, 104–45.
19. For an in-depth discussion of the dynamics of these discourses, see Scott, "Work Identities for Men and Women."
20. Chauvet, *Les Ouvriers du livre en France*, 90–95.
21. Thérenty and Vaillant, *1836, L'an 1 de l'ère médiatique*, 26.
22. Pinkney, *The French Revolution of 1830*, 277–78.
23. "Commission Municipale-Paris le 31 juillet 1830-Habitans de Paris!" *Le Moniteur universel*, supplément extraordinaire au n° du 31 juillet (Edition du soir). Cited in Marrinan, *Painting Politics for Louis-Philippe*, 32.
24. Ladvocat, "Note pour Monsieur le ministre de l'intérieur sur les ouvriers imprimeurs," September 4, 1830. Reprinted in Chauvet, *Les Ouvriers du livre en France*, 645–48.
25. Parmentier, *Paris; ou, Le Livre des cent-et-un: Anthologie*, 52.
26. Arago and Duvert, *27, 28 et 29 juillet* (first performed at the Vaudeville theater August 17, 1830). Republished in Muret, *L'Histoire par le théâtre*, 3:24.
27. The subscription service, run by Jean Louis of Dessau, was called *Théâtre français moderne: Choix de pieces de Theatre Nouvelles représentées avec succès sur les théâtres de Paris*, and its different numbers included Victor Hugo's *Marion de Lorme*, Alfred de Vigny's *Chatterton* (both in 1835), and many others. Arago's vaudeville appeared in the first series, livraison XII, in 1830.

28. Toulotte, *Etienne Arago*, 100.
29. Eymery, *Les Enfants de Paris; ou, Les Petits Patriotes, scènes de courage, de présence d'esprit, de magnanimité, de grandeur d'âme et de désintéressement de la jeunesse parisienne pendant les journées des 27, 28, 29 juillet 1830*, n.p. This image is available on the French National Library website: https://gallica.bnf.fr/ark:/12148/bpt6k5452370n/f8.item#.
30. Marrinan, *Painting Politics for Louis-Philippe*, 37.
31. Cuvillier, *Hommes et idéologies de 1840*, 95.
32. Sewell, *Work and Revolution in France*, 219.
33. Marx and Engels, "Manifesto of the Communist Party," 14.
34. Maza, "The Failure of 'Bourgeois Monarchy,'" 162, 166.
35. *Le Maitron dictionnaire biographique mouvement ouvrier mouvement social*, s.v. "SAINT-SIMON Claude, Henri. (Claude-Henri de Rouvroy, comte de Saint-Simon)," last modified December 18, 2013, https://maitron.fr/spip.php?article24357.
36. Saint-Simon, "Lettre sur l'établissement du parti de l'opposition," *Le Censeur; ou, Examen des actes et des ouvrages qui tendent à détruire ou à consolider la Constitution de l'Etat*, edited by Charles Comte and Charles Dunoyer, 1815. Republished in *Œuvres complètes*, 2:1306–15.
37. Say's note in *Des principes de l'économie politique, et de L'impôt par M. David Ricardo, traduit de l'anglais par F. S. Constancio avec des notes explicatives et critiques, par M. Jean-Baptiste Say*, 7.
38. Examples of this phenomenon can be found in Christen-Lecuyer, "Les Caisses d'épargne et la littérature dans la première moitié du XIX siècle"; and Harrison, "Patronage: Emulation for the Working Class."
39. Rosanvallon, *Le Moment Guizot*, 95, 162.
40. For an in-depth discussion of this, see Goldstein, "An A Priori Self for the Bourgeois Male: Victor Cousin's Project," in *The Post-Revolutionary Self*, 139–81.
41. Mirecourt, *Guizot*, 55.
42. Jules Vinçard, "Aux fondateurs de *La Ruche*," *La Ruche populaire*, December 1841, 5.
43. Cited in Frobert, "What Is a Just Society?," 297.
44. For an in-depth investigation of how employers used coercive tactics to encourage bourgeois values and behaviors among their employees, see Harrison, "Patronage: Emulation for the Working Class."
45. Dupin, *Forces productives et commerciales de la France*, iii.
46. Published as the "Premier extrait de *L'Organisateur*" in 1819.
47. Lyon-Caen, *La Lecture et la vie: Balzac*, 145.
48. Benjamin, "Exposé of 1935," trans. Eiland and McLaughlin, 6.
49. Stiénon, *La Littérature des physiologies*, 58.
50. Durand and Glinoer, *Naissance de l'éditeur*, 81.

51. For a complete listing of the numerous literary *physiologies* published between 1840 and 1845, see Lhéritier, *Les Physiologies*.
52. Balzac, "Lettre adressée aux écrivains français du XIXe siècle," 63.
53. These themes are explored in Mathias, "'L'esprit, le coeur et les bras': Rethinking Art as Labour in George Sand"; and in White, "George Sand, Digging."
54. Texier, *Physiologie du poète*, 12.
55. Angenot, "La Littérature populaire au dix-neuvième siècle," 94–95.
56. Sand, *The Journeyman Joiner; or, The Companion of the Tour of France*, trans. Shaw, 24.
57. Planche, "La Journée d'un journaliste," in *Paris; ou, Le Livre des cent et un*, vol. 6 (Paris: Ladvocat, 1832), 149–50. Cited in Glinoer, "Classes de textes et littérature industrielle dans la première moitié du xixe siècle," n.p.
58. Gautier, "Préface," in *Mademoiselle de Maupin*, 20.
59. Dumasy, "Introduction," in *La Querelle du roman-feuilleton: Littérature, presse et politique un débat précurseur (1836–1848)*, 5–21.
60. O'Neil-Henry, *Mastering the Marketplace*, 151.
61. Jasinski, *Les Années romantiques de Th. Gautier*, 171.
62. Vaillant, *L'Histoire littéraire*, 117.
63. Furet and Ozouf, *Reading and Writing: Literacy in France from Calvin to Jules Ferry*, 117.
64. Allen, *In the Public Eye*, 331.
65. Richter, "Les Bibliothèques populaires et la lecture ouvrière," 516.
66. Richter, "Les Bibliothèques populaires et la lecture ouvrière," 519–20.
67. Pigoreau, *Cinquième supplément*, iii. Cited in Glinoer, "Classes de textes et littérature industrielle dans la première moitié du xixe siècle."
68. Voilquin, *Souvenirs d'une fille du peuple*, 65.
69. Parent-Lardeur, *Lire à Paris au temps de Balzac*, 260.
70. Lyon-Caen, *La Lecture et la vie*, 203–4.
71. Lyons, *Readers and Society in Nineteenth-Century France*, 21.
72. Nadaud, *Mémoires de Leonard*, 90.
73. Thérenty and Vaillant, *1836, L'an 1 de l'ère médiatique*, 46–47.
74. Vigier, *La Seconde République (Que sais-je?)*, 22.
75. Agulhon, *The Republican Experiment*, 45–55.
76. Vigier, *La Seconde République (Que sais-je?)*, 21.
77. *Les Pommes de terre au boisseau*, n.d., 1.
78. Vigier, *La Seconde République (Que sais-je?)*, 40–42.
79. Girardin, "Introduction," *Le Droit au travail au Luxembourg et à l'Assemblée nationale*, xx–xxxv.
80. Garnier, "Introduction," *Le Droit au travail à l'Assemblée nationale*, xix.
81. Cited in Bouchet, "Le droit au travail sous le 'masque des mots,'" 601.
82. *Les Pommes de terre au boisseau*, 3.

2. Balzac's Literary Labor Theory of Value

1. Mortimer, *For Love or for Money*, 8; Pasco, *Balzac, Literary Sociologist*, 241.
2. Balzac, *History of the Thirteen*, trans. Herbert Hunt, 318.
3. Moreau de la Sarthe, "Idée générale du système du docteur Gall," 49–50.
4. Moreau de la Sarthe, "Idée générale du système du docteur Gall," 50.
5. See Stiénon, *La Littérature des physiologies*, and, in particular, her chapter titled "Contextualisation: Un siècle physiologique," 21–60.
6. Smith, *An Inquiry into the Nature and Causes of the Wealth of Nations*, 23.
7. Say, "Chapitre XXIII. Origine de la valeur des monnaies," in *Traité d'économie politique*, n.p. (no pages in e-book edition).
8. Jacoud, *Jean Baptiste Say and Political Economy*, 220.
9. Breton, "Les Économistes, le pouvoir politique et l'ordre social," 236.
10. Cole, *The Power of Large Numbers*, 71–101.
11. Brix, *Le Romantisme français*, 275–84.
12. Staël, *Corinne; ou, L'Italie*, 1049.
13. Riot-Sarcey, "Le Passé du présent," 80.
14. Balzac, *The Physiology of Marriage*, 186.
15. Thompson, "The Moral Economy of the Crowd in the Eighteenth Century," 78.
16. Balzac, *Eugénie Grandet*, trans. Marriage, 138.
17. *La Comédie humaine*, ed. Pierre-Georges Castex (Paris: Gallimard, 1979): 10:660. All subsequent references to this multivolume edition (Bibliothèque de la Pléiade) are cited in the text as CH followed by volume and page number.
18. Sieyès, *What Is the Third Estate?*, 171.
19. Barbéris, *Le Monde de Balzac*, 222–23.
20. Balzac, *The Wild Ass's Skin*, trans. Hunt, 251.
21. Rosanvallon, *Le Moment Guizot*, 160.
22. Régnier, "Les Saint-Simoniens, le prêtre et l'artiste," 36.
23. Cole, *The Power of Large Numbers*, 123
24. Thiher, *Fiction Rivals Science*, 41–42.
25. Balzac, *The Physiology of Marriage*, 142–43.
26. Ambrière, "Balzac et l'énergie," 44.
27. Balzac, "Gobseck," trans. Wormeley, 7.
28. Balzac, *History of the Thirteen*, 311–12.
29. Thiher, *Fiction Rivals Science*, 67.
30. The classic study of Balzac's understanding of the scientific theories of his day remains Le Yaouanc, *Nosographie de l'humanité balzacienne*, first published in 1959.
31. Vila, *Suffering Scholars*, 156.

32. *Le Dictionnaire de l'Académie française*, 16th ed. (1835), s.v. "mouvement," https://artflsrv04.uchicago.edu/philologic4.7/publicdicos/navigate/13/5710. Interestingly, the 1835 definition says nothing about social or political movements.
33. Diaz, "La Société des choses," 53.
34. Nesci, "Epilogue: Les Corsets d'Ida ou la femme au travail," in *Le Flâneur et les Flâneuses*, 161–68.
35. For more on the *grisette*, and how the cultural representations of this social type evolve over the course of the Romantic era, see Lescart, *Splendeurs et misères de la grisette*.
36. For an in-depth look at this phenomenon, see DeGroat, "Virtue, Vice, and Revolution: Representations of Parisian Needlewomen in the Mid-Nineteenth Century."
37. Balzac, *The Country Doctor*, trans. Marriage, 1–2.
38. Balzac, *The Unknown Masterpiece*, trans. Marriage, 10–12.
39. Rabinbach, *The Human Motor*, 56–61.
40. Goldstein, *The Post-Revolutionary Self*, 159–60.
41. Andréoli, "Balzac, Cousin et l'éclectisme," 80.
42. Balzac, *The Wild Ass's Skin*, 52
43. Jameson, "*La Cousine Bette* and Allegorical Realism," 244.
44. Piketty, "Inequality and Concentration: Preliminary Bearings," 238–40.
45. Bordas, "Balzac et la lisibilité de l'argent romanesque," 119.
46. *Le Dictionnaire de l'Académie française*, 16th ed. (1835), s.v. "frai," https://artflsrv04.uchicago.edu/philologic4.7/publicdicos/navigate/12/19544.
47. Say, "Chapitre XXIX. Ce que devraient être les monnaies," in *Traité d'économie politique*, n.p.
48. Spang, *Stuff and Money in the Time of the French Revolution*, 269.
49. Smith, *Wealth of Nations*, 13–14.
50. Ricardo, *On the Principles of Political Economy and Taxation*, n.p.
51. Say, "Chapitre XXVII. Que la monnaie n'est ni un signe ni une mesure," in *Traité d'économie politique*, n.p.
52. Marx, *Capital: A Critique of Political Economy*, vol. 1, trans. Fowkes, 128.
53. Harvey, *A Companion to Marx's Capital*, 24.
54. Lafargue, *Karl Marx, His Life and Work*, 11.
55. Marx, *Capital: A Critique of Political Economy*, vol. 3, trans. Untermann, 52.

3. The Worker as Hero

1. Vergé, "Séance du 9 Mai 1840," 6.
2. Buret, *De la misère des classes laborieuses en Angleterre et en France*, 1:42.
3. Frégier, *Des classes dangereuses de la population dans les grandes villes, et des moyens de les rendre meilleures*, 1:334.

4. Vergé, "Séance du 9 Mai 1840," 5.
5. Vergé, "Séance du 9 Mai 1840," 4.
6. *Report from His Majesty's Commissioners*, 3.
7. Dupin, *Forces productives et commerciales de la France*, 75.
8. Balzac, *History of the Thirteen*, 309–10.
9. Frégier, *Des classes dangereuses*, 1:84.
10. Goulet, *Optiques: The Science of the Eye and the Birth of Modern French Fiction*, 68.
11. Villermé, *Tableau de l'état physique et moral des ouvriers*, 1:29.
12. Foucault, *Discipline and Punish*, trans. Sheridan, 138.
13. Dupin, *Du travail des enfants qu'emploient les ateliers, les usines et les manufactures*, xv.
14. Kalifa, "Enquête et 'culture de l'enquête' au XIXe siècle," 11.
15. Lyon-Caen, "Enquêtes, littérature et savoir sur le monde social en France dans les années 1840," 104.
16. Craiutu, *Liberalism Under Siege: The Political Thought of the French Doctrinaires*, 77.
17. Furet and Ozouf, *Reading and Writing: Literacy in France from Calvin to Jules Ferry*, 116.
18. Rosanvallon, *Le Moment Guizot*, 96.
19. Craiutu, *Liberalism Under Siege*, 224.
20. Guizot, *Discours académiques*, cited in Craiutu, *Liberalism Under Siege*, 224.
21. Delmas, *Instituer des savoirs d'état*, 86.
22. Institut Royal de France, Académie des sciences morales et politiques, *Règlement 1833*, 24.
23. Rosanvallon, *Le Moment Guizot*, 227.
24. Chevalier, *Laboring Classes and Dangerous Classes*, trans. Jellinek, 365.
25. Picot, *Concours de l'Académie: Sujets proposés, prix et récompenses décernés, liste des livres couronnés ou récompensés, 1834–1900*, 12.
26. Picot, *Concours de l'Académie*, 15.
27. Picot, *Concours de l'Académie*, 18.
28. Picot, *Concours de l'Académie*, 5.
29. Picot, *Concours de l'Académie*, 11.
30. Buret, *De la misère des classes laborieuses en Angleterre et en France*, 1:113, 260.
31. For the remainder of the chapter, I will refer to these texts respectively as *The Journeyman Joiner* and *Travels*. Citations are given in text and, unless otherwise noted, are taken from the following translations: Etienne Cabet, *Travels in Icaria*, trans. Leslie Roberts (Syracuse, NY: Syracuse University Press, 2003); and George Sand, *The Journeyman Joiner; or, The Companion of the Tour of France*, trans. Francis George Shaw (1847; rpt., New York: H. Fertig, 1976). Citations refer to the reprint edition.
32. Furst, *The Contours of European Romanticism*, 42, 43.

33. Nadaud, *Mémoires de Léonard, ancien garçon maçon*, 282–86.
34. Fourn, "L'Utopie ou la barbarie," 209–10.
35. Sutton, *Les Icariens*, 32–34.
36. *Revue de progres*, October 1, 1840. Cited in Johnson, *Utopian Communism in France*, 76.
37. Johnson, *Utopian Communism in France*, 74–82.
38. Fourn, "L'Utopie ou la barbarie," 210.
39. Daniel Stern (pseudonym for Marie d'Agoult), "Le Compagnon du Tour de France de George Sand (Variétés)." Cited in Bourgeois, "Introduction," in *Le Compagnon du Tour de France*, 14.
40. Durocher (pseud. Louis Reybaud), review of *Le Compagnon du Tour de France*, *Le National* [no date given]. Cited in Lerner, *Inventing the Popular*, 112.
41. Watrelot, "Introduction," in Sand, *Le Compagnon du Tour de France*, 7–34.
42. This is according to the catalog of the BnF, https://catalogue.bnf.fr/rechercher.do?index=TIT3&numNotice=13505564&typeNotice=s.
43. Perdiguier, *Correspondance inédite avec George Sand et ses amis*, 67–69. Cited in Ribard, "De l'écriture à l'événement."
44. Watrelot, "Réception du *Compagnon du Tour de France* au XIXe siècle," in Sand, *Le Compagnon du Tour de France*, 495–511.
45. This practice inspired the title of Jacques Rancière's foundational study of the worker-poets *La Nuit des prolétaires* (1981), first translated into English as *Nights of Labor* (1989).
46. For example, in a moment of overwhelming emotion, Pierre confides to his friend Amaury, "I love the men of my race, and I am unhappy because they hate each other" (80). Later on, the count will remark that the artisans who work for him are "specimens of a noble race" (167).
47. *Dictionnaire de l'Academie Francaise*, 16th ed. (1835), s.v. "noble," https://artflsrv04.uchicago.edu/philologic4.7/publicdicos/navigate/13/6315. Definition 1 and 3 are both nouns: "He who, by right of birth or letters of the prince, is a part of the distinguished class of the state [*Qui, par droit de naissance ou par lettres du prince, fait partie d'une classe distinguée dans l' État*]," and "He who has, or who signals greatness, elevation, and superiority [*Qui a ou qui annonce de la grandeur, de l'élévation, de la supériorité.*]." The fact that the figurative sense of the word is circumscribed in the second entry leads us to conclude that definitions 1 and 2 are to be understood literally.
48. Larousse, *Grand Dictionnaire universel du XIXe siècle: Français, historique, géographique, mythologique, bibliographique, littéraire, artistique, scientifique* (1876), 9:379, s.v. "honneur."
49. Cohen, *The Sentimental Education of the Novel*, 128.
50. Schor, *George Sand and Idealism*, 93.
51. Marx and Engels, "Manifesto of the Communist Party," 33.

52. Leroux, *De l'humanité, de son principe et de son avenir*, 1:95.
53. Bénichou, *Le Temps des prophètes: Doctrines de l'âge romantique*, 327.
54. Riot-Sarcey, *Le Réel de l'utopie*, 217–18.
55. Sipe, *Text, Image, and the Problem with Perfection in Nineteenth-Century France*, 80.
56. For more on this ancient tradition see Millot, "Tradition(s) et Evolution: Les Chansons du compagnonnage."

4. A Literary Identity for the Worker-Writer

1. Puech, *La vie et l'œuvre de Flora Tristan*, 10. The addition of "ouvrière" to her job title indicates that this is low-paid unskilled labor.
2. Chauvet, *Les Ouvriers du livre en France*, 76–81.
3. Lerner, *Inventing the Popular*, 42.
4. Zancarini-Fournel, *Les Luttes et les rêves*, 261.
5. McIlvanney, *Figurations of the Feminine in the Early French Women's Press*, 223.
6. Rabine, "Feminist Texts and Feminist Subjects," in *Feminism, Socialism, and French Romanticism*, 85–86.
7. *Le Maitron dictionnaire biographique mouvement ouvrier mouvement social*, s.v. "VOILQUIN Suzanne, née MONNIER," by Philippe Régnier, last modified August 6, 2021, https://maitron.fr/spip.php?article24365.
8. *Le Maitron dictionnaire biographique mouvement ouvrier mouvement social*, s.v. "REBOUL Jean [Gard]," last modified May 20, 2017, https://maitron.fr/spip.php?article36845.
9. Dumas, "Une visite à Nîmes," 14.
10. Tristan, *Mephis*, 95.
11. Hustache, "*Méphis*, Entre roman populaire et roman moral," 53.
12. Puech, *La Vie et l'œuvre de Flora Tristan*, 11.
13. Michaud, *Flora Tristan*, 27.
14. Watrelot, "La Réception du roman *Le Compagon du Tour de France*," 164.
15. Membres de la comité, Untitled, *La Ruche populaire*, December 1839.
16. *Le Dictionnaire de l'Académie française*, 6th ed. (1835), s.v. "littérateur," https://artflsrv04.uchicago.edu/philologic4.7/publicdicos/navigate/13/2972. Decades later, Littré would offer this precision: "Someone who is occupied with literature, that is, whose profession is to create works or to study or analyze works by others." Littré, *Dictionnaire de la langue française* (1863–1873), s.v. "littérateur," https://www.littre.org/definition/litt%C3%A9rateur.
17. To borrow an apt formulation of the phenomenon from Anne O'Neil-Henry.
18. Chapuys-Montlaville, "Discours à la chambre des députés, 13 juin 1843," 81.
19. Kalifa and Régnier, "'Séparatismes' médiatiques 1: Identités de classe," in *Civilisation du Journal*, 1438.

20. Oberthür and Millot, "La Poésie populaire et la chanson face à la censure et à la répression," 93.
21. Sainte-Beuve, "De la littérature industrielle," 675.
22. Sainte-Beuve, "De la littérature industrielle," 691.
23. A. Dutacq, Gérant du *Siècle*, "Prospectus," *Le Siècle*, June 23, 1836.
24. Thérenty and Vaillant, *1836, L'an 1 de l'ère médiatique*, 31–32.
25. "Introduction," *Revue des deux mondes: Table général (1831–1874)* (Paris, 1875), ii.
26. Thérenty and Vaillant, *1836, L'an 1 de l'ère médiatique*, 31–32.
27. Preiss, *De la poire au parapluie*, iv.
28. Baudouin, "Justice, presse et politique," 332.
29. Balzac, "Lettre sur le procès de Peytel, notaire à Belley," *Le Siècle*, September 28, 1839.
30. Baudouin, "Justice, presse et politique," 336.
31. See note 42 in Badouin, "Justice, presse et politique": "Bibliothèque Lovenjoul, A 114, f° 140: lettre de Vineur [sic], fabricant de mesures linéaires à Paris, 2 octobre 1839."
32. Vinçard, "Lettre adressée à M. Dutacq, gérant du journal *Le Siècle*," *La Ruche populaire*, December 1839, 29.
33. De La Fontaine, "The Raven and the Fox," trans. Wright, 1.
34. Vinçard, "Lettre adressée à M. Dutacq," 29–30.
35. Hugo, "Réponse de M. Victor Hugo, à la lettre écrite le 26 février 1841, par Savinien Lapointe," *La Ruche populaire*, March 1841, 24.
36. Quoted in Rancière, "Le Prolétaire et son double; ou, Le Philosophe inconnu," 25. Cited in Ribard, "De l'écriture à l'événement."
37. Vinçard, "De la populace. A propos du discours académique de M. Victor Hugo," *La Ruche populaire*, June 1841, 1–5.
38. Vinçard, "Aux fondateurs de La *Ruche*," *La Ruche populaire*, December 1841, 3–4.
39. Harrison, "Patronage: Emulation for the Working Class," 126.
40. Ribard, "De l'écriture à l'événement," 89.
41. Boissy, "Aux philosophes," *La Ruche populaire*, January 1840, 22.
42. Varin, "A tous," *La Ruche populaire*, December 1839, 5.
43. Desplanches, tailleur, "Le Peuple," *La Ruche populaire*, December 1839, 9–10.
44. Vannostal, typographer, "Aux travailleurs," *La Ruche populaire*, January 1840, 4.
45. Roly, "L'Amour de la gloire," *La Ruche populaire*, March 1841, 27–28.
46. Bowman, *Le Christ des barricades, 1789–1848*, 264.
47. Tourte, "L'Épée et le Marteau," *La Ruche populaire*, May 1841, 22.
48. Rodrigues, *Poésies sociales des ouvriers*, vii-viii.
49. Lerminier, "La Littérature des ouvriers," 976.

50. "Introduction," *L'Atelier*, September 1840.
51. Vinçard, "Aux fondateurs de *La Ruche*," *La Ruche populaire*, December 1841, 2.
52. Vinçard, "Aux fondateurs de *La Ruche*," 2.
53. Vinçard, "Aux fondateurs de *La Ruche*," 5.
54. Vinçard, "De L'importance du journalisme," *La Ruche populaire*, December 1842, 3.
55. "Programme," *La Ruche populaire*, December 1844, n.p.
56. "Concours pour le prospectus de *La Ruche*," *La Ruche populaire*, March 1845, 78.
57. Paton, P. J., railroad worker, "Simple exposé," *L'Union*, December 1843, n.p.
58. Chapuys-Montlaville, "Discours à la chambre des députés, 14 mars 1845," 96.
59. Dumasy-Queffélec, "Le Feuilleton," 936.
60. Paton, railroad worker, "Poésies sociales. *Le Chantier*. Poésies de Charles Poncy, de Toulon, ouvrier maçon. (Troisième article)," *L'Union*, April 1844, 3.
61. Vinçard, "Chronique," *L'Union*, March 1844, 4.

5. Building Character

1. Lyons, "Les Bestsellers," 409, 416.
2. Thiesse, "Le Roman populaire," 509.
3. For the remainder of the chapter, I will refer to this text as *Mysteries*. Unless otherwise noted, citations are taken from the following edition: *The Mysteries of Paris*, 3 vols., translator unknown (New York: Peter Fenelon Collier & Son, 1900). References are given in the text as *MP* followed by volume and page.
4. This is the title of Chevasco's study of the explosion of attention and emulators that Sue's novel received in Great Britain. More recently, Marie-Ève Thérenty has demonstrated the global scope of this phenomenon in "Mysterymania: Essor et limites de la globalisation culturelle au XIXe siècle."
5. For the remainder of the chapter, I will refer to this text as *The Wandering Jew*. Unless otherwise noted, citations are taken from the following edition: *The Wandering Jew*, 3 parts, translator unknown (London and New York: George Routledge and Sons, 1889). References are given in the text as *WJ* followed by part and chapter (no page numbers in the e-book edition).
6. Lyons, "Les Bestsellers," 425.
7. The Collier translation skips over these details.
8. Ernestine Dumont to Eugène Sue, July 1843. Cited in Lyon-Caen, *La Lecture et la vie*, 9.
9. Chaisemartin, *La Caractérisation des personnages de roman*, 511.
10. Forster, *Aspects of the Novel*, 65–67.

11. Woloch, *The One vs. the Many*, 307.
12. Woloch, *The One vs. the Many*, 219.
13. Pezard, "Le Romantisme 'frénétique': Histoire d'une appellation générique et d'un genre dans la critique de 1821 à 2010."
14. Lhéritier, *Les Physiologies*, 11.
15. Villermé, *Tableau de l'état physique et moral des ouvriers*, 1:90, 364.
16. Balzac, *The Country Doctor*, trans. Marriage, 99–100.
17. The Routledge translation does not list out these tasks as fully as the original French.
18. Rancière, "The Myth of the Artisan," trans. Lake, 2.
19. Sue, *Les Mystères de Paris*, vol. 1, pt. 2, chap. 10. https://www.gutenberg.org/cache/epub/18921/pg18921-images.html.
20. Eugène Sue to Ernest Legouvé, October 1841, in *Correspondance générale d'Eugène Sue*, ed. Galvan, 2:70–71.
21. Honoré de Balzac to Madame Hanska, June 16, 1846, in *Lettres à Madame Hanska*, ed. Pierrot, 2:213.
22. *Lettres à Madame Hanska*, June 15, 1846.
23. O'Neil-Henry, *Mastering the Marketplace*, 109.
24. Robb, *Balzac*, 328.
25. Maurois, *Prométhée*, 535.
26. *Lettres à Madame Hanska*, July 22, 1846, 2:270.
27. Maurois, *Prométhée*, 536.
28. *Lettres à Madame Hanska*, February 6, 1844, 1:83.
29. *Lettres à Madame Hanska*, October 5 and November 7, 1846, 2:370, 409.
30. Lorant, *Les Parents pauvres d'Honoré de Balzac*, 335.
31. This is Fredric Jameson's argument in "*La Cousine Bette* and Allegorical Realism."
32. Weinstein, *The Literature of Labor and the Labors of Literature*, 23.
33. Marron, *La Revue Indépendante*, January 25, 1847, cited in Lorant, *Les Parents pauvres d'Honoré de Balzac*, 323.

Epilogue

1. Pyat, *Le Chiffonnier de Paris*, 924.
2. Muret, *L'Histoire par le théâtre*, 3:297.
3. Quoted in Sabatier, *Le Mélodrame de la République sociale et le théâtre de Félix Pyat*, 1:319.
4. Compagnon, *Les Chiffonniers de Paris*, 226.
5. Galvan, "Chronologie," in *Correspondance d'Eugène Sue*, 2:23.
6. *Compte-rendu des séances par le Moniteur et des documents imprimés par ordre de l'Assemblée Nationale Constituante.* Cited in Sabatier, *Le Mélodrame de la République sociale et le théâtre de Félix Pyat*, 1:320.

7. [Anon.], "Assemblée Nationale. Séance du 3 novembre," *Le Charivari*, no. 308, November 2 and 3, 1848.
8. Agulhon, *The Republican Experiment*, 50.
9. Perrot, *George Sand, politique et polémiques*, 529–42.
10. Ministère de l'intérieur, "En Guise de préface," *Bulletins de la République*, v.
11. Ministère de l'intérieur, *Bulletin de la République*, no. 19 (April 22, 1848). Cited by Perrot, *George Sand, politique et polémiques*, 406–9.
12. Galvan, "Introduction," in *Correspondance d'Eugène Sue*, 2:11.
13. Balzac, "Lettre sur le travail," 17.
14. Balzac, "Lettre sur le travail," 15.
15. *Lettres à Madame Hanska*, February 25, 1848, 2:718.
16. *Lettres à Madame Hanska*, February 29, 1848, 2:726–27.
17. *Lettres à Madame Hanska*, March 17, 1848, 2:754.
18. Mombert, "Action politique et fiction Romanesque," 171.
19. Dumas, "Aux travailleurs," March 15, 1848.
20. Hayat, *Quand la République était révolutionnaire*, 342–44.
21. Haubtmann, *Pierre-Joseph Proudhon: Sa vie et sa pensée*, 787.
22. Proudon, "Aux électeurs du Doubs," in *Correspondance de P.-J. Proudhon*, ed. Langlois, 2:302.
23. Castelton, "Pierre-Joseph Proudhon: Seul contre tous," 279.
24. Hayat, *Quand la République était révolutionnaire*, 343.
25. Proudhon, "Ce que la révolution doit à la littérature," *Le Représentant du peuple*, May 28, 1848.
26. Proudhon, "Lettre de candidature à la pension Suard," in *Oeuvres complètes de P.-J. Proudhon*, ed. Bouglé and Moysset, 4:15–16.
27. Dumas, "Ce que la révolution doit à la littérature," *La France nouvelle*, June 4, 1848.
28. Pouillaude, ouvrier peintre en bâtiment, to Eugène Sue, June 5 or 6, 1848, in *Correspondance d'Eugène Sue*, ed. Galvan, 3:476–77.
29. Baudelaire to Narcisse Ancelle, March 5, 1852, in *Correspondance*, ed. Pichois, 188.
30. Charles Baudelaire, "The Swan," in *The Flowers of Evil*, trans. McGowan, 175.

BIBLIOGRAPHY

Agulhon, Maurice. *The Republican Experiment, 1848–1852*. Translated by Janet Lloyd. Cambridge: Cambridge University Press, 1983.
Allen, James. *In the Public Eye: A History of Reading in Modern France, 1800–1940*. Princeton: Princeton University Press, 1991.
Ambrière, Madeleine. "Balzac et l'énergie." *Romantisme*, no. 46 (1984): 43–48.
Andréoli, Max. "Balzac, Cousin et l'éclectisme." *L'Année balzacienne* (1971): 37–81.
Angenot, Marc. "La Littérature populaire au dix-neuvième siècle." In *Les Dehors de la littérature: Du roman populaire à la science-fiction*. Paris: Honore Champion, 2013.
Balzac, Honoré de. *La Comédie humaine* [CH]. Edited by Pierre-Georges Castex. Vols. 1, 5, 7, 10, and 12. Paris: Gallimard, 1976–81.
Balzac, Honoré de. *The Country Doctor, The Quest of the Absolute, and Other Stories*. Translated by Ellen Marriage. Philadelphia: John D. Morris, 1899?
Balzac, Honoré de. *Eugénie Grandet*. Translated by Ellen Marriage. 1907. Reprinted New York: Knopf, 1992.
Balzac, Honoré de. "Gobseck." In *The Comedy of Human Life*. Translated by Katharine Prescott Wormeley. Boston: Roberts Brothers, 1896.
Balzac, Honoré de. *History of the Thirteen*. Translated by Herbert Hunt. Middlesex, UK: Penguin Books, 1987.
Balzac, Honoré de. "Lettre adressée aux écrivains français du XIXe siècle." *Revue de Paris* 11 (1834): 62–82.
Balzac, Honoré de. *Lettres à Madame Hanska*. Edited by Roger Pierrot. 2 vols. Paris: Laffont, 1990.
Balzac, Honoré de. "Lettre sur le procès de Peytel, notaire à Belley." *Le Siècle*, September 28, 1839.
Balzac, Honoré de. "Lettre sur le travail." Undated, sometime between February and June 1848. *Revue des deux mondes*, September 1, 1906. Reprinted *Revue des deux mondes*, February 2009, 13–24.
Balzac, Honoré de. *The Physiology of Marriage*. Translated by [unattributed] with Introduction by Sharon Marcus. Baltimore: The Johns Hopkins University Press, 1997.
Balzac, Honoré de. *The Unknown Masterpiece and Other Stories*. Translated by Ellen Marriage. New York: Macmillan, 1901.
Balzac, Honoré de. *The Wild Ass's Skin*. Translated by Herbert J. Hunt. Harmondsworth, UK: Penguin Books, 1977.

Barbéris, Pierre. *Le Monde de Balzac*. Paris: Arthaud. 1973.
Barrault, Emile. *Aux artistes: Du passé et de l'avenir des beaux-arts (Doctrine de Saint-Simon)*. Paris: Alexandre Mesnier, 1830.
Barthes, Roland. *Le Degré zéro de l'écriture: Suivi de nouveaux essais critiques*. Paris: Éditions du Seuil, 1972.
Baudelaire, Charles. *Correspondance*. Edited by Claude Pichois. Paris: Gallimard, 1993.
Baudelaire, Charles. "The Swan." In *The Flowers of Evil*. Translated by James McGowan. Oxford: Oxford University Press, 1993.
Baudouin, Patricia. "Justice, presse et politique." *Revue d'histoire du XIXe siècle* 26/27 (2003): 331–48.
Bénichou, Paul. *Le Temps des prophètes: Doctrines de l'âge romantique*. Paris: Gallimard, 1977.
Benjamin, Walter. "Exposé of 1935." In *The Arcades Project*. Translated by Howard Eiland and Kevin McLaughlin. 3–13. Cambridge, MA: Belknap Press of Harvard University Press, 1999.
Boissy. "Aux philosophes." *La Ruche populaire*, January 1840, 22.
Bordas, Eric. "Balzac et la lisibilité de l'argent romanesque." In *La Littérature au prisme de l'économie: Argent et roman en France au XIXe siècle*, edited by Francesco Spandri, 117–33. Paris: Classiques Garnier, 2014.
Bouchet, Thomas. "Le Droit au travail sous le 'masque des mots': Les Économistes français au combat en 1848." *French Historical Studies* 29, no. 4 (Fall 2006): 595–619.
Bouchet, Thomas. *Un jeudi à l'assemblée: Politiques du discours et droit au travail dans la France de 1848*. Cap-Saint-Ignace: Editions Nota Bene, 2007.
Bourdieu, Pierre. *The Rules of Art*. Translated by Susan Emanuel. Cambridge: Polity Press, 1996.
Bourgeois, René. "Introduction." In *Le Compagnon du Tour de France*, by George Sand. Grenoble: Presses Universitaires de Grenoble, 1988.
Bowman, Frank Paul. *Le Christ des barricades, 1789–1848*. Paris: Les Editions du Cerf, 1987.
Breton, Yves. "Les Économistes, le pouvoir politique et l'ordre social en France entre 1830 et 1851." *Histoire, économie et société* 4, no. 2 (1985): 233–52.
Brix, Michel. *Le Romantisme français: Esthétique platonicienne et modernité littéraire*. Louvain-Namur: Editions Peeters, 1999.
Buret, Eugène. *De la misère des classes laborieuses en Angleterre et en France, de la nature de la misère, de son existence, de ses effets, de ses causes, et de l'insuffisance des remèdes qu'on lui a opposés jusqu'ici: avec l'indication des moyens propres à en affranchir les sociétés*. 2 vols. Paris: Paulin, 1840.
Cabet, Etienne. *Travels in Icaria*. Translated by Leslie Roberts. Syracuse, NY: Syracuse University Press, 2003.

Castelton, Edward. "Pierre-Joseph Proudhon: Seul contre tous." In *Quand les socialistes inventaient l'avenir 1825–1860*, edited by Thomas Bouchet, Vincent Bourdeau, Edward Castelton, Ludovic Frobert, and François Jarrige, 278–92. Paris: La Découverte, 2015.

Chaisemartin, Amélie de. *La Caractérisation des personnages de roman sous la monarchie de juillet: Créer des types*. Paris: Classiques Garnier, 2020.

Chapuys-Montlaville, Benoît-Marie. "Discours à la chambre des députés, 13 juin 1843." Reprinted in *La Querelle du roman-feuilleton: Littérature, presse et politique un débat précurseur (1836–1848)*, by Lise Dumasy, 80–86. Grenoble: ELLUG Université Stendhal, 1999.

Chapuys-Montlaville, Benoît-Marie. "Discours à la chambre des députés, 14 mars 1845." Reprinted in *La Querelle du roman-feuilleton: Littérature, presse et politique un débat précurseur (1836–1848)*, by Lise Dumasy, 95–103. Grenoble: ELLUG Université Stendhal, 1999.

Chauvet, Paul. *Les Ouvriers du livre en France, de 1789 à la constitution de la Fédération du Livre*. Paris: Marcel Rivière, 1956.

Chevalier, Louis. *Laboring Classes and Dangerous Classes in Paris during the First Half of the Nineteenth Century*. Translated by Frank Jellinek. New York: Fertig, 1973.

Chevasco, Berry. *Mysterymania*. Bern: Peter Lang UK, 2003.

Christen, Carole, Caroline Fayolle, and Samuel Hayat. *S'Unir, travailler, résister: Les Associations ouvrières au XIX siècle*. Villeneuve d'Ascq: Presses universitaires du Septentrion, 2021.

Christen-Lecuyer, Carole. "Les Caisses d'épargne et la littérature dans la première moitié du XIX siècle." In *Économie et littérature: France et Grande-Bretagne, 1815–1848*, edited by François Vatin and Nicole Edelman, 219–41. Paris: Éditions le Manuscrit, 2007.

Cohen, Margaret. *The Sentimental Education of the Novel*. Princeton: Princeton University Press, 2002.

Cole, Joshua. *The Power of Large Numbers: Population, Politics, and Gender in Nineteenth-Century France*. Ithaca, NY: Cornell University Press, 2000.

Compagnon, Antoine. *Les Chiffonniers de Paris*. Paris: Gallimard, 2017.

Craiutu, Aurelian. *Liberalism under Siege. The Political Thought of the French Doctrinaires*. Lanham, MD: Lexington Books, 2003.

Cuvillier, Armand. *Hommes et idéologies de 1840*. Paris: M. Rivière, 1956.

DeGroat, Judith. "Virtue, Vice, and Revolution: Representations of Parisian Needlewomen in the Mid-Nineteenth Century." In *Famine and Fashion: Needlewomen in the Nineteenth Century*, edited by Beth Harris, 201–14. New York: Routledge, 2005.

De La Fontaine, Jean. "The Raven and the Fox." In *The Fables of La Fontaine*. Translated by Elizur Wright. London: William Smith, 1842.

Delmas, Corinne. *Instituer des savoirs d'état: L'Académie des sciences morales et politiques au xixe siècle.* Paris: L'Harmattan, 2006.

Deluermoz, Quentin, and Anthony Glinoer, eds. *L'Insurrection entre histoire et littérature, 1789–1914.* Paris: Publications de la Sorbonne, 2015.

Démier, Francis. "Droit au travail et organisation du travail en 1848." In *1848: Actes du colloque international du cent cinquantenaire, tenu à l'Assemblée nationale à Paris, les 23–25 février 1998,* edited by Jean-Luc Mayaud, 159–82. Paris: Créaphis, 2002.

Desplanches, tailleur. "Le Peuple." *La Ruche populaire,* December 1839, 9–10.

Diaz, José-Luis. "La Société des choses." In *Usages de l'objet—Littérature, histoire, arts et techniques, XIXe–XXe siècles,* edited by Marta Caraion, 41–54. Seyssel: Champs Vallon, 2014.

Duchet, Claude, and Ruth Amossy. "Entretien avec Claude Duchet." *Littérature,* no. 140, Analyse du discours et sociocritique (December 2005): 125–32.

Dumas, Alexandre. "Aux travailleurs." (March 15, 1848). In "1848 Alexandre Dumas dans la Révolution," *Cahiers Alexandre Dumas,* no. 25 (November 1999): 332–34.

Dumas, Alexandre. "Ce que révolution doit à la littérature." *La France nouvelle,* June 4, 1848.

Dumas, Alexandre. "Une visite à Nîmes." Introduction to *Poésies,* by Jean Reboul. Brussels: E. Laurent, 1836.

Dumasy, Lise. *La Querelle du roman-feuilleton: Littérature, presse et politique un débat précurseur (1836–1848).* Grenoble: ELLUG Université Stendhal, 1999.

Dumasy-Queffélec, Lise. "Le Feuilleton." In *Civilisation du journal,* edited by Dominique Kalifa, Philippe Régnier, Marie-Eve Thérenty, and Alain Vaillant, 925–36. Paris: Nouveau Monde Editions, 2011.

Dupin, Charles. *Du travail des enfants qu'emploient les ateliers, les usines et les manufactures: Considéré dans les intérêts mutuels de la société, des familles et de l'industrie.* Paris: Bachelier, 1840.

Dupin, Charles. *Forces productives et commerciales de la France.* Paris: Bachelier, 1827.

Durand, Pascal, and Anthony Glinoer. *Naissance de l'éditeur: L'Édition à 'âge Romantique.* Paris: Les Impressions nouvelles, 2005.

Durocher (pseud. Louis Reybaud). "Review of *Le Compagnon du Tour de France.*" *Le National* [n.d.].

Duveau, Georges. "L'Illusion lyrique." In *1848: Le Livre du centenaire,* edited by Georges Bourgin, Georges Duveau, and Charles Moulin, 49–64. Paris: Atlas, 1948.

Duveau, Georges. *1848, the Making of a Revolution.* Translated by Anne Carter. New York: Pantheon Books, 1967.

Eymery, Alexis. *Les Enfants de Paris; ou, Les Petits Patriotes, scènes de courage, de présence d'esprit, de magnanimité, de grandeur d'âme et de désintéressement de la*

jeunesse parisienne pendant les journées des 27, 28, 29 juillet 1830. Paris: Nepveu and Eymery, 1831.
Flaubert, Gustave. *Sentimental Education*. Translated by Helen Constantine. Oxford: Oxford University Press, 2016.
Forster, E. M. *Aspects of the Novel*. London: E. Arnold, 1958.
Foucault, Michel. *Discipline and Punish: The Birth of the Prison*. Translated by Alan Sheridan. New York: Vintage Books, Random House, 1995.
Fourn, François. "L'Utopie ou la barbarie: Contre la violence révolutionnaire: *Le Populaire* de Cabet." In *Quand les socialistes inventaient l'avenir 1825–1860*, edited by Thomas Bouchet, Vincent Bourdeau, Edward Castelton, Ludovic Frobert, and François Jarrige, 203–16. Paris: La Découverte, 2015.
Frégier, Antoine. *Des classes dangereuses de la population dans les grandes villes, et des moyens de les rendre meilleures*. 2 vols. Paris: Baillière, 1840.
Frobert, Ludovic. "What Is a Just Society? The Answer According to the Socialistes Fraternitaires Louis Blanc, Constantin Pecqueur, and François Vidal." *History of Political Economy* 46, no. 2 (2014): 281–306.
Furet, François, and Jacques Ozouf. *Lire et Écrire: L'Alphabétisation des Français de Calvin à Jules Ferry*. Paris: Les Editions de Minuit, 1977.
Furet, François, and Jacques Ozouf. *Reading and Writing: Literacy in France from Calvin to Jules Ferry*. Cambridge: Cambridge University Press, 1982.
Furst, Lilian R. *The Contours of European Romanticism*. Lincoln: University of Nebraska Press, 1979.
Galvan, Jean-Pierre, ed. *Correspondance générale d'Eugène Sue*. 5 vols. Paris: Honoré Champion, 2010.
Garnier, Joseph. *Le Droit au travail à l'Assemblée nationale: Recueil complet de tous les discours prononcés dans cette mémorable discussion. Introduction et notes de M. Joseph Garnier*. Paris: Guillaumin et Cie., 1848.
Gautier, Théophile. "Préface." In *Mademoiselle de Maupin*. Paris: Classiques Garnier, 2018.
[Gay], Jeanne-Désirée. [Untitled article]. *La Femme Libre*, [n.d.], 1832.
Girardin, Emile de. "Introduction." In *Le Droit au travail au Luxembourg et à l'Assemblée nationale / par MM. De Lamartine, Thiers, Louis Blanc, Duvergier de Hauranne, de Tocqueville, Wolowski, Ledru-Rollin, etc. etc*. Paris: Michel Levy Frères, 1849.
Glinoer, Anthony. "Classes de textes et littérature industrielle dans la première moitié du xixe siècle." *COnTEXTES* (2009). http://journals.openedition.org/contextes/4325.
Goldstein, Jan. *The Post-Revolutionary Self*. Cambridge, MA: Harvard University Press, 2005.
Goulet, Andrea. *Optiques: The Science of the Eye and the Birth of Modern French Fiction*. Philadelphia: University of Pennsylvania Press, 2006.
Guizot, François. *Discours académiques*. Paris: Didier, 1862.

Harrison, Carol E. "Patronage: Emulation for the Working Class." In *The Bourgeois Citizen in Nineteenth-Century France: Gender, Sociability, and the Uses of Emulation*, 123–56. Oxford: Oxford University Press, 1999.
Harvey, David. *A Companion to Marx's Capital*. London: Verso, 2010.
Haubtmann, Pierre. *Pierre-Joseph Proudhon: Sa vie et sa pensée, 1809–1849*. Paris: Beauchesne, 1982.
Hayat, Samuel. *Quand la République était révolutionnaire: Citoyenneté et représentation en 1848*. Paris: Seuil, 2014.
His Majesty's Commissioners. *Report from His Majesty's Commissioners for Inquiring into the Administration and Practical Operation of the Poor Laws*. London: B. Fellowes, Ludgate Street, 1834.
Horn, Jeff. *The Path Not Taken: French Industrialization in the Age of Revolution, 1750–1830*. Cambridge, MA: MIT Press, 2008.
Hugo, Victor. "Réponse de M. Victor Hugo, à la lettre écrite le 26 février 1841, par Savinien Lapointe." *La Ruche populaire*, March 1841.
Hustache, Pascale. "*Méphis*, Entre roman populaire et roman moral." In *Flora Tristan, George Sand et Pauline Roland: Les Femmes et l'invention d'une nouvelle morale 1830–1848*, edited by Maurice Agulhon and Stéphane Michaud, 49–60. Paris: Créaphis, 1994.
Institut Royal de France. Académie des sciences morales et politiques. *Règlement 1833*. Paris: Imprimerie de Firmin Didot Frères, 1833.
Jacoud, Gilles. *Jean Baptiste Say and Political Economy*. New York: Routledge, 2017.
Jameson, Fredric. "*La Cousine Bette* and Allegorical Realism." *PMLA* 86, no. 2 (1971): 241–54.
Jarrige, François. "The Contested Productivitity of the Baker's Body: Technology, Industrialization, and Labor in Nineteenth-Century France." In *Histories of Productivity: Genealogical Perspectives on the Body and Modern Economy*, edited by Peter-Paul Baniger and Mischa Suter, 92–112. New York and London: Routledge, 2017.
Jarrige, François, and Thomas Le Roux. *La Contamination du monde: Une histoire des pollutions à l'âge industriel*. Paris: Points, 2020.
Jasinski, René. *Les Années romantiques de Th. Gautier*. Paris: Vuibert, 1929.
Johnson, Christopher. *Utopian Communism in France: Cabet and the Icarians, 1839–1851*. Ithaca, NY: Cornell University Press, 1974.
Kalifa, Dominique. "Enquête et 'culture de l'enquête' au XIXe siècle." *Romantisme* 3, no. 149 (2010): 3–23.
Kalifa, Dominique, and Philippe Régnier. "'Séparatismes' médiatiques 1: Identités de classe." In *Civilisation du Journal*, edited by Dominique Kalifa, Philippe Régnier, Marie-Eve Thérenty, and Alain Vaillant, 1429–42. Paris: Nouveau Monde Editions, 2011.

Kaplan, Steven L. *Bread, Politics, and Political Economy in the Reign of Louis XV.* The Hague: Martinus Nijhoff, 1976.
Ladvocat, François. "Note pour Monsieur le ministre de l'intérieur sur les ouvriers imprimeurs." September 4, 1830. Reprinted in Chauvet, *Les Ouvriers du livre en France*, 645–48.
Lafargue, Paul. *Karl Marx, His Life and Work.* New York: International Publishers, 1943.
Lamartine, Alphonse de. "Du droit au travail et de l'organisation du travail." In *La France Parlementaire (1834–1851)*, 4:103–21. Paris: A. Lacroix, Verboeckhoven et Cie., 1865.
Larousse, Pierre. *Grand Dictionnaire universel du XIXe siècle: Français, historique, géographique, mythologique, bibliographique, littéraire, artistique, scientifique*, vol. 9. Paris: Administration du grand dictionnaire universel, 1876.
Le Hir, Marie-Pierre. "The *Société des Gens de Lettres* and French Socialism: Association as Resistance to the Industrialization and Censorship of the Press." *Nineteenth-Century French Studies* 24, nos. 3–4 (1996): 306–18.
Leroux, Pierre. *De l'humanité, de son principe et de son avenir, où se trouve exposée la vraie définition de la religion et où l'on explique le sens, la suite et l'enchaînement du mosaïsme et du christianisme.* 2nd ed. 2 vols. Paris: Perrotin, 1845.
Lerminier, Eugène. "La Littérature des ouvriers." *Revue des deux mondes* 28 (1841): 955–76.
Lerner, Bettina. *Inventing the Popular: Printing, Politics, and Poetics.* New York: Routledge, 2018.
Lescart, Allan. *Splendeurs et misères de la grisette: Évolution d'une figure emblématique.* Paris: Honoré Champion, 2008.
Le Yaouanc, Moïse. *Nosographie de l'humanité balzacienne.* Paris: Librairie Maloine, 1959.
Lhéritier, Andrée. *Les Physiologies.* Paris: Université de Paris, Institut français de presse, 1958.
Lichtlé, Michel. "Balzac à l'école du droit." In *Balzac, le texte et la loi*, edited by Sophie Vanden Abeele, 137–56. Paris: Presses de l'université Paris-Sorbonne, 2012.
Littré, Émile. *Dictionnaire de la langue française.* Paris: Hachette, 1863–73.
Locke, John. "The Second Treatise on Civil Government" (1689). In *Two Treatises of Government and a Letter Concerning Toleration*, edited by Ian Shapiro. New Haven: Yale University Press, 2003.
Lorant, André. *Les Parents pauvres d'Honoré de Balzac. La Cousine Bette. Le Cousin Pons. Étude historique et critique.* Geneva: Droz, 1967.
Lyon-Caen, Judith. "Enquêtes, littérature et savoir sur le monde social en France dans les années 1840." *Revue d'histoire des sciences humaines* 2, no. 17 (2007): 99–118.

Lyon-Caen, Judith. *La Lecture et la vie: Les Usages du roman au temps de Balzac.* Paris: Tallandier, 2006.

Lyons, Martyn. "Les Bestsellers." In *Histoire de l'Edition française*, vol. 3, *Le Temps des éditeurs: Du romantisme à la Belle Epoque*, edited by Roger Chartier and Henri-Jean Martin 409–37. Paris: Fayard, 1989.

Lyons, Martyn. *Readers and Society in Nineteenth-Century France: Workers, Women, Peasants.* New York: Palgrave, 2001.

Le Maitron dictionnaire biographique mouvement ouvrier mouvement social (online resource). https://maitron.fr.

Marrinan, Michael. *Painting Politics for Louis-Philippe: Art and Ideology in Orléanist France, 1830–1848.* New Haven: Yale University Press, 1988.

Marx, Karl. *Capital: A Critique of Political Economy*, volume 1. Translated by Ben Fowkes. London: Penguin Classics, 1990.

Marx, Karl. *Capital: A Critique of Political Economy*, volume 3. Edited by Frederick Engels, translated by Ernest Untermann. Chicago: Charles H. Kerr & Company Classics, 1909.

Marx, Karl. *The Class Struggles in France (1848–1850).* London: Martin Lawrence, 1895.

Marx, Karl, and Frederick Engels. "Manifesto of the Communist Party." In *Marx/Engels Selected Works*, 1:98–137. Translated by Samuel Moore in cooperation with Frederick Engels. Moscow: Progress Publishers, 1969. https://www.marxists.org/archive/marx/works/1848/communist-manifesto/.

Mathias, Manon. "'L'esprit, le coeur et les bras': Rethinking Art as Labour in George Sand." *Modern Language Review* III, no. 1 (January 2016): 104–20.

Maurois, André. *Prométhée; ou, La vie de Balzac.* Paris: Flammarion, 1974.

Maza, Sarah. "The Failure of the 'Bourgeois Monarchy.'" In *The Myth of the French Bourgeoisie: An Essay on the Social Imaginary, 1750–1850*, 161–91. Cambridge, MA: Harvard University Press, 2005.

McIlvanney. Siobhán. *Figurations of the Feminine in the Early French Women's Press, 1758–1848.* Liverpool: Liverpool University Press, 2019.

Michaud, Stéphane. *Flora Tristan, 1803–1844.* Paris: Editions ouvrières, 1984.

Millot, Hélène. "Tradition(s) et Evolution: Les Chansons du compagnonnage." In *La Poésie populaire en France au XIXe siècle: Théories, pratiques et reception*, edited by Hélène Millot, Nathalie Vincent-Munnia, Marie-Claude Shapira, and Michele Fontana, 68–73. Tusson: Éditions du Lérot, 2005.

Millot, Hélène, and Corinne Saminadayar-Perrin, eds. *1848, une révolution du discours.* Saint-Etienne: Editions des Cahier intempestifs, 2001.

Ministère de l'intérieur. "En Guise de préface." In *Bulletins de la République émanés du Ministère de l'intérieur du 13 mars au 6 mai 1848: Collection complète avec une préface par un haut fonctionnaire en activité.* Paris: Bureau central, 1848.

Mirecourt, Eugène de. *Guizot.* Paris: G. Havard, 1855.

Mombert, Sarah. "Action politique et fiction Romanesque: La Révolution impossible d'Alexandre Dumas." In *1848, une révolution du discours*, edited by Hélène Millot and Corinne Saminadayar-Perrin, 171–89. Saint-Etienne: Editions des Cahier intempestifs, 2001.
Moreau de la Sarthe, Louis-Jacques. "Idée générale du système du docteur Gall." In *L'Art de connaître les hommes par la physionomie de Gaspard Lavater*. Paris: Depelafol, 1820.
Mortimer, Armine Kotin. *For Love or for Money: Balzac's Rhetorical Realism*. Columbus: Ohio State University Press, 2011.
Moses, Claire G., and Leslie W. Rabine. *Feminism, Socialism, and French Romanticism*. Bloomington: Indiana University Press, 1993.
Muret, Théodore. *L'Histoire par le theatre 1789–1851*. 3 vols. Paris: Amyot, 1865.
Nadaud, Martin. *Mémoires de Leonard, ancien garçon maçon*. Bourganeuf: A. Duboueix, 1895.
Nesci, Catherine. *Le Flâneur et les Flâneuses: Les Femmes et la ville à l'époque romantique*. Grenoble: Université Stendhal, 2007.
Oberthür, M., and Hélène Millot. "La Poésie populaire et la chanson face à la censure et à la répression." In *La Poésie populaire en France au XIXe siècle: Théories, pratiques et réception*, edited by Hélène Millot, Nathalie Vincent-Munnia, Marie-Claude Shapira, and Michele Fontana, 90–98. Tusson: Éditions du Lérot, 2005.
Oehler, Dolf. *Juin 1848, Le Spleen contre L'Oubli : Baudelaire, Flaubert, Heine, Herzen, Marx*. Paris: La Fabrique éditions, 2017.
Offen, Karen. *The Woman Question in France, 1400–1870*. Cambridge: Cambridge University Press, 2017.
O'Neil-Henry, Anne. *Mastering the Marketplace: Popular Literature in Nineteenth-Century France*. Lincoln: University of Nebraska Press, 2017.
Parent-Lardeur, Françoise. *Lire à Paris au temps de Balzac: Les Cabinets de lecture à Paris, 1815–1830*. Paris: EHESS, 1999.
Parmentier, Marie. *Paris; ou, Le Livre des cent-et-un: Anthologie*. Paris: Honoré Champion, 2015.
Pasco, Allan. *Balzac, Literary Sociologist*. New York: Palgrave Macmillan, 2016.
Paton, P. J., railroad worker. "Poésies sociales. *Le Chantier*. Poésies de Charles Poncy, de Toulon, ouvrier maçon. (Troisième article)." *L'Union*, April 1844.
Paton, P. J., railroad worker. "Simple exposé." *L'Union*, December 1843.
Perdiguier, Agricol. *Correspondance inédite avec George Sand et ses amis*. Edited by Jean Briquet. Paris: Éditions Klincksieck, 1966.
Perrot, Michelle. *Enquêtes sur la condition ouvrière en France au 19e siècle*. Paris: Microeditions Hachette, 1972.
Perrot, Michelle. *George Sand, politique et polémiques*. Paris: Imprimerie nationale, 1996.

Pezard, Emilie. "Le Romantisme 'frénétique': Histoire d'une appellation générique et d'un genre dans la critique de 1821 à 2010." PhD diss., University of Paris–Sorbonne, 2012.

Picot, Georges. *Concours de l'Académie: Sujets proposés, prix et récompenses décernés, liste des livres couronnés ou récompensés, 1834–1900.* Paris: Imprimerie Nationale, 1901.

Pigoreau, Alexandre-Nicolas. *Cinquième supplément à la Petite bibliographie biographico-romancière.* Paris: Pigoreau, February 1823.

Piketty, Thomas. "Inequality and Concentration: Preliminary Bearings." In *Capital in the Twenty-First Century*, 237–70. Cambridge, MA: Harvard University Press, 2014.

Pinkney, David. *The French Revolution of 1830.* Princeton: Princeton University Press, 1972.

Planche, Gustave. "La Journée d'un journaliste." In *Paris; ou, Le Livre des cent et un*, vol. 6. Paris: Ladvocat, 1832.

Les Pommes de terre au boisseau, 1848–49. Bibliothèque nationale de France, Tolbiac, rez-de-jardin. FOL-LC2–1957. http://ark.bnf.fr/ark:/12148/cb3284 1092k.

Pouillaude, ouvrier peintre en bâtiment. Letter to Eugène Sue (Paris, June 5 or 6, 1848). In *Correspondance d'Eugène Sue*, edited by Jean-Pierre Galvan, 3:476–77. Paris: Honoré Champion, 2010.

Preiss, Nathalie. *De la poire au parapluie: Physiologies politiques.* Paris: Honoré Champion, 1999.

Proudhon, Pierre-Joseph "Aux électeurs du Doubs." In *Correspondance de P.-J. Proudhon*, edited by J.-A. Langlois, 2:299–304. Paris: A. Lacroix et Cie, 1875.

Proudhon, Pierre-Joseph. "Ce que la révolution doit à la littérature." *Le Représentant du peuple*, May 28, 1848.

Proudhon, Pierre-Joseph. *Oeuvres complètes de P.-J. Proudhon.* 15 vols. Edited by C. Bouglé and H. Moysset. Paris: M. Rivière, 1926.

Puech, Jules. *La Vie et l'œuvre de Flora Tristan: 1803–1844.* Paris: Marcel Rivière, 1925.

Pyat, Félix. *Le Chiffonnier de Paris. Drame. Edition originale du 24 février 1848, non censurée par la Royauté.* In *Anthologie du mélodrame classique*, edited by Peter Brooks and Myriam Faten Sfar, 867–1054. Paris: Classiques Garnier, 2011.

Rabinbach, Anson. *The Human Motor: Energy, Fatigue, and the Origins of Modernity.* New York: Basic Books, 1990.

Rancière, Jacques. *Mute Speech: Literature, Critical Theory, and Politics.* Translated by James Swenson. New York: Columbia University Press, 2011.

Rancière, Jacques. "The Myth of the Artisan: Critical Reflections on a Category of Social History," trans. David H. Lake, *International Labor and Working-Class History* 24 (1983): 1–16.

Rancière, Jacques. "Le Prolétaire et son double; ou, Le Philosophe inconnu." In *Les Scènes du peuple* 21–33. Lyon: Horlieu éditeur, 2003.
Reboul, Jean. *Poésies*. Brussels: E. Laurent, 1836.
Régnier, Philippe. "Les Saint-Simoniens, le prêtre et l'artiste." *Romantisme*, no. 67 (1990): 31–46.
Ribard, Dinah. "De l'écriture à l'événement: Acteurs et histoire de la poésie ouvrière autour de 1840." *Revue d'histoire du XIXe siècle*, no. 32 (2006): 79–91.
Ricardo, David. *On the Principles of Political Economy and Taxation*. 3rd ed. London: John Murray, 1821. https://www.econlib.org/library/Ricardo/ricP.html?chapter_num=2#book-reader.
Richter, Noé. "Les Bibliothèques populaires et la lecture ouvrière." In *Histoire des bibliothèques françaises*, vol 3, *Les Bibliotheques de la Revolution et du XIXe siècle 1789–1914*, edited by Dominique Varry, 513–36. Paris: Éditions du Cercle de la librairie, 2009.
Riot-Sarcey, Michèle. "Le Passé du présent." In *Balzac et le politique*, edited by Boris Lyon-Caen and Marie-Ève Thérenty, 73–82. Saint-Cyr-sur-Loire: Pirot, 2007.
Riot-Sarcey, Michele. *Le Réel de l'utopie*. Paris: Bibliothèque Albin-Michel, 1998.
Robb, Graham. *Balzac*. London: Picador, 1994.
Rodrigues, Olinde. *Poésies sociales des ouvriers*. Paris: Paulin, 1841.
Roly, Michel. "L'Amour de la gloire." *La Ruche populaire*, March 1841, 27–28.
Rosanvallon, Pierre. *Le Moment Guizot*. Paris: Gallimard, 1985.
Rosanvallon, Pierre. *The New Social Question: Rethinking the Welfare State*. Translated by Barbara Harshav. Princeton: Princeton University Press, 2000.
Rousseau, James. *Physiologie de la portière*. Paris: Aubert, 1841.
Sabatier, Guy. *Le Mélodrame de la République sociale et le théâtre de Félix Pyat*. 2 vols. Paris: L'Harmattan, 1999.
Sainte-Beuve, Charles Augustin. "De la littérature industrielle." *Revue des deux mondes* 19 (1839): 675–91.
Saint-Simon, Henri. *Œuvres complètes*. Edited by Juliette Grange, Pierre Musso, Philippe Régnier, and Frank Yonnet. 4 vols. Paris: Presses universitaires de France, 2012.
Samson, Véronique, and Mathieu Roger-Lacan. *1848 et la littérature*. Paris: Colloques Fabula, 2021. https://www.fabula.org/colloques/sommaire6982.php.
Sand, George. *The Journeyman Joiner; or, The Companion of the Tour of France*. Translated by Francis George Shaw. New York: H. Fertig, 1976.
Say, Jean-Baptiste. Notes on *Des principes de l'économie politique, et de L'impôt par M. David Ricardo, traduit de l'anglais par F. S. Constancio avec des notes explicatives et critiques, par M. Jean-Baptiste Say*. Paris: Chez J. P. Aillaud, 1819.
Say, Jean-Baptiste. *Traité d'économie politique; ou, Simple exposition de la manière dont se forment, se distribuent et se consomment les richesses*. 1803. E-book by Institut Coppet, 2011. https://www.institutcoppet.org/wp-content/uploads/2011/12/Traite-deconomie-politique-Jean-Baptiste-Say.pdf.

Schor, Naomi. *George Sand and Idealism*. New York: Columbia University Press, 1993.
Scott, Joan Wallach. "Work Identities for Men and Women: The Politics of Work and Family in the Parisian Garment Trades in 1848." In *Gender and the Politics of History*, 93–112. Rev. ed. New York: Columbia University Press, 1999.
Sewell, William Hamilton. *Work and Revolution in France: The Language of Labor from the Old Regime to 1848*. Cambridge: Cambridge University Press, 1980.
Sieyès, Emmanuel-Joseph. "What Is the Third Estate?" Translated by M. Blondel and edited by S. E. Finer. London: Phaidon Press Ltd., 1964. Reprinted in *University of Chicago Readings in Western Civilization*, volume 7, *The Old Regime and the French Revolution*, edited by Keith M. Baker, 154–79. Chicago: University of Chicago Press, 1987.
Sipe, Daniel. *Text, Image, and the Problem with Perfection in Nineteenth-Century France: Utopia and Its Afterlives*. London: Routledge, 2016.
Smith, Adam. *An Inquiry into the Nature and Causes of the Wealth of Nations*, 1776. E-book edition by Jonathan Bennett, 2017. https://www.earlymoderntexts.com/assets/pdfs/smith1776_1.pdf.
Spang, Rebecca. *Stuff and Money in the Time of the French Revolution*. Cambridge, MA: Harvard University Press, 2015.
Spary, Emma. *Feeding France: New Sciences of Food, 1760–1815*. Cambridge: Cambridge University Press, 2014.
Staël, Germaine de. *Corinne; ou, L'Italie. Œuvres*. Edited by Catriona Seth. Paris: Gallimard, 2017.
Stearns, Peter. "Patterns of Industrial Strike Activity in France during the July Monarchy." *American Historical Review* 70, no. 2 (1965): 371–94.
Stern, Daniel (pseud. Marie d'Agoult). "Le Compagnon du Tour de France de George Sand (Variétés)." *La Presse*, January 9, 1841.
Stiénon, Valérie. *La Littérature des physiologies: Sociopoétique d'un genre panoramique, 1830–1845*. Paris: Classiques Garnier, 2012.
Sue, Eugène. *The Mysteries of Paris* [*MP*]. 3 vols. Translated by [unattributed]. New York: Peter Fenelon Collier & Son, 1900. https://catalog.hathitrust.org/Record/012468851.
Sue, Eugène. *The Wandering Jew* [*WJ*]. 3 parts. Translated by [unattributed]. London and New York: George Routledge and Sons, 1889. https://www.gutenberg.org/cache/epub/3350/pg3350-images.html.
Sutton, Robert P. *Les Icariens: The Utopian Dream in Europe and America*. Urbana and Chicago: University of Illinois Press, 1994.
Texier, Edmond. *Physiologie du poète*. Paris: Aubert, 1842.
Thérenty, Marie-Ève. "Mysterymania: Essor et limites de la globalisation culturelle au XIXe siècle." *Romantisme* 160, no. 2 (2013): 53–64.

Thérenty, Marie-Ève, and Alain Vaillant. *1836, L'an 1 de l'ère médiatique: Étude littéraire et historique du journal* La Presse *d'Emile de Girardin*. Paris: Nouveau monde, 2001.
Thiesse, Anne-Marie. "Le Roman populaire." In *Histoire de l'Edition française*, vol. 3, *Le Temps des éditeurs: Du romantisme à la Belle Epoque*, edited by Roger Chartier and Henri-Jean Martin, 509–25. Paris: Fayard, 1989.
Thiher, Allen. *Fiction Rivals Science: The French Novel from Balzac to Proust*. Columbia: University of Missouri Press, 2001.
Thompson, E. P. "The Moral Economy of the Crowd in the Eighteenth Century." *Past and Present* 50, no. 1 (1971): 76–136.
Tilly, Louise, and Joan Wallach Scott. *Women, Work, and Family*. New York and London: Routledge, 1987.
Toulotte, Muriel. *Etienne Arago, 1802–1892: Une vie, un siècle*. Perpignan: Publications de l'Olivier, 1993.
Tourte, Francis. "L'Épée et le Marteau." *La Ruche populaire*, May 1841.
Tristan, Flora. *Mephis*. Paris: Éditions Indigo & Côté Femmes, 1996.
Vaillant, Alain. *L'Histoire littéraire*. 2nd ed. Paris: Armand Collin, 2017.
Vannostal, typographer. "Aux travailleurs." *La Ruche populaire*, January 1840, 4.
Varin, Emile. "A tous." *La Ruche populaire*, December 1839.
Vergé, Charles-Henri. "Séance du 9 Mai 1840." In *Séances et travaux de l'Académie des sciences morales et politiques: Comptes rendus publiés dans le Moniteur Universel par MM. Ch. Vergé et Loiseau. Années 1840 et 1841*. Paris: Alphonse Picard et Fils, 1893.
Verley, Patrick. *La Révolution industrielle*. Paris: Gallimard, 1997.
Vigier, Philippe. *La Seconde République (Que sais-je?)* 8th ed. Paris: Presses Universitaires de France, 2001.
Vila, Anne C. *Suffering Scholars: Pathologies of the Intellectual in Enlightenment France*. Philadelphia: University of Pennsylvania Press, 2018.
Villermé, Louis-René. *Tableau de l'état physique et moral des ouvriers employés dans les manufactures de coton, de laine et de soie: Ouvrage entrepris par ordre et sous les auspices de l'Académie des sciences morales et politiques*. 2 vols. Paris: Jules Renouard et cie., 1840.
Vinçard, [Jules]. "Aux fondateurs de *La Ruche*." *La Ruche populaire*, December 1841.
Vinçard, [Jules]. "Chronique." *L'Union*, March 1844.
Vinçard, Jules. "De la populace: A propos du discours académique de M. Victor Hugo." *La Ruche populaire*, June 1841.
Vinçard, [Jules]. "De l'importance du journalisme." *La Ruche populaire*, December 1842.
Vinçard, [Jules]. "Lettre adressée à M. Dutacq, gérant du journal *Le Siècle*." *La Ruche populaire*, December 1839.

Voilquin, Suzanne. *Souvenirs d'une fille du peuple; ou, La Saint-simonienne en Egypte*. Introduction by Lydia Elhadad. Paris: F. Maspero, 1978.

Watrelot, Martine. "Introduction" and "Réception du *Compagnon du Tour de France* au XIXe siècle." In George Sand, *Le Compagnon du Tour de France*, critical edition by Martine Watrelot, 7–34 and 495–511. Paris: Honoré Champion, 2022.

Watrelot, Martine. "La Réception du roman *Le Compagon du Tour de France.*" In Le Compagnon du Tour de France *de George Sand*, edited by Martine Watrelot and Michèle Hecquet, 155–67. Lille: Éditions du Conseil scientifique de l'Université Charles-de-Gaulle–Lille, 2009.

Weinstein, Cindy. *The Literature of Labor and the Labors of Literature: Allegory in Nineteenth-Century American Fiction*. Cambridge: Cambridge University Press, 1995.

White, Claire. "George Sand, Digging." In *The Labour of Literature in Britain and France, 1830–1910*, edited by Marcus Waithe and Claire White, 61–78. London: Palgrave, 2018.

Woloch, Alex. *The One vs. the Many: Minor Characters and the Space of the Protagonist in the Novel*. Princeton: Princeton University Press, 2003.

Zancarini-Fournel, Michelle. *Les Luttes et les rêves: Une histoire populaire de la France de 1685 à nos jours*. Paris: Zones, 2016.

INDEX

Illustrations are indicated by italicized page numbers.

Académie des science morales et politiques, 18; creation of fictional social group by, 93–94; on ending of slavery, 93; *enquêtes* compared to fiction of Cabet and Sand, 111; goal to cultivate docile and orderly workforce, 93, 111; governance and membership of, 91–92; Guizot reinstituting, 90; industrial mentality of, 15; influence of, 90, 93; liberal focus on suffering of laboring classes, 92; literary allusions in reports published by, 85–88; situating labor at intersection of morality and political economy, 94; workers as focus of, 2

Académie française, conservative stance on linguistic change, 12. See also *Dictionnaire de l'Académie Française, Le*

Agulhon, Maurice, 8

allegories in Balzac's work, 19, 59, 67, 77, 166–71

Angenot, Marc, 39

Arago, Etienne: political positions held by, 175; "La République et les artistes," 30; *27, 28 et 29 juillet, tableau épisodique des trois journées* (vaudeville), 29–30, 41, 175, 185n27

aristocracy: Balzac's character Henri de Marsay (*La Fille aux yeux d'or*), 49, 60, 65, 68, 73; Balzac's critique of (*La Duchesse de Langeais*), 75; Balzac's origins, 3; bourgeoisie's displacement of, 56, 75, 129; Guizot's view of new elite as, 34, 91; Louis-Philippe's origins, 28; Saint-Simon's origins, 32; in Sand's and Cabet's work, 104, 106, 107; in Tristan's *Mephis*, 117, 118

Artisan, L,' journal de la classe ouvrière (The artisan: Journal of the laboring class), 114, 115, 119

artistic creation and genius: artistic motivation, 73; labor and, 70–71; in Romanticism, 54; valuing of, 54–55

Art pour l'Art, L' (Art for Art's Sake) movement, 40–41

Assemblée Constituante, 46–47, 174

Assemblée Nationale, 175

Atelier, L' (newspaper), 35, 113, 130, 133

ateliers nationaux (national workshops), 46–47, 175

ateliers sociaux (social workshops), 46

audience. See readership

average man. See *homme moyen*

Balzac, Honoré de: allegories, use of, 19, 59, 67, 77, 166–71; bestseller status never achieved by, 169; Brillat-Savarin as influence on, 55; as Catholic, 3; characters from different classes in, 147; *Le Chef-d'œuvre inconnu* (The Unknown Masterpiece), 70–71; compared to Sue, 166–70; competitive streak of, 160–62; as contributor to Ladvocat's series, 29; critical reception of, 169; *La Cousine Bette*, 160, 163–67; *Le Cousin Pons*, 160, 162–64; deviating from pro-industry climate in France, 169; *La Duchesse de Langeais*, 75; Dumas as competitor of, 38, 162; Dumas's characters copied by, 164; *Eugénie Grandet*, 55–56, 74; *La Fausse Maitresse*, 161; *Ferragus*, 65–68; as *feuilletoniste*, 19, 160–61; *La Fille aux yeux d'or*, 49–50, 65; *Gobseck*, 60, 62;

211

Balzac, Honoré de (*continued*)
Illusions perdues, 40–41; knowledge reached through empirical science, reason, and blind faith, 58; on laborer as "*un moyen*," 146; "Lettre adressée aux écrivains," 49, 59, 69; "Lettre sur le travail" (posthumously published), 4, 11, 55, 176–77; Madame Hanska and, 160–61, 162, 177–78; *Le Médecin de campagne* (*The Country Doctor*), 69–70, 151; *Modeste Mignon*, 161; as monarchist, 3; obsession with money and economics, 49–50, 55, 56, 74, 160–61; *La Peau de chagrin* (*The Wild Ass's Skin*), 57–59, 60, 64, 72–73, 77, 78, 166–67; *Le Père Goriot*, 74; Peytel Affair (1839) and, 124–25; physiological reading of subjects' bodies and facial features, 51–52, 67, 86, 90; *La Physiologie du mariage*, 51, 55, 57, 59–60; on political economy, 55–56; *La Recherche de l'absolu* (*The Quest of the Absolute*), 56, 60–61, 64; Romanticism of, 8, 146; on social problems of his day, 162, 176; *Splendeurs et misères des courtisans*, 161–62; Sue's formula adopted by, 160–62, 164, 169, 170; "La Théorie de la démarche," 62, 67, 72; "La Théorie de la volonté," 73; *Thirteen* trilogy, 65, 75; "Le Traité de la vie élégante," 68–69, 74–75; unifying all of humanity through theory of energy, 59; *La Vieille Fille*, 141; working-class characters created by, 68, 82, 160–63, 170; on working-class movement, 177; writers' union, founding of, 38, 122, 161; on writing as labor, 19, 38, 39, 169. See also *Comédie humaine, La*; literary labor theory of Balzac; *Parents pauvres, Les*; "Physionomies parisiennes"

Barba, J. N., 29
Barbéris, Pierre, 56
Barillot (lithographer-songwriter), 137
Barrault, Emile, 138; *Aux artistes*, 17
barricades in Paris, 30, 47
Barthes, Roland, 6–9, 181

Baudelaire, Charles, 9, 182; "Le Cygne" (the swan), 182
Bénichou, Paul, 109
Benjamin, Walter, 37, 148
Benoît, Joseph, 98
Béranger, Pierre-Jean de, 99, 114–15, 121, 137
Biard, Gustave, 128
biblical analogies, 105, 110, 130–31
Bichat, Xavier, 12, 62
Blanc, Louis, 3; *ateliers sociaux* (social workshops) and, 46; on Cabet, 98; "Declaration of the *droit au travail*," 22; on guarantee of work, 14; on moral order, 36; *L'Organisation du travail*, 14, 31, 36, 46, 93, 177, 184n28; in Provisional Government, 184n28; as socialist, 32, 45. See also Luxembourg Commission
Blanqui, Adolphe, 32
Blanqui, Auguste, 31, 32
Boccaccio, Giovanni, 147
Boissy (artisan), "Aux philosophes" (To the philosophers), 128–29
Bonhomme, Claude. See Saint-Simon, Henri de Rouvoy de
boulanger, equating creative artist with, 1–2
Bourbon monarchy, end of, 2, 27–28, 30
Bourbon Restoration (1814–30), 43, 53, 75, 177
Bourdieu, Pierre, 7–8; *The Rules of Art*, 7
bourgeoisie: attitude toward working classes, 92, 127; as audience, 10, 140; Balzac's fascination with, 56; in Balzac's social system, 73, 124–25; "bourgeois emulation," 127; as constructor of modern society, 70; Doctrinaires and, 34; expansion in eighteenth and nineteenth centuries, 147; Louis-Philippe's association with, 28, 32; meaning of, 32; political economy and, 56; printworkers and, 114–15; rise of, 31–37; *La Ruche* and, 127, 134; Vinçard and, 113
bourgeoisies, value of productivism and, 145
Bowman, Frank Paul, 131

Boyer, Adolphe, 132
Brillat-Savarin, Jean Anthelme, *Physiologie du gout; ou, Méditations de gastronomie transcendante* (*The Physiology of Taste; or, Meditations on Transcendent Gastronomy*), 51, 55
Brisset, M.-J., *Le Cabinet de lecture*, 44
Britain: abolishment of slavery in colonies of, 93; fashionable society in, 68; industrialization in, 23–24, 26; patrimonial wealth system in, 74; political economists on value in, 77; Poor Laws (1834), 84; poverty in, 82
British Modernism, 147
Brix, Michael, 54
Broussais, François, 62
Buchez, Philippe, 130
Buffon, comte de, 57
Bulletins de la République, 176
Buret, Eugène: award for study of French pauperism, 81; hyperbole, use of, 85; literacy and, 43; literary tools enabling reconciliation of harms of labor with benefits of labor, 89; *De la misère des classes laborieuses en Angleterre et en France . . .* (On the misery of the working classes in England and France . . .), 81–85, 94, 97; theatrical scenes in reports by, 90; Villermé and, 86
Byron, Lord, 95

Cabet, Etienne, 18, 32, 44; Buret compared to, 97; as communist, 98, 112; Fourier's influence on, 108; influence of, 98; labor as mark of honor for, 104–5; mainstream Left and moderate newspapers ignoring, 98–99; public reception of new worker-hero of, 97–98; Romantic hero and, 95–96, 107; as social progressive valuing individuals for the good they bring to society, 103; solidarity promoted between workers and writers, 111; utopianism of, 31, 98, 107–9, 146; weekly salon held by, 98. See also *Populaire, Le*; *Voyage en Icarie*

cabinets de lecture (reading rooms), 43–44
Carnot, Sadi, 59, 71
Catholic Church, libraries established by, 43
Cavaignac, Louis-Eugène, 47
censorship, 2, 7, 28–29, 31, 114
Chaisemartin, Amélie de, 146–47, 160
Chaptal, Jean-Antoine, 23
Chapuys-Montlaville, Benoît-Marie, 120, 136
character development, 146–54; Balzac's physiological reading of subjects' bodies and facial features, 51–52, 67, 86, 90; *chiffonnier* as ubiquitous stereotype in novels, 174; fictional vs. sociological, 146–47; Forster's characters, classic distinctions of, 147; in literary works of 1830s and 1840s as "types," 146–47; *portière* as ubiquitous stereotype in novels, 148–49, 162; round vs. flat, 147–49, 153, 154, 157, 160, 164–65, 169; shrinking significance of hero in nineteenth-century novels, 147; Sue's mastery of, 145, 148, 152. See also *Juif errant, Le*; *Mystères de Paris*; Romantic hero; working-class hero
Charivari, Le (newspaper), 175
Charles X (French king), 2, 28
Chassériau, Théodore, *Une forge au Creusot* (The forge at Le Creusot), 24–25, 25
Chateaubriand, 54, 116, 117, 137; *René*, 95, 146
Chaucer, Geoffrey, 147
Chevalier, Louis, 92
Chevasco, Berry, 141, 194n4
chiffonnier as ubiquitous stereotype in novels, 174
child labor, 88–89
chômeurs (unemployed workers), 47
Cixous, Hélène, *The Laugh of the Medusa*, 115
class alienation: Reboul and, 117; Sand's Pierre in *Travels* experiencing, 105–6; utopianism offered as solution to, 108; Vinçard accusing Balzac of, 125

Cohen, Margaret, 106
Cole, Joshua, 54
collective duty, 20, 106
colportage, 140
Comédie humaine, La (*The Human Comedy*; Balzac), 50, 161–62; "Avant-Propos" to, 36, 57–58, 162; Marx planning to write book on, 79; metaphysics and, 61; money's relationship with social distinctions, 76; no social justice in, 164; tragic heroes as moral paragons in, 79; worker as "winch" or mere type in, 146; working classes absent from, 68
commercial literature. See "Industrial Literature"
commodities: Marx on valuation of, 79; Smith on valuation of, 52, 77; social context of, 79; value determined by labor to create, 77–78
communism, 98, 107–8, 112
Compagnon du Tour de France, Le (*The Journeyman Joiner; or, The Companion of the Tour of France*; Sand), 31, 39, 94–100, 102–11; balance of Pierre's desire to learn and duty to work, 102; critical reception of, 99; honor as part of nobility, 105–6; hope for society's future in, 111; incomplete love story of Pierre (carpenter) and Yseult (aristocrat), 96–97; nobility as part of Pierre's working-class heroism, 102–5; Perdiguier's work providing inspiration for, 100; Pierre as epitome of working-class virtue and attractiveness, 97; Pierre compared to Jesus Christ, 97, 105, 106, 130–31; Pierre's ability to recognize truth, 103–4; Pierre's intellectual superiority, 102; Pierre viewed as idealized character of proletarian sublime, 107; realism in, 109–10; Romantic hero in, 95, 96–97; as success and in multiple printings, 99; Tristan and, 119; utopianism in, 107, 111; working-class audience for, 99–100; Yseult's Christian virtues, 110

compagnonnage, 100, 121
competition in literary marketplace, 159–62, 170
Comte, Auguste, 41; *First Course on Positive Philosophy*, 179
Condillac, Etienne Bonnot de, 34
Condorcet, Nicolas de, *Troisième Mémoire sur l'instruction publique*, 42
confection (piecework), 26
conservative politicians (1848), 14, 21, 99
Constant, Benjamin, 54
Constituent Assembly (*Assemblée Constituante*), 46–47, 174
Constitution (France, 1848), 14, 47–48, 175
Constitutionnel, Le (newspaper), 28, 136; Balzac publishing letter of candidature in, 177; Sue's *Le Juif errant* published as serial in, 136, 141–42
copyright and reuse of other's literary creation: collective action to pursue, 3, 183n7; government's enforcement failure, 2, 3; modifying existing tropes as common practice, 161, 174
Coriolis, Gaspard-Gustave, 71
Cormenin, Louis de, 43
Cottin, Sophie, 106
Courrier français, Le (newspaper), 141
Cousin, Victor, 34, 72–73, 76, 92
Craiutu, Aurelian, 90
creative artists. *See* artistic creation and genius; literary authors
creative destruction, 58, 60–61, 64
Creusot, Le, 25–26
cross-class solidarity, 4, 19; *cabinets de lecture* (reading rooms) and, 43–44; Provisional Government and, 23
Curmer, Léon, 43
currency, instability of, 74–76
Cuvier, Georges, 57
Cuvillier, Armand, 31

d'Agoult, Marie, 99
Dante, *Inferno*, 85
Daumier, Honoré, 38, 148
dehumanization, 24, 81, 89

Delacroix, Eugène, 99
Delessert, François, 43
Delmas, Corinne, 91
democratization, 9, 19, 83, 91, 120, 147
desire: arbitrary value of object of, 77; Cabet's concept of society and, 109; as destructive force, 73–74, 77; as most powerful human faculty, 76
deskilling, 3, 26–27, 41, 105
Desplanche (tailor), as founder of *L'Union* with Vinçard, 129–30
de Staël, Germaine (Madame), 41, 54; *Corinne; ou, L'Italie*, 54, 71, 146
Destutt de Tracy, Antoine, 91–92
Dézamy, Théodore, 98
Dickens, Charles, 147
Dictionnaire de l'Académie Française, Le: on *"littérateur,"* 120, 192n16; on *"mouvement,"* 63, 189n32; on *"noble,"* 103, 191n47; on *"travail,"* 11–12
difficulty of authorship, 7
Doctrinaires (political party), 24, 32, 34, 58, 72, 90–91
drinking habit, as vice of working classes, 66, 67, 85, 89
droit au travail (right to work), 11–14, 47–48; derivation of word *"travail,"* 11; of equal importance to writer as to manual laborer, 175; Lamartine offering support for, 175; Marxism and, 31–32; as Revolution of 1848 issue, 3, 22
droit du travail (Turgot), 11
Duchet, Claude, 6–7
Dufoux (farmer), "Le Songe" (The dream), 128–29
Dumas, Alexandre: "Aux Travailleurs," 179; Balzac as competitor of, 38, 162; Balzac copying characters of, 164; "Ce que la révolution doit à la littérature," 180; *Comte de Monte Cristo*, 141, 161, 164; as politician, 39, 178–80; Proudhon on, 179–80; Reboul and, 116, 117, 126, 138; serial novels and melodramas by, 39, 141; *Les Trois Mousquetaires*, 141; Vinçard and, 138–39

Dumont, Ernestine, 145
Dunoyers, Charles, 36
Dupin, Charles: on child labor, 88; *Forces productives*, 33, 36–37, 84; on morality and nobility of industry, 36–37; *Petit Producteur français*, 34; on taxonomic understanding of *travail* and productive forces, 33
Duquenne (*ouvrier imprimeur*), 128
Duras, Claire de, 41, 106
Dutacq, Armand, 40, 120, 122, 124–26. See also *Siècle, Le*
Duveau, Georges, 5–6, 8, 13–14, 45, 183n11

economic liberalism, 3, 27, 34, 52, 53, 91
écriture, Barthes on, 6–7
education: attainment level of French men, 42; Cousin's design of national curriculum, 72; Enquête Guizot (1833) to investigate primary schools, 91
empirical studies, 15, 36, 50, 58, 84–87, 89–93, 111
energy: Balzac's fascination with, 62–63; conservation vs. *mouvement*, 63; diversion of rebellious energy into manual labor, 88; economy of, 59–77; Helmholtz's discovery of *Kraft* as universal force, 71; labor energy, 63, 71, 105; limited vital energy, 62; metaphysical nature of, 61; *Organicistes* vs. *Vitalistes*, 61–62; Paris neighborhoods characterized by, 65; Sand adopting Balzac's logic of labor energy, 105; scarcity of, 60; science of, 12, 57–59
Enfantin, Prosper, 115
Enfants de Paris, Les; ou, Les Petits Patriotes (children's book), 30
Engels, Friedrich, 31; Balzac as inspiration for, 79–80; *The Communist Manifesto* (with Marx), 108; on utopianism and French communism, 107–8
England. *See* Britain
Enlightenment, 11, 12, 41, 51, 108
Enquête Guizot (1833), 91
enquêtes, 86–91, 100, 111

factory system, 27; factory workers, 2, 25–27, 41, 42, 86; labor organization's influence on, 93
February Revolution. *See* Revolution of 1848
Femme de l'avenir, La (newspaper), 115
Femme libre, La (newspaper), 22, 115
Femme nouvelle, La (newspaper), 115
Fénelon, François, *Télémaque*, 140
Fessart, Auguste, 161
feuilletons. *See romans-feuilletons*
Féval, Paul: Balzac viewing as rival, 161; *Les Mystères de Londres*, 141
Flaubert, Gustave, 5–9; Balzac compared to, 7–8, 9; Bourdieu on, 7; *L'Education sentimentale*, 5; *Madame Bovary*, 5; on priceless nature of his work, 7; Revolution of 1848 and, 8, 9, 180; socialism and, 9
Flemish people, Balzac's assessment of, 56
Fleury, Elisa, 131
Flocon, Ferdinand, 184n28
Forster, E. M., 147, 151, 160
Foucault, Michel, 88
Fourier, Charles, 32; *Le Nouveau Monde industriel*, 108; *Théorie des quatre mouvements et des destinées générales*, 108; as utopian thinker, 108–9
Fourierists as utopians, 108–9
Français peints par eux-mêmes, Les (panoramic works), 38
France Nouvelle, La (newspaper), 180
Franklin, Benjamin, *Poor Richard's Almanac*, 42
Frégier, Antoine: *Des classes dangereuses de la population dans les grandes villes, et des moyens de les rendre meilleures* (Of the dangerous classes of the population in large cities, and how to improve them), 83–85, 89–90, 93–94; Villermé and, 86
French Revolution (1789): excesses of, 34; guilds outlawed by, 100; monetary collapse following, 75; motivation for, 1, 74; Saint-Simon and, 16, 32

Fugère, Henri, 128
Furst, Lilian, 95, 97

Gall, Franz Joseph, 51
Garnier, Joseph, 47–48
Garnier-Pagès, Louis, 22
Gauny, Gabriel, 39, 126
Gautier, Théophile, 39–41
Girardin, Emile de: benefiting from cheap literary labor, 40; on improved working conditions, 47; literacy and, 43; on literature's association with commerce, 120. *See also Presse, La*
Goethe, Johann von, *The Sufferings of Young Werther*, 95–96
Goldstein, Jan, 72
Goulet, Andrea, 86
Greppo, Louis, 175
grisettes, 66–67, 102, 145, 150, 152, 189n35
guilds, 11, 27, 100
Guizot, François, 28, 34–35, 53, 90–91. *See also* Doctrinaires
Guizot Law (1833), 42, 91

Habermas, Jürgen, 114
Hanska, Madame, 160–61, 162, 177–78
Harrison, Carol E., 127
Haussmann, Georges Eugène (baron), 65
Hawthorne, Nathaniel, "The Birth Mark," 168–69
Hayat, Samuel, 8
Heine, Heinrich, 9
Helmholtz, Hermann von, 71–72
hero. *See* Romantic hero; working-class hero
high society, 68–69, 75
homme moyen (average man), 53, 68, 146
honor of working-class hero, 104–6
Huart, Louis, *Physiologie de la grisette*, 66
Hugo, Victor: as contributor to Ladvocat's series, 29; language use of, 5; letter exchanges with *La Ruche* contributors, 126–27; *Marion de Lorme*, 185n27; *Les Misérables*, 30; *Orientales* (poetry), 42; Proudhon on, 179; Romanticism and,

8, 42, 126; satirized by Texier, 38–39; support for worker-poets, 39; Vinçard and, 127, 138
human capital, energy as part of, 59
human faculties, Cousin's categorization of, 72
humanism, 82
humanity, 108

idlers, 16, 67, 68, 73
illiterate workers: reading aloud to, 44, 98; songs as way to spread messages to, 121
individualism, 52, 53, 106
industrialization, 23–26; allegory genre and, 168; artistic representation of, 24–25, 25; bourgeois and, 32; of literature, 39; national importance of, 36; productivity increase and, 79; unregulated, effects of, 81–82
"Industrial Literature," 40, 120, 122, 133
inheritance and pension, in Balzac's *La Cousine Bette* and *Le Cousin Pons*, 160, 163–65, 167
Institut de France, 83, 91
instructive books, 42
invisible hand theory, 52

Jameson, Fredric, 74
Jesuits, 142, 144
Journal des débats, Le: Balzac publishing letter of candidature in, 177; Dumas's *Les Trois Mousquetaires* published as serial in, 141; as popular daily, 135; replacing Balzac with Dumas, 161; Sue's *Mystères de Paris* published as serial in, 141, 174
Journal des économistes, 53
Journal des ouvriers, Le (The laborers' journal), 114
Juif errant, Le (*The Wandering Jew*; Sue): Balzac seeking to capitalize on success of, 163; as critique of criminal justice system, 144, 170; as critique of labor's failure to organize, 144, 170; direct dialogue and realist descriptions, 167–68; first published as serial in *Le Constitutionnel*, 136, 141–42; La Mayeux as worker-poet, 156; La Mayeux's frugality and industriousness, 152–53; La Mayeux's physical disability, 152, 156; La Mayeux's poverty despite quality of work production, 152–53, 154, 156; pathos heightened by La Mayeux's purity of heart, 156; plot summary, 142; success of, 158; women-workers as underpaid, 152, 156–57
July Monarchy (1830–48), 2; Balzac's criticism of, 3; character study of great interest in, 146; complexity of literary environment associated with, 10; economic policy, 35, 60; industrialization and, 3, 24, 26; literacy and, 43; Napoleon III compared to, 8; newspapers in, 122; novelists and, 38; popular publications reinforcing imagery of, 30; Say in, 53; social movements of, 5; sociopolitical world's relationship with literature in, 7, 27, 41, 170; worker-writers' productions and, 114–19, 138; working classes and, 30, 113
July Revolution (1830), 2, 18, 27–31, 114, 119
June Days (June 22–26, 1848), 4, 8, 9, 14, 47

Kalifa, Dominique, 89
Kock, Paul de: as contributor to Ladvocat's series, 29; *portière* as ubiquitous stereotype in novels of, 148–49

labor: abstract notion of value of, 77; *Arbeitskraft* as term for power of workforce, 71–72; artistic efforts as, 70–71; Balzac's treatment compared to Sue's, 164–65, 170; Bette's (in Balzac's *La Cousine Bette*) ability to avoid, 165; broad definition of, 70, 80, 94; child labor, 88–89; decay resulting when nonexistent, 66; destructive effects on human body, 87, 89, 151; in discourse of

labor (continued)
Balzac's day, 2; *droit du travail* and, 11; as economically and socially fruitless, 153, 154; as form of energy, 59–71; hard work as a virtue, 56, 70, 145; identities created by, 64; intellectual work as, 70, 72, 79, 111; at intersection of morality and political economy, 84, 94; legitimacy to rule and, 111; life and beauty created by, 66; Locke on, 12; as marker of exceptional character in Sand and Cabet, 94, 97–98, 103–6, 145, 171; Marx viewing as fungible good, 79; moral improvement and, 35–36, 67, 69–70, 72; pathos of, 154–60; physical disfigurement from, 151; poorly rewarded for Sue's and Balzac's characters, 152–56, 162–63; Sand's conception of, 110; social status ignored by, 66; as source of value, 57, 78; Stendhal on, 55; transformation from drudgery, 12, 71; value of commodities determined by, 77; well-being of humanity improved through, 15, 64, 69–72; "winch" image used by Balzac to describe workers, 68, 82, 90, 95, 146. See also *droit au travail; travail*; wages; writers' labor
labor organizations, 39, 93, 114; writers' union, 38, 122, 161. See also guilds
labor rallies and revolts: government ban on, 21; Lyon silk workers' revolts (1831, 1834), 30–31; Société des Saisons uprising (1839), 31; strikes (1839), 21; *L'Union* newspaper calling for revolt, 129. See also Revolution of 1848
labor theory of value, 77–80, 131
Ladvocat, Pierre-François, 28–29; *Paris; ou, Le Livre des cent-et-un*, 29, 38
Lafayette, marquis de, 28
La Fontaine, Jean de, *Fables*, 140
laissez-faire economics, 2, 82–83
Lamarque, Jean Maximillien, 30
Lamartine, Alphonse de: advocating for right to work, 175; alliance with newest literary celebrities, 137; Dumas on, 180; Marche and, 13; Martin and, 23; in Provisional Government, 27, 184n28; Reboul and, 116, 117; revolutionary delegation confronting, 22; as unifying force in early Republic, 5–6
Lamennais, Félicité de, 137
Lapointe, Savinien: dedicating poem to Hugo, 126; Hugo's printed exchange with, 127; in literary alliance with newest literary celebrities, 137; in *Poésies sociales* (collection), 131, 138; review of poetry collection by, 137; "Une voix d'en bas" (poetry collection), 126, 137; Vinçard and Roly founding paper *L'Union* with, 135; as worker-poet, 39, 128
Larousse, Pierre: *Dictionnaire universel*, 174; *Grand Dictionnaire*, 106
Lavater, Johann Kaspar, 57; *Essai sur la physiognomie: Destiné à faire connaitre l'homme et à le faire aimer (Essays on Physiognomy: For the Promotion of the Knowledge and the Love of Mankind)*, 51
law as protection of creative endeavors, 2. See also copyright and reuse of other's literary creation
laws of physics, 60, 61, 63, 65, 71, 76
Ledru-Rollin, Alexandre, 176, 184n28
Leftists, 46–47
leisure class, 68–69, 95
Lemaître, Frédérick, 173–74
Lerminier, Eugène: in *La Revue des deux mondes*, 133; Vinçard and, 138; on workers' literature, 131–33
Lerner, Bettina, 114; *Inventing the Popular: Printing, Politics, and Poetics*, 10
Leroux, Pierre, 108
liberal ideals and reform: Académie des sciences morales et politiques and, 83, 89; Doctrinaires and, 34; guilds and regulation of work vs., 11; in July Monarchy, 53; Say and, 53; well-being of society tied to production, 15
literacy rates, 42
literary allusions in economic and social studies, 85–90

literary authors: allegories used by, 166–71; *L'Atelier* opposed to publishing articles by, 133; Balzac as first to define labor as part of modern society, 19; "brain work" of, 12; definition of, 16; shunning topics of everyday life in early nineteenth century, 54; social and economic value recognized by, 16, 179; social change and, 7, 37–44, 180; solidarity with physical laborers, 19, 23, 29–31, 39, 69, 94, 111, 131–32, 139, 169–70, 177, 181. *See also* "Industrial Literature"; writers' labor; *specific authors*

literary labor theory of Balzac, 18, 49–80; economy of energy and, 59–77; labor as constant and productive way of measuring value, 50; labor theory of value and, 56–57, 77–80; science of energy and, 12, 57–59; scientific understanding of society and, 50–57

literary studies, Revolution of 1848's effect on, 6–7, 9

littérateur: in alliance with manual laborers, 14, 19, 39; attempts to translate literary popularity into political power, 176; Balzac's use of term, 125; definition of, 120, 192n16; as distinct from *enquêteurs*, 90; as identity assumed by different social groups, 42; political power of, 175–76; Proudhon's use of term, 179; in Saint-Simon's *Parabole*, 16–17, 37; Vinçard's attitude toward, 120, 133–35, 138

littérature: association with commerce, 120; close relationship with journalism in its publication in newspapers, 137–38; criticism of "workers' literature," 130–33; Dumas vs. Proudhon disagreeing over productive nature of, 180; multiple meanings and types of, 41–42, 44; popularity of, 140; productive value of, 180; Romantic view of writing as natural endowment, 54; *L'Union*'s focus on, 135; working-class identity created by, 132–33. *See also* literary authors; *littérateur*

Locke, John, 11, 12, 86
Loi Guizot. *See* Guizot Law
Louis XV (French king), 2
Louis-Philippe I (French king), 2; as "Citizen King" or "Bourgeois King," 28; as constitutional monarch, 28; Doctrinaires and, 24; industrial progress and, 24; Peytel's *Physiologie de la poire* and, 124–25; pro-industry policies of, 3; repressive measures, 31; Say and, 53; toppling of, 20, 181

Luxembourg Commission, 45–47; as de facto ministry of labor, 22–23; as symbol of class cooperation, 23

Lyon-Caen, Judith, 90
Lyons, Martyn, 140–41, 169
Lyon silk workers: revolts by (1831, 1834), 30–31; work-related disfigurement of, 151

male breadwinner model, 27
Malthus, Thomas, 52; in Académie des science morales et politiques, 92; Balzac and, 55, 58; Buret on, 81; criticism of, 83; *Essay on the Principle of Population*, 58

marchandage (wage bargaining), 26
Marche (revolutionary worker), 13–14, 22
Marrast, Armand, 14, 175
marriage as economic institution, 73–74
"Marseillaise, La," 174
Martin, Albert, 23
Marx, Karl, and Marxism, 56, 91; Balzac as source of inspiration for, 79–80; *Capital*, 79; *Class Struggles in France*, 4; *The Communist Manifesto* (with Engels), 108; June Revolution (1848) and, 4; labor theory of value and, 77; Revolution of 1848 and, 4–5, 8, 17, 31–32, 45, 180; on utopianism and French communism, 107–8

materialism, 8, 34–35, 51, 58, 61, 62
McIlvanney, Siobhain, 115
Mercier, Louis-Sébastien, *Tableau de Paris*, 37–38
Mesmer, Franz, 62

metaphysics, 51, 57–62, 71–72, 74, 78
Michaud, Stéphane, 119
Michelangelo, 107
Michelet, Jules, 6, 41, 99, 121; *Histoire de la Révolution française*, 42
middle class. *See* bourgeoisie
Mirecourt, Eugène de, 35
monarchists: Balzac's origins, 3; in Constituent Assembly, 46; Reboul as, 113, 116, 129; Saint-Simon's opposition to, 32
monetary value, 74–76; worth of object measured in, 77
Monfalcon, Jean-Baptiste, 151
Moniteur universel, Le (newspaper), 34–35
Monnier, Henry, *Les Grisettes dessinées d'après nature*, 66
moral economy, 55, 74
morality and moral improvement, 35–36, 58, 67, 69–70, 72, 86; breakdown of morality shown by popularity of *roman-feuilleton*, 136; labor as tool to promote, 93, 111; labor at intersection of morality and political economy, 84, 94; *misère* meaning poverty experienced morally, 94; *La Ruche populaire* and, 120; as solution to social disorder, 92
More, Thomas, 109
Moreau de la Sarthe, Louis-Jacques, 51
mouvement: conservation vs., 63; definition of, 63, 189n32; horizontal vs. vertical, in society, 65
music and songs, 110, 121, 174
mutual aid societies, 127
Mystères de Paris (*The Mysteries of Paris*; Sue), 18; Balzac seeking to capitalize on success of, 163, 164; direct dialogue and realist descriptions, 167–68; *grisette* Rigolette, 150; Madame Hanska praising to Balzac, 162; Madame Pipelet as stock character *portière*, 148–49, 162; morality of labor in, 149; Morel disfigured from intense physical labor, 151; Morel family as proletarian, 150–51, 156; Pipelet's and Morel's labor poorly rewarded, 154–55, 162; plot summary, 142; psychological complexity of Morel's character, 152; published in *Journal des débats* as serial, 141, 174; Pyat's work copied in, 174; rise of literary *physiologie* and, 148–52; success of, 158; trustworthiness of Pipelets, 149–50; vigilante justice in response to corrupt legal system, 143–44; working classes in, 149, 165
"Mysterymania," 141, 194n4

Nacquart, Jean-Baptiste, 61–62
Nadaud, Martin, 42, 44, 98
Napoleon I (Bonaparte), 23, 53
Napoleon III (Louis-Napoleon Bonaparte), 5, 8, 182
National, Le (newspaper), 98–99
National Guard, 14, 29, 174
naturalists, 52, 57, 167
Navier, Claude-Louis, 71
Nesci, Catherine, 66
newspapers: blurring of fact and fiction in, 45, 136–38; elitist in July Monarchy, 122–23; emergence of cheap newspapers, 8, 122–23, 159; layout with *roman-feuilleton* as below the line, 123, 135–36; moral responsibility of, 126; press industry workers' demands for improved working conditions, 28–29; worker-run, 114, 133. *See also romans-feuilletons; specific titles of newspapers*
nobility: debt to physical labor, 19, 131; definition of "noble," 101, 103, 191n47; Dupin on, 36–37; social duty and sense of honor associated with, 104–6; working-class hero's nobleness, 101–4
North American colonies and utopianism, 108

Oehler, Dolf, *Le Spleen contre L'Oubli*, 9
Old Regime, 27, 56, 74, 103; currency of, 76; "honor" defined without reference to, 106
O'Neil-Henry, Anne, *Mastering the Marketplace*, 10
Organicistes, 61–62

panoramic literature, 37–38, 80, 148
Parents pauvres, Les (*The Poor Relations*; Balzac), 4; as allegories, 166–67; characters driven to destruction by their quests, 166; compared to Sue's works, 166–70; inheritance and pension in, 160, 163–65, 167; published first as *romans-feuilletons*, 160–61; revenge in *La Cousine Bette*, 163–64, 166; social justice in, 162–64; social structure creating zero-sum game in, 166–67
Paris: *ateliers nationaux* (national workshops) in, 46–47; cutthroat literary market of, 41; described in Balzac's "Physionomies parisiennes," 85; difference from provinces, 5, 41, 46, 55, 69, 116, 124–25; ingenuity and deceit of, 61; renovations and modernization of, 65; as site of revolutionary drama, 4, 28, 30, 176–78; social character of neighborhoods in, 15, 65, 75
Parny, Evariste de, 115
Paton, Jules, 134–38
Perdiguier, Agricol, 39, 99–100, 121; Lerminier's criticism of, 132; *Le Livre de compagnonnage*, 100; Sand and, 127
Perrot, Michelle, 15
Perrotin, Charles, 99
Peuple, Le, journal général des ouvriers rédigé par eux-mêmes (The people: A common laborers' journal, written by themselves), 114, 121
peuple, le, meaning of, 112–13, 127
Peytel, Sébastien, *Physiologie de la poire* (*Physiology of the Pear*), 124–25
Peytel Affair (1839), 124–25
physics. *See* laws of physics; metaphysics
physiologies (pseudoscientific literary genre), 38, 51–52, 146, 148, 187n51; *Physiologie de la grisette* (Huart), 66; *Physiologie de la poire* (*Physiology of the Pear*; Peytel), 124–25; *Physiologie du gout; ou, Méditations de gastronomie transcendante* (*The Physiology of Taste; or, Meditations on Transcendent Gastronomy*; Brillat-Savarin), 51, 55; *La Physiologie du mariage* (Balzac), 51, 55, 57, 59–60; *Physiologie et hygiène des hommes livres aux travaux de l'esprit* (*The Physiology and Hygiene of Men Devoted to the Labors of the Mind*; Reveillé-Parise), 13, 38
physionomie (para-scientific analysis), 50–51, 146; *Essai sur la physiognomie: Destiné à faire connaitre l'homme et à le faire aimer* (*Essays on Physiognomy: For the Promotion of the Knowledge and the Love of Mankind*; Lavater), 51
"Physionomies parisiennes" (Balzac): desire's potential to cause devastation and, 73; economic use of energy in, 60; explanation of *physionomie* in relation to, 50–52; industrialized Paris described in, 85; labor energy of working classes in, 63–65; later published as part of *La Fille aux yeux d'or*, 49–50, 65; "lifetime of labors," value of, 78–79; metaphor of wealth to fish reproduction and upriver migration, 75–76; realistic depiction of Parisian living space, 150; sentence structure in, 63–64; types of labor and resulting productivity, 64, 68, 72
Pigoreau, Alexandre, 43
Piketty, Thomas, 74
Pillot, Jean-Jacques, 98
Planche, Gustave, 39
Platonic ideal, 54
pleasure: as human motivation, 73; value of good based on, 76–77
Poe, Edgar Allan, "The Man That Was Used Up," 168–69
poetry: on laborer as objects of contemplation and moral goodness, 130; published above the line in *L'Union*, 137; in *La Ruche*, 128, 130–31; Vinçard's recognition of usefulness of, 121; worker-writer identity and, 131. *See also* Reboul, Jean
Polignac, Jules de, 28

political economy, 52–53, 55–56, 75, 77–78, 81, 84
political instability, 74
politics: labor's importance in, 80; literature and, 17, 178; nonviolent means of asserting rights, 129; Second Republic politicians, authors as, 7, 39, 175, 178–80; uselessness of, 129; varied politics of *La Ruche* contributors, 129
Poncelet, Jean-Victor, 71
Poncy, Charles, 39, 137, 138
populace, meaning of, 127
Populaire, Le (newspaper), 44, 98–99
population growth, 58
Potatoes by the Bushel (newspaper), 47–48
Pouillaude (artist), 181
Poussin, Nicolas, 70–71
poverty: Buret's study on, 81–82, 84, 94; English Poor Laws (1834), 84; free-market commerce and, 36; Frégier on moral vs. material causes of, 94; *misère* meaning poverty experienced morally, 94; mortality rates and, 15; overpopulation as cause of, 58
pragmatism, 34, 47, 90, 138
Presse, La (newspaper), 40, 44, 99, 122–23, 135
press laws. *See* censorship
printworkers: exposure and sympathy to bourgeois ideology, 114–15; labor protests by, 2, 114; opposition to censorship, 114; steam-powered printing press, effect of, 114
production and productivism: bourgeois value of productivism, 145; definition of productivism, 15–16; industrialization increasing, 79; labor as source of, 15, 90; productivist worldview, 33–37, 45, 83; Romanticism's approach to productivity, 55; success measured by productivity, 35; success of author measured by pathetic descriptions evoking readers' emotions, 154; writers realizing need to produce something valuable in society, 169

proletarians: in Balzac's social system, 65, 69, 73; bonding of, 41; Chevalier on history of term, 92; legal protections for, 2; Lerminier targeting "workers' literature" by, 132; literary writers as, 44, 45, 69; as owners of only their own labor, 31, 63; pan-proletarian class consciousness, 114; Revolution of 1848 and, 5; in Sand's *Le Compagnon du Tour de France*, 107; society of things and, 64; in Sue's *Mystères de Paris*, 151, 156
Proudhon, Pierre-Joseph, 4–5, 45, 178–80; "Ce que la révolution doit à la littérature" (What the revolution owes to literature), 179–80; *What Is Property?*, 31, 178–79
Provisional Government (Second Republic, 1848), 13–14; Blanc in, 14, 22, 45; *Bulletins de la République* issued by, 176; egalitarianism and, 45; Lamartine in, 23, 175, 184n28; libraries requested from, 181; Martin in, 175; members of, 21, 184n28; Proudhon's critique of, 178; Pyat as *commissaire général*, 174; *républicains du lendemain* as members, 21
Pyat, Félix: *Le Chiffonnier de Paris* (*The Ragpicker of Paris*), 173–74; *Les Deux Serruriers*, 42, 174; dramas by, 41; political career of, 174–75

Quetelet, Adolphe: on *homme moyen* (average man), 68, 146; *Physique sociale; ou, Essai sur le développement des facultés de l'homme*, 53–54

Rabinbach, Anson, 15
Rabine, Leslie, 115
"race" used to mean "class" by Sand, 102, 191n46
railroads, 23–24, 25
Rancière, Jacques, 9
Raphael, 107
readership: audience size as determinative of success, 159; Balzac's failure to achieve bestseller status, 169; book

sales in France of 1840s, 140–41; borrowing successful tropes of other authors in effort to attract, 160–62, 164, 169, 170, 174; bourgeoisie as, 10, 140; cheap newspapers, effect of, 8, 122–23, 159; *romans-feuilletons* as reason to buy newspaper, 136; Sand reaching popular audience, 99; Sand vs. Cabet, 97–98; working classes as audience, 10, 99–100, 170

reading aloud to illiterate fellow workers, 44, 98

reading rooms. See *cabinets de lecture*

realism, 109–10, 146, 166, 167

reason, 34, 57, 58, 76, 87, 90–91, 179

Reboul, Jean: "L'Ange et L'Enfant" (The angel and the child), 116; Dumas and, 116, 117, 126, 138; as monarchist, 113, 116, 129; *Poésies* (collection), 116–17; as worker-writer, 116–17

Réforme, La (newspaper), 98–99, 174

Représentant du peuple, Le (newspaper), 178

Restoration. See Bourbon Restoration

retirement funding. See inheritance and pension

Reveillé-Parise, Joseph-Henri, 13, 38, 54; *Physiologie et hygiène des hommes livres aux travaux de l'esprit*, 13, 38

revenge: in Balzac's *La Cousine Bette*, 163–64, 166; in Dumas's *Comte de Monte Cristo*, 164

Revolution of 1789. See French Revolution

Revolution of 1830. See July Revolution

Revolution of 1848: Balzac as firsthand observer, 177; Barthes on, 6–9; cross-class solidarity of, 4; failure of, 5, 6, 180; Flaubert on, 5; literary authors and, 16, 45; literary production generated from, 6; literary world's role in, 4–5, 10, 14, 17, 19, 180–81; as "Lyrical Illusion," 5, 8, 14, 180; Marx on, 4–5, 8; right to work and, 3, 13, 47–48; *roman-feuilleton* view of, 19; significance of, 8; sociopolitical world's relationship with literature in, 45; unity of workers after, 22; victory of the people in, 173–74

Revue de Paris, La, 122–23; Balzac letter to French writers of nineteenth century (1834), 1, 49; Sainte-Beuve as writer for, 122

Revue des deux mondes, La, 122–24, 133, 135

Revue indépendante, La (newspaper), 132

Rey, Louis, 124–25

Reybaud, Louis, 99

Ribard, Dinah, 127–28

Ricardo, David: Balzac and, 55, 78; Buret on, 81; *On the Principles of Political Economy and Taxation*, 33, 77–78; refuting labor as abstract notion, 77–78; Say and, 33; Smith and, 78

right to assistance, 47–48, 175

right to vote, 14, 45–46, 129

right to work. See *droit au travail*

Roberts, Leslie, 101

Rodrigues, Olinde, 16; *Poésies sociales* (collection of worker poetry), 131–32

Rollinat, François, 99

Roly, Michel (worker-poet): "L'Amour de la gloire" (The love of glory), 130; in literary alliance with newest literary celebrities, 137; in *Poésies sociales* (collection), 131; Vinçard and Lapointe founding paper *L'Union* with, 135

romans-feuilletons (serial novels in newspapers), 19, 37, 40; Balzac's final novels (*La Cousine Bette* and *Le Cousin Pons*) as, 160–61; Balzac's *La Vieille Fille* considered first novel published as, 141; characters from different classes in, 147; integral role with journalism, 45, 136–38; lowering price of newspaper by including, 122; most common way readers consume literature in 1840s, 44, 141–42; pathos as literary device in, 154; presentation and layout in daily newspapers, 123, 135–36; as reason to buy newspaper, 136; Sainte-Beuve's criticism of, 122, 123–24; simultaneous rise

romans-feuilletons (continued)
  of literary *physiologie* and panoramic literature, effect of, 148; solutions to social problems offered in, 144–45; Sue as "king" of, 142
Romantic hero, 95–97, 106, 117, 146, 148
Romanticism: artist as instrument of higher power in, 54; Balzac and, 8, 146; canonical authors of, 8; definition of literary writing including, 45; end of, 8, 38; Flaubert and, 5; genius and, 71; Hugo and, 8, 42, 126; imagination and emotions as focus of, 18, 148; influence of, 9; Lamartine and, 23; on nature's beauty, 101, 116; political beliefs and, 5–6, 54; Rancière on, 9; Reboul and, 116–17; reflected in reading tastes of 1840s France, 159; Sand and, 107, 176; second wave of, 54; worker-writers' relations with, 10, 127
Rosanvallon, Pierre, 92
Rousseau, James, *La Physiologie de la portière*, 148
Rousseau, Jean-Jacques, 12
Ruche populaire, La (newspaper), 31, 35, 80; *L'Atelier* as direct competitor of, 133; bourgeoisie and, 127, 134; cessation as working-class paper, 134; different regional backgrounds of contributors to, 128; first issue showing worker-writer's place in media landscape, 119–20; goals of, 133; Hugo, letter exchanges with, 126–27; on literature's association with commerce, 120–21; Paton taking director's role from Vinçard, 134–35; poetry in, 130–31; Saint-Simonian contributors, 131, 132; shift of paradigm to *L'Union*'s treatment of literature, 138; Sue's character Rodolphe quoted in, 145; *L'Union* as successor of, 134–38; varied political positions of contributors to, 129; Vinçard's letter on Balzac advocating for Peytel's release, 124, 125; Vinçard's role as director, 113, 119, 133–34; worker-writers as contributors to, 121–22

rural vs. urban French: literary tastes of, 140; Paris, difference from provinces, 5, 41, 46, 55, 69, 116, 124–25; in Peytel Affair, 124–25; voting trends, 46; worker-writers' different social experiences based on, 128–29

Sainte-Beuve, Charles-Augustin: criticism of daily newspapers by, 123; criticism of modern literary practices by, 135, 138, 159, 179; on "Industrial Literature," 40, 120, 122, 133; Société des gens de lettres and, 122–24; Vinçard and, 121, 124, 126, 133, 138
Saint-Hilaire, Geoffroy, 57
Saint-Ouen, Madame de, *Histoire de France*, 140
Saint-Pierre, Bernardin de, *Paul et Virginie*, 140
Saint-Simon, Henri, 16–17; assuming name Claude Bonhomme, 32; as bourgeois, 32; *Nouveau Christianisme* (*The New Christianity*), 34, 70; *La Parabole de Saint-Simon*, 16, 37; on production, 33; term "*littérateur*" used by, 120; as utopian thinker, 108–9; working-class movement and, 32–33
Saint-Simonians and Saint-Simonianism: Barrault and, 138; feminists of, 22, 27, 113, 115–16; Leroux and, 108; *prolétaires saint-simoniennes* and newspaper production, 115; Rodrigues and, 131; synthesis of materialism and spiritualism by, 58; utopianism and, 108; Vinçard as, 113, 119, 144; Voilquin as, 113, 115–16; women's exclusion from hierarchy (Enfantin), 115; worker-poets and worker-writers associated with, 131, 132
Sand, George, 18; audience of, 99; Balzac viewing as rival, 161; *Bulletins de la République* written by, 176; Buret compared to, 97; Cabet's followers and, 98; comparing writing to labor of farmers, 38; critical reception of, 99; "Dialogue familier sur la poésie des prolétaires" (articles), 132; honor as interest of, 106;

influence of, 99; labor as mark of honor for, 105–6; labor energy of Balzac and, 105; Ledru-Rollin and, 184n28; Lerminier targeting for promoting "workers' literature," 132; Leroux and, 108; in literary alliance with newest literary celebrities, 137–38; on manual labor, 80; Perdiguier and, 127; public office refused as unsuitable for woman, 176; public reception of new worker-hero of, 97–98; "race" used to mean "class" by, 102; Reboul and, 116; Romanticism and Romantic hero in, 95, 96–97, 107, 176; Saint-Simon's influence on, 108; as social progressive, 103; solidarity promoted between workers and writers, 111; utopianism of, 31, 107–9, 146; Vinçard and, 138; working-class writers and, 39. See also *Compagnon du Tour de France, Le (The Journeyman Joiner)*

satire, 31, 38, 42, 47–48, 124, 175

Say, Jean Baptiste: Balzac and, 75, 78; in Bourbon Restoration, 53; British economists' influence on, 52; Buret on, 81; *Catéchisme d'économie politique (Catechism of Political Economy)*, 34, 52–53, 70, 78; on labor views of Smith and Ricardo, 33, 54; on political economy, 52–53; on postrevolutionary monetary system, 76–78; on production, 33; *Treatise on Political Economy*, 52–53; on value, 77, 78; on women's role, 27

Schneider, Adolphe and Eugène, 25

Schor, Naomi, 107

science of energy, 12, 57–59

scientific study of society, 55, 57

Scott, Joan, 8

Second Empire (1852–70), 7, 182. See also Napoleon III

Second Law of Thermodynamics, 15

Second Republic (1848–52): authors as politicians in, 7, 39, 175, 178–80; Balzac's criticism of, 177; colportage in, 140; establishment of, 20; failure of, 4, 8; library request not fulfilled, 181; Marche and, 13; new chapter in literary history marked by, 7–8, 181–82; Pyat's *Le Chiffonnier de Paris* performed at start of, 173–74; right to work, demand for recognition of, 13; sociopolitical world's relationship with literature in, 45. See also Provisional Government

secret societies, 31, 47

September Laws (1835), 31

serial novels. See *romans-feuilletons*

Sewell, William, 8

Siècle, Le (newspaper), 40, 44, 116, 122–23; Balzac's articles seeking Peytel's release, 124–25; Dumas's *Les Trois Mousquetaires* published as serial, 141; *L'Union* adopting layout of, 135

Sieyès, Emmanuel Joseph (abbé), 56, 103

Sipe, Daniel, 109

slavery, abolishment of, 93

Smith, Adam: Balzac and, 55, 75, 78; division of art and industry based on, 39; invisible hand theory, 52; Ricardo and, 78; Say and, 33, 52–53; *The Wealth of Nations*, 77–78

Smith, Eliza Jane, *Literary Slumming: Slang and Class in Nineteenth-Century France*, 10

social cohesion: after Revolution of 1848, 22–23; political differences in how to achieve, 129

social discourse analysis, 7

socialists: Balzac in common cause with, 3; bourgeoisie as, 32; canonical authors identifying with, 9; as Constituent Assembly minority (1848), 46; Jesus as socialist hero, 131; newspapers as vehicle for, 45, 113; in Second Republic, 45–46; Sue as, 145, 174, 176

social justice and reform: Balzac's compared to Sue's approach, 162–63, 166; literary pleas for, 18, 35; moral improvement and, 35–36, 84; political economy and, 84; Sue advocating for, 143–45, 162, 166, 170, 176; well-being and, 64

social norms and structure, 55; characters facing zero-sum game based on, 167; dress distinctions of social classes, 75;

social norms and structure (*continued*) literature disseminating, 42; of modern society, based on manual labor, 111; in Sand's *Le Compagnon du Tour de France*, 106, 110; value of objects and, 78. *See also specific classes*
Société des amis du peuple, 31
Société des droits de l'homme, 31
Société des gens de lettres, 38, 122–24, 161, 183n7
Société des Saisons uprising (1839), 31
society of things, 64, 68
sociocriticism movement, 7, 9
solidarity: of bourgeois social thinkers, 111; cross-class, 19, 23, 26, 30, 137–38; cross-gender, 27; of workers and writers, 19, 23, 29–31, 39, 69, 94, 111, 131–32, 139, 169–70, 177, 181
songs and singing, 110, 121, 174
Spang, Rebecca, 76
spiritualism, 58, 130–31
"starving journalist" imagery, 40
Stendhal, 8; *Le Rouge et le Noir: Chronique de 1830*, 55, 146
Sue, Eugène: ability to evoke feelings of pathos, 154–60; ambiguity in depictions of working class in, 153; Balzac borrowing from, 160–62, 164, 169, 170; Balzac compared to, 166–70; Balzac viewing as rival, 161; Cabet's followers and, 98; *cabinets de lecture* (reading rooms) and, 44; as champion of working class, 145; character development contributing to appeal of, 145, 148; characters from different classes in, 147; direct dialogue and realist descriptions in, 167–68, 169; as *feuilletoniste*, 19, 141–42, 145, 154; labor as positive force in character development, 145, 153, 154; labor organizations and, 39, 144, 170; labor shown to be economically and socially fruitless, 153–54, 170; labor's negative effects on body, 151; Lerminier targeting for promoting "workers' literature," 132; *Mathilde*, 161; as politician, 176; poverty of pre-success life, 158; Pyat borrowing from, 174; reprinting workers' letters within his *feuilleton*, 144; as socialist, 145, 174, 176; on social problems of his day, 143–45, 162, 176; success of, 142, 145, 159, 169, 174; on superiority of writers to physical laborers, 154, 158–59, 170; surpassing his competition, 159; on vigilante justice in response to corrupt legal system, 143; Vinçard and, 138. *See also Juif errant, Le*; *Mystères de Paris*
synthesis, 17, 58, 103

Tastu, Amable, 99
taxonomy of human society, 57
Terror, Reign of (1793–94), 34
Texier, Edmond, *Physiologie du poète*, 38–39
"other" as danger to society, 93
Thérenty, Marie-Ève, 194n4
Thiher, Allen, 59, 61
Third Estate, 56
Thomas, Emile, 46–47
Thompson, E. P., 55
Tocqueville, Alexis de, *Recollections*, 22
Tourte, Francis, poetry by, 131
tragedy and tragic characters, 6, 9, 60, 79, 142, 162, 180
travail: *droit du travail* (Turgot), 11; new definition of, 19; as production, 15–18; Say arguing for *industrie* instead of *travail*, 33; social definition of, 20; writers' work as, 38. *See also* labor; production and productivism
travail, droit au. *See droit au travail*
Tribune des femmes, La (newspaper), 43, 115, 119
Tristan, Flora, 39, 99; as idealist, 118; life of, 118; *Mephis*, 117–19; as *ouvrière*, 113, 192n1; *Pérégrinations d'une paria* (Peregrinations of a pariah), 119; *Promenades dans Londres* (Promenades in London), 119; social theory of, 118; "Tour de France," 99; types of writing by, 118–19; *L'Union ouvrière* (The workers' union), 119

Trois Glorieuses. *See* July Revolution
Turgot, Anne Robert Jacques, 2, 11
twentieth-century literary studies of 1848 Revolution, 6

unemployed workers: role in June Days, 47; Sue proposing philanthropic bank for, 144; unemployment insurance, right to assistance as, 47–48, 175
Union, L' (newspaper): blending above-the-line journalism and below-the-line literature, 137–38; collaboration with bourgeois *littérateurs*, 138; focus on contemporary literature and embracing profession of *littérateur*, 135; founded by Vinçard, Roly, and Lapointe, 113, 135, 145; layout like popular dailies, 135; Paton explaining split between factual articles and literature in, 136; Paton joining, 135; on uselessness of politics, 129
universal suffrage for male citizens, 45–46
utility as determinant of value, 78
utopianism, 17, 31, 98, 107–9, 146

value. *See* literary labor theory of Balzac; monetary value
Vannostal, L. J., 128, 129–30
Varin, Emile, 129–30
vaudeville. *See* Arago, Etienne
vice and corruption, 67, 69
Vigier, Philippe, 183n11
Vigny, Alfred de, *Chatterton*, 38, 54–55, 95, 185n27
Villermé, René, 18; in Académie des sciences morales et politiques, 92; on child labor and child neglect, 89; on destructive effects of labor on human body, 151–52; on industrial workers, 100; on labor as means to creating compliant and docile citizens, 111; as liberal, 112; on mortality rates in Paris neighborhoods, 15; political influence of, 90; on statistical measures to analyze social problems, 84; *Tableau de l'état physique et moral des ouvriers employés dans les manufactures de coton, de laine et de soie* (Study of the physical condition of cotton, wool, and silk workers), 86–89; on working-class hero, 112
Vinçard, Jules: founding paper *L'Union* with Roly and Lapointe, 135; Hugo and, 127, 138; on Hugo-Lapointe exchange, 127; as *La Ruche* contributor after stepping down from director role, 135; literary allies of, 138; "littérateur" description and, 120–21, 134, 192n16; newspaper production and, 35, 119, 129; poetry by, 131; removing himself as *La Ruche* director, 133–34, 145; on sacred role of worker-writer, 133–34; Sainte-Beuve and, 119, 124, 126, 133; as Saint-Simonian, 113, 119, 144; Sue reprinting letters by, 144–45; as worker-poet, 35, 39, 113, 119, 128, 180. *See also Ruche Populaire, La; Union, L'*
vis humana, 61–63, 72
Vitalistes, 62
Voilquin, Suzanne, 43, 113, 115–16
Voix des femmes, La (newspaper), 22, 27
Voltaire, 12, 16–17, 41, 109
Voyage en Icarie (Travels in Icaria; Cabet), 31, 94–105, 107–9; Cabet's followers called Icarians, 98; Carisdall as Byronic hero in, 95, 96; Carisdall providing eyes to view new society, 96; French painter Eugène's genius in, 101, 103–4; honor as part of nobility in, 104–5; hope for society's future in, 111; nobility, new definition of, 101; published under pseudonym Francis Adams, 95; realism in, 109; Romantic hero in, 95–96; utopianism in, 98, 107; Valmor as true hero in, 96; Valmor's superiority to Carisdall, 100–101; working-class heroes' nobility in, 103–5, 107
Vulcan, 61

wages: deskilling and, 26–27; industrialization depressing, 79; laborer newspapers advocating for, 114; Sainte-Beuve's criticism of writers' union's pursuit of, 122;

wages (*continued*)
122; Sue advocating for, 144; women as underpaid workers, 152, 156–57
water imagery, 66–67
Watrelot, Martine, 100
wealth: creation of, as public virtue, 153; as human motivation, 73–74; patrimonial wealth system, 74; Say on, 52
Weinstein, Cindy, 168
Woloch, Alex, 147–48
women: burdened by collective duty, 106; Enfantin's exclusion from Saint-Simonianism's hierarchy, 115; exclusion from workforce, 27; as factory workers, 88; as *grisettes*, 66–67, 102, 145, 150, 152, 189n35; hunger fears of, 2; industrialization and, 27; observed for erotic pleasure of men, 49, 66, 88; political emancipation to be achieved through economic independence, 115; primping as labor of, 66; as Saint-Simonian feminists, 22, 27, 113–16, 176; Sue's belief that women possess less literary talent than men, 157; Sue's readership predominantly lower-middle-class women, 157; as underpaid workers, 152, 156–57; vice and labor's relationship depicted through, 67
worker-writers, 35; alliance of worker-poets and bourgeois writers, 137–38; Balzac complaining of being overlooked in discourse on labor rights, 177; Hugo's support for, 126; Lerminier criticizing, 131–32; literary identity of, 112–39; pan-proletarian class consciousness of, 114; popular interest in, leading to monetary benefits for, 139; Proudhon identifying with, 180; shared identity despite disparate politics, 113, 128; Vinçard as worker-poet, 35, 39, 113, 119, 128, 180; women as, 115. *See also* writers' labor; *specific authors*
working classes, 2; anti-working-class sentiment, 4; authors recognizing audience of, 10, 99–100; Balzac's treatment of, 68, 82, 160–61, 170; Blanc's empowerment of, 46; bourgeois attitude toward, 92, 127; as creative force of new society, 18; disillusionment leading to rebellion, 45–47; group identity based on types of performed manual labor, 112–13; guarantee of work in Revolution of 1848, 14; identity of, 128–33; improved working conditions for, 28–29, 47; industrialization and, 24; labor energy of, 63–65; literacy of, 42–43, 140; mutual aid societies and, 127; newspapers of, 35; Pyat as supporter of, 175; redefinition of, 112–13; roles throughout literary history, 147; singing and, 121, 174; Sue as champion of, 145, 158; "vicious" portion described by Frégier, 85; writers' role in creating identity of, 112–39; writers' shared anxieties with, 11. *See also* labor; labor rallies and revolts
working-class hero, 18, 29, 82, 94–111; in Cabet, 97–98, 103–5, 107, 146; fictional presentation of, 94–100, 112; nobleness of, 103–4; in Sand, 97–98, 102–5, 146; sense of honor of, 104–6; Sue's characters as, 146; suffering of labor and, 110; utopian works celebrating, 31, 107
writers' labor: Balzac on, 19, 38, 39, 69; borrowing from work of others, 161; as "brain work," 1, 12; challenges to make a living, 11, 158, 160–61; equated with manual labor, 70, 72, 79, 111, 112, 117; French philosophers' interest in, 12; as "missionary work," 127; moral value of, 13; pitfalls of comparing literary and manual labor, 41, 45, 171; Saint-Simon on value of, 37; superiority to physical labor, 112, 113, 154, 158–59, 170
writers' union, 38, 122. *See also* Société des gens de lettres

www.ingramcontent.com/pod-product-compliance
Lightning Source LLC
Chambersburg PA
CBHW032057230426
43662CB00035B/590